The study of dress history

MANCHESTER
1824
Manchester University Press

general editor:
CHRISTOPHER BREWARD

founding editor:
PAUL GREENHALGH

The study of dress history

Lou Taylor

Manchester University Press

Published by Manchester University Press
Altrincham Street, Manchester M1 7JA, UK
www.manchesteruniversitypress.co.uk

British Library Cataloguing-in-Publication Data is available

Library of Congress Cataloging-in-Publication Data is available

ISBN 978 0 7190 4065 8 paperback

First published 2002

This edition reprinted in 2015, 2017

The publisher has no responsibility for the persistence or accuracy of URLs for any external or third-party internet websites referred to in this book, and does not guarantee that any content on such websites is, or will remain, accurate or appropriate.

Printed by Bell and Bain Ltd, Glasgow

Contents

Illustrations

Figures

Colour plates

Acknowledgements

I have many people to thank for their generous help over the completion of this book, especially my husband, Joe, for his support and patience throughout its long period of incubation. From the curatorial world, I thank first Revel Oddy who taught me to respect objects and understand the care needed to look after and exhibit them, a long time ago, at the Royal Scottish Museum in Edinburgh, now part of the National Museums of Scotland. My sincere and grateful thanks go to other colleagues in the museum world who have put up with my incessant enquiries, particularly Rebecca Quinton at the Museum of Brighton and also Anne Buck, Valerie Mendes, Santina Levey, Amy de la Haye, Emma Young, Ann Wise, Naomi Tarrant, Liz Arthur, Helen Proctor, Tessa Sidey, Christine Stevens, Sheila Shreeve, Elizabeth Dell, Rory O'Connell and Joanna Marschner. Monica Brewis and Louise Tucker at St Peter's House Library, University of Brighton, have given me constant, invaluable help over many years; in France, Germany, the USA, Canada and Australia, I thank Valerie Guillaume, Dominique Veillon, Evelyne Gaudry, Alice and Asia Almeida, Elizabeth Ann Coleman, Sarah Johnson, Susan Michelman, Alexandra Palmer and Margaret Maynard. Amongst my university colleagues David Crowley, Jill Seddon, Louise Purbrick and Frank Gray helped me develop the themes in this book. I thank Linda Rozmovits, Mike Hill of the University of Brighton for help over computer glitches and I owe thanks too to Ann Saunders, Christopher Breward, to my sister, Jo Gladstone and to several generations of undergraduate and postgraduate students at the University of Brighton for their perceptive questions and encouragement.

For Joe

Introduction

The Crown has outlasted the head.
The hand has lost out to the glove
The right shoe has defeated the foot.

As for me, I am still alive, you see.
The battle with my dress rages on.
It struggles, foolish thing, so stubbornly!
Determined to keep living when I am gone! (Wislawa Szymborska)[1]

OVER the past ten years the field of dress history has finally broken free of the shackles that have held it back for far too long. It has benefited from what Ralph Samuel described as 'the Balkanisation' of history, 'the multiplication of sub-disciplines, a phenomenon of the last twenty-five years, [which] has produced a new crop of specialisms, each with its own society, its schisms and secessions'.[2] Dress history is now beginning to benefit from new methodologies which are pulling these 'secessions' together through innovative cross-disciplinary academic approaches.

Because of the multi-faceted 'levels' at which clothing functions within any society and any culture, clothing provides a powerful analytical tool across many disciplines. Yet the four hundred years of development of dress history in Europe and the United States have taken place outside the boundaries of 'academic respectability' and the residues of this prejudice remain a debated issue. Even Angela McRobbie, a feminist sociologist with a deep interest in fashion, still felt obliged to justify her interest in the field as late as 1998. In her *British Fashion Design – rag trade or image industry* she felt it necessary to write that her book 'is based upon the assumption that fashion, despite its trivialised status, is a subject worthy of study'.[3] Here she is facing up to attitudes that were dominant in the once largely male academic world of 'real' history. Here 'clothes', especially those related to Western European feminine fashions, were considered to be a frivolous and ephemeral characteristic of society. As such, to study them would therefore be to trivialise history itself and the subject was seen as an unworthy vehicle for 'serious' academic research. Happily over the last ten years, dress history and dress study have blossomed as new generations of far more open-minded ethnographers, consumption historians and dress/textile specialists have developed fresh approaches to theory and research which are identified and explored in this book.

This has, however, been a hard-fought battle. The study of dress and its related textile history has long been full of tensions and strains which can be laid at the door of the subject itself. Dress and textile history attracts the passions of an extraordinarily wide group of specialists and enthusiasts. Obsessive collectors with a profound knowledge of one artefact may take no interest in examining the social and cultural forces from which these objects grew. An economic historian investigating the export of nineteenth-century British cotton prints may not even be able to date their design or even have considered the issue of their design to be of any relevance. A researcher whose eye is fixed on the cultural 'meanings' of clothes may well take no interest in learning the detailed style and manufacturing minutiae of the garments. In reverse, the meanings of the clothing s/he cares for may well never be considered by an object-based specialist. Between these groups a state of warfare or sullen indifference has existed. The problem is far from new. In 1821 Dr Samuel Rush Meyrick and Charles Hamilton-Smith wrote that costume history was burdened with 'the intemperate and hasty charge of carrying with it the inferiority of not being worthy of consideration of a man of letters'.[4]

This book focuses on the development of current approaches and practices to be found within the field of dress history and dress studies. Through examination of basic methodological approaches and the views of those working in the field, this study assesses the current condition and future directions of dress history.

Notes

1 Extract from 'Museum' by Wislawa Szymborska, *View with a Grain of Sand: selected poems* (Faber and Faber, London, 1995) with thanks to Prof. Elsbieta Tarkowska and the kind permission of Faber and Faber.

2 R. Samuel, *Theatres of Memory*, vol. 1 of *Past and Present in Contemporary Culture* (Verso, London, 1994), p. 3.

3 A. McRobbie, *British Fashion Design – rag trade or image industry* (Routledge, London, 1998), p. 15.

4 S. Rush Meyrick, *Costume of the Original Inhabitants of the British Islands from the Earliest Periods to the Sixth Century* (Thomas M'Lean, London, 1821), preface.

1 ✧ Artefact-based approaches: collection, identification, conservation

Too much concentration on every flounce, pleat, button and bow. (Ben Fine and Ellen Leopold)[1]

Introduction

DRESS historians who work from a base of analysing surviving dress/textile artefacts are criticised for their 'descriptive' concentration on the minutiae of clothing. The economic and social historians Ben Fine and Ellen Leopold describe a series of dress history studies dating from the 1950s through to the 1980s by the Cunningtons, De Marly, Ewing, Kidwell, Ribeiro, Taylor, Tozer and Levitt as 'in the wholly descriptive "catalogue" tradition of costume history, which typically charts in minute detail over the course of several centuries the addition or deletion of every flounce, pleat, button and bow, worn by every class on every occasion'.[2]

Comments such as these confirm the strong feeling within the dress history profession that their expertise and indeed their whole field has still not been properly acknowledged in 'academic' circles. Naomi Tarrant, Curator of Costume and Textiles for the National Museum of Scotland in Edinburgh, wrote in 1994 that in the museum world

> costume is at present being marginalised. Art-based departments view the topic with distrust. For social history departments costume is a very small part of an overall picture and the élite nature of many surviving objects is regarded with suspicion by some curators.[3]

Object-based research does indeed centre on examination of minute detail, channelled through a series of patiently acquired skills and interpretative methods which are underrated or perhaps misunderstood within comments such as those of Fine and Leopold. The professional practice of artefact-based dress history involves first finding the clothing object, followed by its identification, conservation, display and finally interpretation.

Finding clothing

Every dress curator/collector has their own story of triumph and disaster connected to finding special items of dress, such as a rare length of 1920s Lyons art deco fashion fabric, possibly by *Maison Ducharne*, found by the author in the 50p scarf bin at an *Age Concern* shop in Midhurst, East Sussex, in the mid-1980s. Unfortunately, because of scant public regard for 'old clothing', stressful stories are more common: 'we threw away all her clothes last year' or 'we kept the samples till the company was taken over' are typical. The author, when working as Curator of Costume at Brighton Museum, received an urgent phone call to a bakery in St Leonards-on-Sea. The retired baker had been forced to clear out the contents of his family's home above the bakery, *William Beck*'s, and was burning piles of clothes in the back yard. The living accommodation above the bakery had been left intact for very many years and still contained, albeit in a sad and filthy state, turn-of-the-century furniture and clothing. Rescued from the blaze were rare examples of a baker's boy's smock (Figure 1), the baker's wife's half-mourning or Sunday best dresses and hats, and even some of the bakery's printed paper bags, all dating from the 1910–15 period.[4]

Liz Arthur, then Curator of Dress and Textiles at Kelvingrove Museum, Glasgow, was summoned in 1975 to a large bourgeois house at Rothesay, on the Isle of Bute. On arrival she too found the house being cleared,

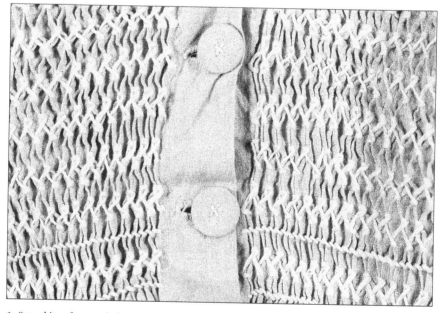

1 Smocking from a baker's boy's smock, about 1900–10

this time by professional removers on behalf of distant relatives of the original owner. She found a large and rare collection of 1830s dresses and accessories. Told she could take whatever she wanted but only right then, she was forced rapidly to collect up what she could remove, wrapping precious dresses up in discarded bedcovers, before everything was taken off to the local dump for burning. Forty garments and textiles were rescued including a lustrous lilac-coloured silk dress of 1830–36 with vast gigot sleeves and an early example of a princess line dress of 1878, in black velvet, labelled *J. White, Regent Street, London.* Liz Arthur now remembers sadly other items she was unable to carry away including an 1850s silk dress with a day and evening bodice, the latter covered in tiny glass acorns.[5] Cecil Beaton's experience was even worse, because he came on his particular nightmare too late to effect any rescues at all: 'A multi-millionaire in Chicago, whose wife, recently dead, had been famous for her clothes, and whose mother before had created a niche in history through the splendour of her apparel, decided that, although many of their dresses, dating from the nineties, had not even been taken out of their Paris boxes, they were of too private a nature. So he committed the great act of vandalism by burning the lot six weeks before I approached him.'[6]

The story is not fortunately always so gloomy. From time to time clothes are kept long after their owners stop wearing them because they become repositories of deeply valued personal memories. Some garments and even collections survive simply because of happy personal associations and because their owners value the quality of design, fabric and making too much to part with them. A deep, joyful emotional attachment rests within certain types of personal clothing such as wedding, party and christening robes, which survive in large numbers, whereas mourning dress and indeed maternity clothes do not. Weybridge Museum has a 'baby boy's embroidered and ribboned cap of the 1890s which was worn in turn by all the five sons of Joseph Tollow, secretary to the local volunteer fire brigade'.[7] Dr Elspeth Clarkson kept her favourite teenage dance dress for twenty years before donating it to Brighton Museum. A pretty 1958 ready-to-wear garment by *Riki Michaels*, Mayfair, it has a short bouffant white nylon and black lace skirt.[8]

More poignantly still, families keep clothing and textiles as memories of much loved, deceased relatives, especially items belonging to those who died before their time. Brighton Museum has two examples. The first is a bedcover which is said to have belonged to a member of the family who ran the famous *Old Bunne Shop* in Pool Valley, Brighton. It is made from red flannel, appliquéd with a patchwork pattern of lozenge shapes in natural linen (Figure 2). Many of these contain short Biblical verses, hand written directly in Indian ink and signed by the writers. All relate to the

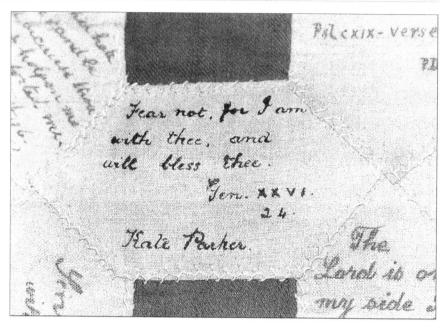

2 Bedcover, 1893, from the bed of a terminally ill girl

themes of young girls and sickness and are dated between 1893 and 1894. A typical verse reads: *Fear not, for I am with thee and will bless thee. Gen. XXVI, 24. Kate Parker.* It is hard not to imagine that this lay on the bed of a terminally ill girl and that it was kept in her memory after her death, before being donated to the museum. The second example from the Brighton Museum is a blue-grey jumper. This was hand knitted in rayon yarn in 1921 by a seventeen year old girl, who died one year later. Her sister kept it for fifty years before donating it to the museum in 1972.[9]

Occasionally whole collections of clothing survive from one family or one shop. One of the oldest and most internationally important groups of clothing in the Victoria and Albert Museum is its Isham Collection of seventeenth-century dress and embroidery. This includes some of the museum's best examples of early English women's garments, one of which is a red figured velvet gown lined with pinked matching silk. This whole collection remained at the Isham family home at Lamport Hall, in Northamptonshire undisturbed for nearly two hundred years. In 1899, the artist Seymour Lucas, who negotiated its purchase on behalf of the museum, noted that it was the antiquarian interests of generations of the family that had led to the happy survival of these beautiful and rare clothes: 'In the store room over the kitchen, commonly called the Wardrobe, are two chests filled with old clothes which the last Sir Justinian and Sir Edward, being lovers of antiquity, set a value upon as showing the Fashions of the time; among them are the clothes made for Sir Thomas Isham's Wedding of 1680.'[10]

These clothes were treasured by descendants of the wearers. Others survive simply by accident. Mrs Katherine Sophia Farebrother, a solicitor's wife from Salisbury, deliberately put all her smart clothes away in trunks when she went into mourning following her husband's death in 1913. Over two dozen items of clothing were found in the attic of her house some sixty years later in the 1970s, leaving us with a clear visual impression of the taste and style of this conventional, upper-middle-class woman. The clothing dates from 1900–14. Mrs Farebrother purchased her grandest dresses and costumes from the top London department stores of *Dickens and Jones*, *Liberty's* and *H. and J. Nichol and Co.* and *Jolly's* of Bath. Her 'Between Maid', Miss E. A. Foan, who first worked for the family in 1903, was still alive and being cared for by the family when Brighton Museum purchased this collection of clothes. Miss Foan was able to confirm that most of the other day-to-day dresses in the collection were made by a local dressmaker who was sometimes paid with a leg of mutton.[11]

Heather Firbank (1888–1954), the daughter of the affluent MP Sir Thomas Firbank and sister of the novelist Ronald Firbank, was much better off than Mrs Farebrother and had her best clothes made at leading London houses such as *Lucile*, *Redfern* and *Mascotte*. Her clothes too, dating from the early 1900s to 1920, were packed into trunks and put into storage in 1921, where they stayed for nearly forty years. In 1960 the Victoria and Albert Museum was given them all – over one hundred items of one wealthy woman's selection of the most exclusive fashions worn in Britain in the early years of the twenty-first century.[12] This group of clothes is so large that Firbank's personal sense of style is very evident – smart, conventional and, as Valerie Mendes notes, with a preference for 'understated pastel-colour day dresses, immaculate tailored suits and evening gowns'. Firbank's clothes were made both by identified couture houses and unknown dressmakers. She favoured the London salon of *Lucile*, ordering a simple grey worsted costume of about 1911, a rare survival since such garments tend to be altered or simply worn out. Another of her dresses is the now famous, neoclassical, draped, cream satin and black velvet dress of 1912–13, much used in the museum's publicity material.[13]

Some sartorial treasures survive by pure accidental chance. One of the most fascinating items in the textile collection at the Victoria and Albert is *A Lady of Fashion, Barbara Johnson's Album of Style and Fabrics*. This is a curious object because it is simply an old accounts ledger, but one into which one woman pinned samples of fabric of all the dresses she wore and then noted alongside details of price, date and occasion for which the dress was made. Even more astonishing is the fact that Miss Johnson did this over a period of nearly eighty years – from 1746, when she was a child, right through to 1823 when she was in her eighties. The album came up for auction at Christies in 1973 and after some desperate fund raising it was purchased for the Victoria and Albert Museum. Natalie Rothstein, then Keeper of Textiles, has since then been able to identify Miss Johnson as a fashion consumer moving on the fringes of London society within the circle of a well-off clerical family. She spent time in London, Norfolk and Bath and never married.[14]

Turning over the pages of this album is almost like hearing Miss Johnson's voice speaking about her clothes, whether they were for weddings, funerals or visits to smart relatives in London and Bath. The note written carefully in black ink alongside a small sample of medium-weight cotton printed with a tiny speckled repeat design in grey and mauve, reads: 'A Stormont Cotten gown and petticoat, ten yards, two shillings a yard. April 1788, mourning for Aunt Johnson.' This modest little print is indeed in the exact etiquette-correct colours of half mourning. Another mourning fabric chosen twenty years later is described as 'a black Chambery muslin, seven yards, half a crown a yard. Made at Bath. June 1808, mourning for my dear friend Mrs Wodhull.' This little note tells us that even when elderly, Miss Johnson was still keeping up with the latest fashion fabrics by turning to the lighter silk and cotton materials fashionable in the early nineteenth century[15] (see Figure 14, p. 77).

The important but as yet largely unseen Messel Collection, now mostly in the keeping of Brighton Museum, contains the clothes of three generations of women from the same family, dating from the 1880s through to the 1960s. It has been loaned by Lord Snowden and includes garments worn by his mother, Ann, Countess of Rosse, of her mother, Maud Messel and of her mother, Marion Sambourne, the wife of the cartoonist, Linley Sambourne, whose home in Staffordshire Terrace in Kensington now belongs to the Victorian Society. Marion's clothes form the first group and include a deep olive-green silk brocaded, bustle-backed dress of the mid-1880s, some mourning bodices and heavy beaver fur jackets. The second, far larger group, was worn by her daughter, Maud Messell and the third was worn by Marion's granddaughter, Ann, the Countess of Rosse. The survival of this clothing (and indeed the contents of the Staffordshire Terrace house, too) is entirely due to the passionate awareness of the late Countess of Rosse of the cultural and aesthetic value of this collection. This collection now contains hundreds of outstanding, innovative garments. When these are finally exhibited, they will enhance our understanding of the very real design strength and national character of English couture and elite dressmaker design in the period from the 1910s to the 1960s.

This collection, under the care of Rebecca Quinton from the late 1990s, goes beyond the Farebrother/Firbank/Johnson collections because it reveals the interlinked generational tastes of one family. Research is further aided by the existence of Marion Sambourne's personal diary.[16] Maud and Ann both married well and were wealthy enough to afford far more expensive clothes than Marion, who was still making family clothes in the 1890s. They both favoured designs by innovative London couture houses for some but not of all their clothes. Both thus wore smart, fashionable but occasionally mildly 'arty' designs. These reflect perfectly Maud's leanings towards mild aestheticism inherited from her upbringing in the Stafford-shire House interior which, as visitors can see today, is also mildly aesthetic in design. Both women were keen gardeners, with an English love for the natural rather than the exotic and chose mostly natural soft colours for their clothes.

Maud Messel dressed conventionally enough at the well-established English couture and top dressmaker houses of *Lucile, Mme Hayward* and *Mme Ross*. She also favoured *Sarah Fullerton Monteith Young* who produced for her a range of fashionable garments showing touches of unconventional aesthetic and Turkish-inspired styling. Usually the touches are moderate but one example of about 1900–10 is an extraordinary grey and purple silk chiffon tea-gown. It has great floating yardages of train but is sleeveless amd held skimpily on to the arms with narrow bands of embroidered ribbon. A second *Monteith Young* design is a pale green cashmere costume of about 1908 with skirt and bolero-styled jacket, trimmed with cream-coloured, spotted silk and braiding. The aesthetic touch to this otherwise high fashion ensemble is the addition of a large gilt scarab clasp fastening on the jacket.[17] Other dresses feature exotic appliquéd embroidery decoration. One, in brick red muslin of about 1905, with entirely handstitched tucking, is decorated with hand-painted panels, probably in imitation of Turkish embroidery (Plate 1). Its origin remains unknown.[18]

Maud had picked up her moderated aesthetic leanings from her mother Marion, whose visitors' book shows the names of Luke Fildes and George du Maurier, her father's colleague on *Punch*. When Maud was in her debutante year in 1895 she attended a grand ball at Ayton Castle. She wrote to her mother Marion, just before the ball, 'I have just come in from the garden where I gathered such a lovely bunch of pink roses to wear tonight with my dress. I am going to be an awful swell.'[19] Her mother, a gifted needlewoman, had made this dress herself – of pink silk from the aesthetically inspired store, *Liberty's*.

The Countess of Rosse continued her mother's practice of patronising unconventional designers by favouring the work of the then young and largely unknown Anglo-American couturier Charles James. She commissioned two evening dresses in pastel silks from him in the early 1930s, with tiny bodices and curiously draped skirts.[20] She commissioned unusual designs from dressmakers and bought elegant garçonne late 1920s styles from Paris fashion houses, remaining a famously elegant dresser into her old age. This exceptionally interesting collection of several hundred dresses has not yet received the proper international recognition it deserves. Even setting aside the socially interesting family history, the Messel Collection is one of the most unusual surviving couture collections of the first half of the twentieth century in Britain. It survives because the Countess of Rosse and her son both appreciated these 'best' clothes for highly personal reasons, aesthetic, sentimental and dynastic, coupled with a clear respect for their quality and period style.

Sometimes clothing survives miraculously in abandoned or neglected retail outlets. Brighton Museum profited from a collection of unsold fashion accessories found in the attic of *Hills*, East Street, which from the early nineteenth century was the smartest retailing street in the town, close to the Royal Pavilion. It had been founded in 1810, according to museum records, as *The Viennese Needlework Shop*. In 1970 boxes covered with dust were found up in the attic containing obviously unsold fans, still tied with their original sale (highly priced) tickets. The fans all dated from about the 1880–1900 period – mostly white silk organdie fan leaves hand painted with flowers and butterflies. One, stamped with the word *France*, had its sticks and guards pierced and gilded and was priced at 84/-, a high price for this period when a ready-to-wear costume could be purchased for 10/6d.[21]

A far more astonishing surviving retail collection is the Hodson Shop Collection highlighted in Suzanne Davies's BBC2 dress history series, *Through the Looking Glass* of 1989–90. This collection of nearly three thousand unsold garments, accessories and paper documents comes from a small dress shop based in the main street of Willenhall, a famous lock-making community near Walsall, in the West Midlands. It is precious because it consists of rarely surviving, cheap ready-to-wear clothing. This shop, at 54 New Road, was owned by two socially ambitious sisters, Flora and Edith Hodson and was run from the ground floor of the family home in a street of tiny terraced houses in an impoverished neighbourhood, where they had lived from 1905.[22] They ran their shop from about 1920 until 1956 and, it would seem, catered for the local women who worked in the lock factories. Neither of the sisters was commercially sharp and they ran the shop in a highly idiosyncratic way. Despairing letters to the sisters from their accountant, a local solicitor, show that the shop never really ran at a profit and was chaotically run.

Unsold stock drifted into storerooms at the back where it piled up over the years, tumbling out of boxes and gathering dust. Amy de la Haye

3 Ready-to-wear clothing of the 1920s from the Hodson Shop Collection, Willenhall

notes that the two sisters stopped trading in 1956 and the stock lay untouched until after the last surviving sister, Flora, died in 1983.[23] All the surviving garments are still priced as if ready for sale. The collection includes a huge selection of underwear, stockings, blouses, hats and sewing threads. Even very rare buyers' catalogues from Birmingham and Leeds wholesale manufacturers survive, such as *Wilkinson and Ridell's* ready-to-wear catalogues of 1931 and 1932. Trading from Cherry Street, Birmingham, in the summer of 1931, this company offered attractive frocks in *Grafton* cotton voile at 13/11d, hats in pull-on shapes in fancy straw at 3/11d and ladies' 'art silk tops' stockings at 17/11d a dozen. Also left in the shop were dozens of perfectly intact, unworn day (and even a few evening) ready-to-wear dresses, dating from the mid-1920s through to utility clothes from the 1942–46 period. The most expensive items left unsold were fine knitted woollen jersey suits at 38/6d, dating from the late 1920s. Typical of these is a design in grey and navy blue with diamond-shaped trimmings, manufactured by the well-known company *St Margaret's* by *Corah's* of Leicester (Figure 3).

The shop passed into the hands of the local history society in the 1980s and the building now houses the Willenhall Lock Museum. The dress collection was of little interest to local historians (mostly retired male workers from the lock trade) and certainly did not fit into their plans for the building. Through the personal energies and single-minded persistence

of Sheila Shreeve, a local dress historian, the entire collection, together
with related archives, was saved, catalogued and finally handed over to
the protection of Walsall Museum in 1993. By 1999 this museum was
planning new displays and a publication which will build on research by
Emma Bryan in 1998. This shows, unexpectedly, that the ready-to-wear
goods sold here were in fact largely too costly for local women in the
interwar period. Instead, the Hodson sisters' clientele came from a wider
geographical area of somewhat better-off customers, though even so many
paid for their garments by instalment.[24] A Lottery award will ensure the
future of this collection but for many museums, short of funds and short
of staff, both finding and purchasing collectable clothing are increasingly
becoming a game of chance.

Identification: 'charting ... the addition or deletion of every flounce, pleat, button and bow'

Once collected, clothing has to be identified. A new and eager volunteer
once asked how it was possible to differentiate by date between pairs in
a jumbled box of similar-looking nineteenth-century women's shoes. The
only possible answer was that dating was dependent upon the term used
so dismissively by Fine and Leopold: 'concentration on every flounce, pleat,
button and bow'. The acquisition of identification skills is a never-ending
learning process and is one of the real pleasures of working as a costume
curator. The challenge is constant both because few garments are ever the
same and because dating mistakes are easy to make. The consumption of
styles lasts far longer in reality than fashion journals ever indicate.

With memory also sometimes an unreliable source, analysis of the
construction and making-up techniques used in clothing and garment
manufacture can certainly help pin down dating. The 'minute detail', which
Fine and Leopold find so boring, is precisely what does in fact give the
required period identification which in turn provides the basis upon which
cultural theory can later be viably applied.

Janet Arnold discussed this in her *Handbook of Costume*, published in
1973,[25] where she explains methods of dating costume from its construction
and sewing techniques. The dater will also need to know when machine
stitching became common, when hooks, eyes, poppers, zips, steel boning,
overlocking, specific fabric types and so on, all came into use, as well as
learning all the minutiae of the cut of fashionable and unfashionable dress.
Naomi Tarrant, of the National Museums of Scotland, Edinburgh, is another
dress historian who stresses the need for an in-depth knowledge of cut
and construction. Both in her 1994 book, *The Development of Costume*, and
in the clothing gallery she created at the National Museum of Scotland in

Edinburgh, she explains the whole process of making clothing, from raw material through cut and construction through to manufacture. Tarrant is consciously using this strongly artefact-based approach as a counterweight to academic approaches where she believes 'clothing studies are contorted to fit some theory without a basic understanding of the properties of cloth and the structure of clothes'.[26]

Arnold and Tarrant's work argues that the shape of a sleeve or even the size of buttons do in fact matter if a garment is to be dated and 'read' properly and that there are no short cuts to the process of learning the cyclical styling of men's and women's clothes, from whatever culture they may be drawn. Assumptions can otherwise be far too easily and dangerously made. McKendrick, using Braudel as his source, for example, seems convinced that 'in Japan, the *kimono* and the *jinbaori* remained virtually unchanged for centuries'.[27] Yet an artefact-based scholar, such as Alan Kennedy, is able to accurately date different periods of kimono design and making because 'there are overlaps and transitions between styles'.[28] These subtle but actual differences centre on elements such as sleeve length and the decorative technique used on the fabric. Artefact study reveals that these never were the style-static garments that McKendrick–Braudel indicate.

Through a detailed examination of the gender variations between the dress of Kalabari men and women, Susan O. Michelman and Tonye V. Erekosima have shown that in this part of Nigeria 'men's dress emphasizes power and social responsibility' whilst 'women's dress draws attention to moral and physical development'. This, they add, 'demonstrates that the contrast of male and female prescribed dress hierarchies relates to this people's interpretation of physical maturity and gendered social roles developed within the context of the Kalabari cultural system'.[29]

Ethnographers with interest in peasant clothing such as Edit Fel and Charles Viski in Hungary can date and identify the exact origins of hundreds of different types of embroidered blouses made by Romanian/Hungarian peasantry which barely look different to the unskilled eye.[30] Susan Conway has exposed a nearly lost eighteenth- and nineteenth-century textile culture from Lan Na in North Thailand. Through meticulous analysis of weaving, embroidery technique, garment styles, temple wall paintings, period photographs and Thai manuscripts and archives, she is able properly to classify textiles once wrongly labelled as 'Burmese' or 'Siamese'.[31]

Following up every possible clue to be found within surviving garments is thus essential within the processes of identification. Dates can be traced, for example, through makers' labels. Where no biography of a garment exists or where dates need to be confirmed, makers' and shop labels can sometimes be useful. To give just one example, the dating of a highly unusual black wedding dress from Aberdeen was confirmed by this method.

Miss Elspeth Brown married Andrew Watt, a farmer from Aberdeen, in 1888. The family story is that her father had died six weeks before the wedding and consequently Miss Brown married in black. A black wedding dress is very rare because this use of full black for a bride was either a defiance of, or more likely a misunderstanding of, socially correct mourning-wedding dress codes. These ruled that such a bride should marry in white with veil, but with black stitching on the back seams of her gloves as the only indication of mourning.

It may well be that Miss Brown could not afford to marry in full white bridal attire, a common enough occurrence, in which case a serviceable plain grey, bottle green or dark brown costume would have been considered the decent and respectable colour to wear. The family story insists, however, that Miss Brown did marry in this black silk bodice and skirt and dating this garment to near the wedding day was therefore vital for verification of the story. It was the label that provided the confirmation. The costume was made by *Andrew Cameron, 19–21 Broad Street*. Street directories indicate that the firm was only at that address from 1888–89.[32]

Interestingly, when using couture dress labels in this same way even more care needs to be taken. After researching Worth couture clothes of the 1860–1900 period in great depth for her Brooklyn Museum exhibition of 1990, *The Opulent Era, Fashions of Worth, Doucet and Pingat*, Elizabeth Ann Coleman warned of the dangers of over-reliance on labels. She had discovered that even then, because of fraudulent copying by other dressmakers, 'among the genuine labels of the 1880s there lurk several suspicious specimens in which neither the quality and cast of the label nor the garments to which it is attached have an authentic air'.[33] When Paul Poiret went to New York in 1913 on the invitation of a 5th Avenue dressmaker he was astonished and furious at the vast amounts of bogus copies of his designs he found in New York, calling this 'the fraudulent side of commerce'. For good financial return, when he was short of money after the First World War, Poiret did, however, license some designs out for the manufacture of specific accessories.[34] Thus a surviving picture hat of 1921, made of natural horsehair trimmed with yellow and white flowers, reveals a licensed manufacturer's label, 'Paul Poiret à Paris, Joseph, New York'.[35]

The oldest label found by Elizabeth Ann Coleman, then Curator of Costume at Brooklyn Museum, was on the petersham waistband of an early 1860s flesh-coloured silk moiré dress. For many years its skirt and two bodices had become separated, but when finally put back together it was clear that this outfit was composed of 'evening and day bodices and a coordinating skirt. The label read *Mme. Olympé*, "a notable New Orleans dressmaker, milliner and general fashion merchandise importer"'. Coleman was curious to know whether, 'because of her frequent buying trips to Paris', this dressmaker was the first in the United States to name-stamp the garments she sold in this way.[36] Labels are sometimes placed in unexpected places. The identification of an Elsa Schiaparelli dress owned by the Museum of Brighton was only discovered when a small label was found stitched on the selvedge edge of a side seam right down at the hemline. This slim mid-1930s black silk evening dress, donated by the family of Lord Gage of Firle Place, Sussex, has a bold print of ballet dancers on a black ground. When imaginatively placed on a Surrealist-inspired mannequin designed by Michael Jones, this dress became the highlight of the museum's fashion gallery which opened in 1981 and closed in 2000 (Plate II).

Attention to minute detail is also vital because styles are so constantly recycled from one period to another – 'post-modern' design has always existed in the world of fashion. The Farebrother family were convinced that a gown in their family collection, in vertically striped Regency-style cotton lawn cut in high waisted Empire style, had to date from the early nineteenth century. Examination soon showed that it was a machine-stitched, early twentieth-century tea-gown, made just when there was a popular Regency revival. The garment was nonetheless interesting and collectable but made one hundred years later.[37]

Identification therefore requires a wide range of specific skills and historical, object-based knowledge. Without examination of this minutiae of raw material, making up and style dating becomes all too easily suspect and prone to error.

Clothing condition

The problem of wear and tear is a serious difficulty when collecting dress and condition is always a critical consideration. Accidental disasters stem from innocent attempts to clean old garments. Delicate wools are matted by washing and brocaded silks washed until colours bleed into watery rainbows. Other typical disasters are caused by the deliberate cutting out of sections of skirts or the centre back of dresses to make cushions and handkerchiefs. Such badly damaged items are not accepted unless they date from the eighteenth century or earlier.

Increasingly, however, some types of altered clothes would now be welcome in recognition of the social and cultural insights that alterations can give us. Igor Kopytoff has stressed the importance of learning about the personal cultural biographies of things, a process which 'can make salient what might otherwise remain obscure'[38] (see Chapter 3). His debate vindicates the 'minute details' approach because detailed analysis of the actuality of clothing can blow apart stereotypic assumptions. Three examples will suffice here to confirm the value of this method.

The first concerns Court dress. There is a commonly held myth that women moving within Court society in eighteenth-century Europe discarded their fashionable clothes on a seasonal basis. Whereas this may have been true at the most elite level of the French Court at Versailles, it certainly was not so in London. In the eighteenth century the cost of certain types of brocaded silks was exorbitant. Even women moving in Court circles in Britain could not afford to (or perhaps also for personal taste reasons chose not to) buy new clothes on a frequent basis. Pamela Clabburn found that Mrs Papendiek, Assistant Keeper of the Royal Wardrobe, made alterations to the same silk dress over a period of twelve years.[39] Janet Arnold (who died in 1999) was a specialist in the analysis of sixteenth- to eighteenth-century garments of both sexes.[40] She was also able to demonstrate from close examination of alterations that the active life of an embroidered ivory silk mantua dating from 1740–45 may have been as long as forty years. It has been altered 'at the waistline at least three times' and was worn again as late as the 1770–80 period.[41]

The second example concerns the remaking of clothing for sentimental

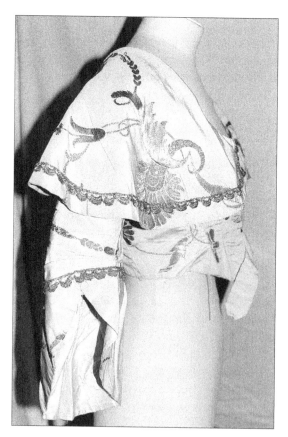

4 Bodice of Court presentation dress of Louisa Chambers in silk of 1742–43, restyled in 1846

reasons. Brighton Museum has a Court presentation dress made of a white Spitalfields silk with a large gilt-metal brocaded flower design. Natalie Rothstein dated this to 1742–43. The skirt and bodice were kept with care within the family until it was restyled one hundred years later in 1846 (Figure 4). It was then worn by Miss Louisa Chambers, daughter of Dr Chambers, whose patients included Queen Victoria and Elizabeth Barratt Browning. Miss Chambers wore the dress to a formal Drawing Room presentation to Queen Victoria. Notes from the young debutante's diary, provided when the dress was presented to the museum in 1974, read: 'we began to dress about 11. o'clock – dress our hair and put on the feathers, ... practising with great long sheets held up behind us'.[42] Her presentation train and Court feathers have not survived. There are indications that this much loved dress may have been altered again in the 1870s.

The last example is Indian woven cashmere, French or Paisley shawls, which were remade into dresses and gowns after they went out of fashion around 1870. This remaking lasted in fashionable society right through to about 1900. In 1999, the *Musée de la Mode de la Ville de Paris* at Palais Galliera, Paris, showed a group of luxury outer garments for women made up from shawls woven in Paris from the 1820s to the 1850s. Their exhibition *Cachemire parisiens: 1810–1880*, curated by Monique Lévi-Strauss, featured a most beautiful display of evening and day wear jackets, pelisses, coats and tea-gowns remade between 1870 and 1890. Many were 'augmented with fringing, braiding and embroidery where the old met the new'. A bustle-backed *visite* of about 1872, for example, was reworked from a precious 1835–40 Paris shawl. Blue and yellow silk fringe and tiny embroidered flowers were added to unify the join where the original woven borders were sewn on to the new grey serge cloth of the new garment, just as described by Lévi-Strauss.[43] The Metropolitan Museum in New York owns an imposing French tea-gown of about 1895 made from pieced panels of a black, orange and grey shawl, woven in Paisley, Scotland, in the 1860–70 period.[44]

Clearly none of these sophisticated reworkings were the result of dire poverty, but close examination of clothing often does reveal alterations undertaken for economic reasons. Indeed such alterations were basic to the wardrobes of working-class and many middle-class women in Europe and North America through to the mid-1950s. Unfortunately all too little of such clothing survives in museum collections. Wartime shortages also trigger the urgent need to alter and remake clothing. An important aspect of the whole social history of British women during the Second World War is exposed through examination of alterations to surviving wartime clothes. Vast numbers of garments were made up from unexpected fabrics – curtains, bedcovers, wall maps, parachutes, blackout sheeting and men's clothes. This was partly as a result of the Government's *Make Do and Mend* campaign, but more probably was simply also an extension of normal working-class practice.[45] Worthing Museum has long owned an extraordinary dressing gown made from a large, rather stiffly gummed printed silk wall map of North Indo-China.[46] Many of these garments came to light as a result of commemoration exhibitions held in 1944–45 to mark the ending of the Second World War. The Warwickshire Museums exhibition *We Wore What We Had* unearthed biographical histories of a winter coat made from a blanket and a skirt from sailor's white cotton trousers and a belt made from cellophane.[47]

Dress curators now recognise that drawing up the 'biography' of altered clothes in this way can sometimes be even more culturally and socially revealing than collecting pristine garments. Ann Wise, Assistant Curator at Worthing Museum, East Sussex, set in place a rare and broad-minded collecting policy at least ten years ago. She accepts altered clothing into her collection without qualm if it fills date gaps and if she feels it makes useful social comment.[48]

Conservation and storage of clothing artefacts

Once clothes have become 'detached' from their wearers and placed for safe keeping in collections they take on quite different semiotic characteristics. As static and empty vessels, they immediately become displaced 'objects' taking on a second life as venerable, valuable and treasured icons. They acquire a new mystique and a new life. Conserved at vast expense, they are wrapped and stored in dust free, air-conditioned environments if they are lucky and then measured and catalogued by experts with extraordinary patience and specialised skills.

The conservation of dress and textiles has become a sophisticated field in its own right involving scientists, specialist professionals and a whole support system of international conferences and publications. Textile and clothing conservation allies highly specific scientific/conservation procedures with patient application of the most delicate of hand skills. Most textile conservators are women and not a few feel their profession to be marginalised into a clichéd corner labelled 'women's work'. The field of textile conservation, as that of the costume curator, has developed outwith the circles of academia and conservators find explaining to the academic world that they do not merely launder and mend old clothes an uphill struggle. Textile and clothing conservation research is published in the *Museums' Association Journal, the Centre International des Textiles Anciens, Textile History, Dress, Costume* and the special publications issued by the Costume Committee of the International Committee of Museums.[49]

In the conservation world, as in fine art and architectural restoration programmes, one 'good practice' debate centres on the extent of the restoration process. Should damage be completely 'repaired' so garments and fabrics look complete again or should damaged areas be left exposed or clearly identifiable? Sarah Lowengard, a textile conservator based in New York, believes that with enough funding available most textile and clothing could be 'restored' to virtually its original condition. No matter how ancient, grounds can in very many cases be dyed and woven to a perfect match and embroidery re-created in perfect simulation of the original. Lowengard has noticed that whilst many private collectors and dealers have a leaning towards this policy, museums would see such extensive 'accurate' reproduction as veering far too heavily towards re-creating rather than conserving fabrics and clothing. Lowengard emphasises that the internationally accepted policy is that 'there should be no attempt at deception'.[50]

This was indeed the conservation policy adopted at the Pitti Palace, Florence, for the rescuing of a rare Spanish doublet and paned trunk hose of crimson satin and velvet, complete with its matching codpiece decorated with gilt metal thread. This had been discovered during an archaeological exhumation in 1947 of the grave of Don Garzia de Medici. The garment dates from 1562. Photographs show the clothes as a crumbled, tattered heap of rags. After years of conservation the garments unfortunately still 'remained in a very precarious state'. A conservation solution was reached when Janet Arnold drew up an accurate pattern and made a toile of the garments. This filled in the missing pieces. A special stand was then built up from this pattern in conservationally acceptable ethafoam and the conserved garments were finally stitched on to this to give 'the required support in order to prolong its future life'.[51] The garment now looks 'whole' and its style can be studied, yet conserved sections are clearly identifiable.

Once conserved, clothing has to be stored safely. The storage of textiles has become another specialist field and is yet another costly process. Looking after a clothing collection throws up immediate problems because garments are at such rapid risk of damage from light, dampness, dryness, moths, dirt, heat. If garments are left suspended on badly designed hangers, they will suffer damage from tearing. Some textile types can even suffer damage from lying flat. Many are so large that they have to be rolled and then stored in such a way that no pressure is exerted on delicate fibres. The very passage of time wreaks havoc which can turn fabrics into mouldering rag heaps or dry ashes. The ideal environment for clothes and textiles is to be safely wrapped in acid free tissue paper, *Tyvec* or calico and kept, gently hung on padded hangers, rolled or placed flat in roomy drawers, in well-ventilated spaces suffused with purified air and in the dark. Fur has to be kept at temperatures below freezing to kill off moths and 'woolly bear' mite infestations.

All this has involved the development of specific storage methods and related 'furniture'. Most museum stores are sadly unable to match the standards set, for example, by the McCord Museum in Montreal. In their air-conditioned textile storage hall, dresses are hung on a conveyer belt fixed to the ceiling with each precious garment gently hung in its own conservationally proper calico bag. At the touch of a button, the hanging line of suspended treasures swings along on its tracks like passengers in a railway carriage waiting to disembark at the correct station. Because of the deep financial restrictions so long impacting on museums, and not only in Britain, most costume stores are far from this calibre though all take professional care as best they can of their precious garments.

Curators are thus tempted to accept damaged artefacts only if the objects are exceptionally unusual or old. Sometimes damage permits a useful view of a garment's construction. Brighton Museum has a woman's cloak, donated by Lady Holford, dating from about 1820–30. In olive green silk, its canary yellow lining has shredded so badly that the inner white cotton padding is visible. This view makes it clear that the garment was hand quilted once the entire cloak had been made up (Figure 5).[52]

5 Early nineteenth-century cloak with damage revealing the inner cotton padding

Conclusion

What does infuriate curators and conservators is to have their professional skills so summarily dismissed by theorists from other fields as merely descriptive or narrow. Tarrant feels strongly that the shoe is on the other foot and that 'a little knowledge of weaving and dressmaking might have made some works' (covering the social history and cultural theory of clothing) 'more relevant to clothing studies'.[53] As Alexandra Palmer, the E. Vaughan Fashion/Costume Curator of the Royal Ontario Museum, Toronto, comments, costume curatorial work is

> very labour intensive and expensive, both on staff time and on mounts. We require it rotates so it is even more problematic, as we are always dealing with it … This is rarely addressed, so in terms of museum budgets, staff etc, we are problematic, expensive and demanding. We do have to reiterate this all the time – the material is delicate, fugitive and demanding and, of course, compelling.[54]

Notes

1 B. Fine and E. Leopold, *The World of Consumption* (Routledge, London, 1993), p. 94.

2 Ibid.

3 N. Tarrant, *The Development of Costume* (Routledge, London, 1994), p. 12.

4 Brighton Museum, the Beck Collection.

5 Correspondence, August 1999; see the Burrell Collection E1975. 107, nos 2 and 1, with thanks to Liz Arthur.

6 C. Beaton, *Fashion: an anthology* (Victoria and Albert Museum, London, 1971), p. 8.

7 A. Lansdell, Costume In a Local History Museum – Weybridge, Surrey (*Costume*, VII, 1973), p. 73.

8 Brighton Museum, no. H112/78.

9 Brighton Museum, nos C003159 and H45/72, donated by Mrs Scully.

10 A. Hart, Men's Dress, in Rothstein, *Four Hundred Years of Fashion*, p. 51.

11 Interviews with the Farebrother family in 1976. Brighton Museum nos H1–23/78.

12 V. D. Mendes, Women's Dress since 1900, in N. Rothstein (ed.), *Four Hundred Years of Fashion* (Victoria and Albert Museum, London, 1984), p. 78.

13 Victoria and Albert Museum, nos T38 and 38A. 1960 and T31. 1960.

14 Victoria and Albert Museum, no. T219. 1973; see N. Rothstein, *A Lady of Fashion: Barbara Johnson's album of style and fabrics* (Thames & Hudson, London, 1987).

15 For further details on these mourning fabrics see Lou Taylor, *Mourning Dress: a costume and social history* (Allen and Unwin, London, 1983), pp. 113–117.

16 S. Nicholson, *A Victorian Household* (Barrie and Jenkins, London, 1988).

17 Brighton Museum, Messell Collection, chiffon tea-gown, about 1910, no. C004203 and Sarah Fullerton Monteith Young costume, about 1908, no. C004229.

18 Brighton Museum, Messel Collection, brick red, muslin costume, no. C004225/1–3.

19 Nicholson, *A Victorian Household*, p. 153.

20 Brighton Museum, Messell Collection, two silk evening dresses by Charles James, early 1930s, pink silk, no. C004211 and black and white silk, C004212.1/2.

21 Brighton Museum, nos H. 53/70 (1–9) with thanks to Emma Young.

22 I am grateful to Suzanne Davies for introducing me to this collection in 1988 and to Sheila Shreeve for her generous help compiling details of the Hodson Shop Collection over the last ten years.

23 A. de la Haye, The Dissemination of Design from Haute Couture to Fashionable Ready-to-Wear During the 1920s – with specific reference to the Hodson Dress Shop in Willenhall (*Textile History*, 24. l, 1993), pp. 39–48.

24 E. Bryan, *From Haute Couture to Ready to Wear? An examination of the process of style diffusion within the British ready-to-wear industry, 1925–1930, with specific reference to the Hodson Shop Collection, Walsall Museum* (B.A. Design History dissertation, University of Brighton, 1998).

25 J. Arnold, *A Handbook of Costume* (Macmillan, London, 1973).

26 N. Tarrant, *The Development of Costume* (Routledge, London, 1994), p. 12.

27 N. McKendrick, The Commercialisation of Fashion, in N. McKendrick, J. Brewer and J. H. Plumb, *The Birth of the Consumer Society* (Europa, London, 1982), p. 36.

28 A. Kennedy, *Japanese Costume: history and tradition* (Adam Biro, Paris, 1990), p. 36.

29 S. O. Michelman and T. V. Erekosima, Kalabari Dress in Nigeria: visual analysis and gender implication, in R. Barnes and J. Eicher (eds), *Dress and Gender* (Berg, Oxford, 1993), p. 179.

30 C. Viski, *L'Art Populaire Hongrois* (Department Ethnographique de Musée National Hongrois, Budapest, 1928).

31 S. Conway, *Dress and Cultural Identity: court costume and textiles in nineteenth century Lan Na* (Ph.D. thesis, University of Brighton, 2000).

32 Taylor, *Mourning Dress*, p. 255.

33 E. A. Coleman, *The Opulent Era: fashions of Worth, Doucet and Pingat* (Thames & Hudson, London, and Brooklyn Museum, New York, 1989), p. 109.

34 P. Poiret, *King of Fashion* (Lipincott, London, 1931), pp. 258–259.

35 The Costume Institute, Metropolitan Museum, New York, no. 1982.281.1.

36 Correspondence with E. A. Coleman, 16 September 1996.

37 Brighton Museum, Farebrother Collection, silk tea-gown about 1910, C003145.

38 I. Kopytoff, The Cultural Biography of Things: commoditization as process, in Arjun Appadurai (ed.), *The Social Life of Things: commodities in cultural perspective* (Cambridge University Press, Cambridge, 1986), p. 100.

39 P. Clabburn, Notes and Queries, quoting Court and Private Life in the Time of Queen Charlotte: being the journal of Mrs Papendiek, Assistant Keeper of the Wardrobe and Reader to her Majesty (*Costume*, Victoria and Albert Museum, London, 6, 1972), p. 6.

40 J. Arnold, *Patterns of Fashions: the cut and construction of clothes for men and women,*

1560–1670 (Macmillan, London, 1985), pp. 48–52; idem, *Patterns of Fashions. 1. Englishwomen's dresses and their construction, 1660–1860* (Macmillan, London, 1972, reprint from 1967); idem, *Patterns of Fashions. 2. Englishwomen's dresses and their construction, 1860–1940* (Macmillan, London, 1972, reprint from 1967).

41 J. Arnold, A Court Mantua (*Costume*, Victoria and Albert Museum, London, 7, 1973), pp. 42–46. This dress is in the collection of the Victoria and Albert Museum, no. T260–1969.

42 Brighton Museum, no. C002528.

43 M. Lévi-Strauss, *Cachemires Parisiens, 1810–1880* (Musée Galliera-Musée de la Mode de la Ville de Paris, Paris Musées, Paris, 1999), p. 100 and museum no. 1962.108.111.

44 R. Martin and H. Korda, *Orientalism – visions of the East in Western dress* (The Metropolitan Museum of Art, Harry N. Abrams, New York, 1994), p. 46; museum no. 1985.39.33.

45 See T. Morgan, *An Assessment of the Make Do and Mend Campaign during the Second World War* (B.A. Hons. Design History dissertation, Brighton Polytechnic, 1986).

46 For an illustration see E. Wilson and L. Taylor, *Through the Looking Glass: a history of dress from 1860 to the present day* (BBC Books, London, 1989), p. 115.

47 M. Wood (ed.), *We Wore What We'd Got: women's clothes in World War 2* (Warwickshire Books, Exeter, 1989), pp. 23–28.

48 Interview, May 1999.

49 A. Buck, ICOM Costume Committee – guidelines for costume collections (*Costume*, 24, 1990), pp. 126–128. This contains an excellent recommended reading list of professional publications related to cataloguing, conservation, storage and display.

50 Interview, 22 August 1996.

51 J. Arnold and M. Westerman Bulgarella, An Innovative Method for Mounting the Sixteenth-Century Doublet and Trunk-Hose Worn by Don Grazia de' Medici (*Costume*, 30, 1996), pp. 47–55.

52 Brighton Museum, no. C002998.1/2.

53 Tarrant, *The Development of Costume*, p. 12.

54 Correspondence, 23 February 1999.

2 ✧ Artefact-based approaches: display and interpretation

So real one believes them to be alive. (*Les Modes* 1911)[1]

Display

CLOTHES escape occasionally from their darkened storerooms to be displayed on specially created mannequins in conservationally sound but unnatural gallery environments – but never again to be seen clothing a human body. Display poses enormous problems for the curator. As Buck explains, 'the beauty of dress, always ephemeral, is so closely connected with the living, moving body which wore it and gave it final expression, that a dress surviving, uninhabited, may appear as an elaborate piece of fabric, an accidental repository of the textile arts, but little more'.[2] The whole range of human experience attached to the wearing of clothes is inevitably lost on the static dummy placed behind glass. The challenge for the curator and exhibition designer is to try and revive it.

Display fabrics and conservation issues

Fashion and fashion textile designers have built their reputations on the fusion of malleable textures and colours as their garments move on the wearer. Indeed garments are created specifically around an understanding of the play of light on textures and fabric in motion. The eighteenth-century silk designers of Lyons deliberately placed a subtle variety of sparkling yarns within one single brocaded design element – a leaf or a flower – using their sophisticated technical understanding of the ways in which rays of light would be differently deflected to enhance the glamour of the wearer. Ellis Miller has shown that Lyons spinners became expert in producing gold and silver flat, plaited, coiled and stamped strip and spun yarns for their famous '*dorures*' cloths. These fabrics which were used in the most costly of all Lyons silks '*les fond or et argent riches*' were for formal Court and church occasions.[3] Brighton Museum has just such an example, dating from the mid-1740s which features large bouquets and meanders woven into purple and variegated gilded yarns on a sky blue ground (Plate III). Arnold also noted this same sparkle effect on a delphinium blue and silver mantua dress of 1760–65 now in the collection at the Metropolitan Museum, New York. She marvelled at the interplay of light between silver thread and flat silver strip used in this design which gives a special 'feeling of depth and texture to each motif ... giving the appearance of beaten silver'.[4]

This highly crafted Lyonnais skill was maintained still within Michel Dubost's famous gilded poppy designs of the mid-1920s, woven into the floppiest of French silk crêpes. Huge drooping poppy heads glint in dull gold on purple or orange silken grounds. Colette wrote that these designs were 'as miraculous as a rainbow, and as beautiful as the eye of an octopus'.[5] In the 1990s the success of *devoré* velvets made from high sheen rayons again revived a vogue for glistering fashion fabrics.

Charles Worth was so convinced of the importance of this play of light upon his evening dresses that his Faubourg St Honoré salon contained a darkened mock-up ballroom, where he could examine the effect of gaslight on his finished creations in the daytime. The walls of his *salon de lumiére* were hung with huge mirrors. 'Hissing gas jets with movable shades lighted the place brilliantly. The lady who there tried on her new *toilette de bal* was seen as she would be seen the following night in the Tuileries.'[6] Lucien Lelong, who introduced many new commercial ideas into his successful couture salon in Paris in the interwar period, revived this sales method in the mid-1920s. During his afternoon shows heavy curtains covered the windows of his salon and an intensity of illumination was achieved with

> batteries of blue tinted gas-filled bulbs which illuminate the stage. It is artificial day-light. Every hue and shade of her gown comes out in its correct tone. Every Lelong gown that is to be worn by day-light is shown in such lighting. When evening gowns come to be displayed ordinary incandescent lights are substituted for the blue ones.[7]

These manufacturers and designers all understood that it takes strong light levels to reveal this carefully created glimmer. However, since conservation-correct museum lighting levels preclude the extended exposure of all fabrics to powerful light these glisters become lost altogether in display. What can the curator do when fabrics fade so very fast under such strong light? Not much, is the answer, when according to the accepted professional standards issued by the International Committee of Museums, a dim level 50 lux is all that is permitted to avoid permanent damage.[8] One solution, as practised by the *Musée de la Mode et du Costume* in the

Palais Galliera, Paris, and by the Fashion Institute of Technology in New York, amongst others, is to hold two temporary exhibitions a year to ensure that precious clothing is never displayed for more than a few months. Even then their lighting levels are dim.

One unusual solution was put in place when Brighton Museum showed their *Mariano Fortuny* exhibition in 1980. The essence of Fortuny's *delphos* dresses and gilded velvets lies in their soft sheen and subtle colour ranges. Proust famously wrote of one Fortuny dress that 'it changed into malleable gold by those same transmutations which before the advancing gondolas, change into flowing metal the azure of the Grand Canal'.[9] Without extra light, there was little sign of 'malleable gold', so small torches were lent to visitors. Many enjoyed watching the fabrics come to life as they played light beams over the gleaming fabrics. In general, however, there seems little that the curator can do to lift the gloomy impression left by conservationally sound dress displays, except to try and educate the viewing public into a more sympathetic understanding of the problem (Figure 11, p. 44).

Display and body movement

The issue of fabric weight and texture in movement is another major design characteristic lost in static displays, where the impact of extra heavy or very fine fabric movement is completely and inevitably lost. The very stiffness enforced on actors in the Japanese Noh theatre by their many layers of decorative silks, for example, is lost in static display of these complex *kosode*. The soft flow in movement of very fine light fabrics, such as silks, chiffons, veiling, pleating and soft feathers is lost too in static display. These have a delicacy in movement relished by designers which is entirely lost on static stands where their cobwebby folds hang limply and forlornly. Thus much of the sophistication of cut and drape of the work of Mmes Vionnet and Grès will never be seen to full advantage through the plate glass of museum cases. Bruce Chatwin was fascinated by the innovative geometric cut of Vionnet's 'tubes of flimsy white material' of the 1920s and 1930s which so confused clients that they 'used to telephone in panic when they could not understand how to put a dress on'. Chatwin commented of Vionnet's work that 'she wanted the body to show itself through the dress. The dress was to be a second or more seductive skin, which smiled when its wearers smiled.'[10] Pity the poor curator trying to re-create all that on a plaster or fibreglass dummy.

Brooklyn Museum, New York, pioneered a moving *Costume Theater* in the late 1960s, where costume figures could be seen 'walking' across a stage. The original concept was proposed by the Museum's Director, Thomas S. Buechner. Elizabeth Ann Coleman, now Curator of Costume at the

Museum of Fine Arts in Boston, worked on this project between 1969 and 1972. Period music and projected slide images of fashionable and historical events were used to help set the time-frame of between 1790 and 1970. Over fifty mannequins, 'fully dressed, appeared from darkness on a V-bend on a conveyer belt track', driven by a one-half horsepower motor. The figures stood 'on circular pallets, thus allowing the audience a two-third view of the garments. The audience sat on carpeted, stepped bleachers.' Coleman remembers that 'the public loved the *Costume Theater*' and that they had even applauded these fibreglass dummies. The *Costume Theater* was closed after Coleman left the museum.[11]

Issey Miyake's *Pleats Please* collections dating from 1993 always cause problems in display. Their heat-set polyester pleats move in an extraordinarily beautiful way, collapsing on themselves like the leaves of folding fans. When a black, grey and white pleated Miyake dress was shown on a static mannequin in the Metropolitan Museum's *East/West* exhibition in New York in 1989 it was transformed in its stillness into a beautiful but stratified stone sculpture and its *raison d'être* was entirely lost.[12] However, when Miyake showed his own clothes at his *Making Things* exhibition at the *Centre Cartier*, Paris, in 1998, he created a sensational moving setting for his latest garments. Perhaps in the early twenty-first century this would, more properly be called 'installation art' rather than a fashion display. Miyake here made certain that the concertina-like flexibility so central to his woven fabrics took centre stage. In a vast, empty, glass-walled space, he suspended his garments from the ceiling on long wires. As visitors entered the hall, their body movement triggered electric pulses. These caused the garments to drop from the ceiling at high speed, like dozens of merry bungee jumpers, making the pleats and ruffles contract and extend as they would on the human body. The impact was funny, witty and clever, revealing the subtle delicacies of Miyake's fashion fabrics.

The Victoria and Albert Museum also addressed the problem in 1999. In 1997–98 Amy de La Haye and Claire Wilcox of the Dress and Textiles department at the Victoria and Albert Museum ran a series of immensely successful study days connected to the museum's own exhibition *The Cutting Edge – forty years of British couture fashion* and with the Craft Council's *Satellites of Fashion*, their first exhibition of avant-garde fashion accessories. Young designers were invited to present the creative ideas behind their latest collections, through lectures, often with videos and even live fashion shows to sell-out audiences. Recognising the popular appeal of this approach, which also related to a policy set on modernising the 'image' of the museum, from the summer of 1999 a *Fashion in Motion* project was launched. This abandoned the use of static models altogether. Live models walked around the museum galleries wearing clothes and hats by

designers whose work was represented in the museum collection. Eager
visitors followed the models, delighted to be able to catch close-up views
of the models and of the work of Philip Treacy, Anthony Price, Shirin
Gild and Alexander McQueen, amongst others. Claire Wilcox explained
that 'the aim is to convey the energy of fashion as performance and to
reveal the beauty of contemporary fashion to a public that is used to
seeing fashion in magazines but has rarely seen such ensembles – or
models – in the flesh'.[13]

Ironically, just as models perambulated the galleries of the Victoria
and Albert Museum in his creations, Alexander McQueen caused a sensation
in Paris by displaying his entire autumn/winter 2000 couture collection
on static models rather than on the backs of the usual supermodels.
Susannah Frankel reported in *The Independent* on 19 July 1999 that

> his haute couture collection for the House of Givenchy was shown on
> showroom mannequins with gleaming Plexiglass heads, which emerged
> from holes in the floor on rotating turntables ... The atmosphere resembled
> nothing more than a cool and serene museum exhibit.

In *The Guardian* on the same day, Laura Craik commented that 'the
spectacle was riveting ... Never have dummies looked so alive ... lending
a futuristic slant to a collection inspired by history.' Believing that the press
attention devoted to fashion models distracts attention from his designs,
McQueen returned to the same static mannequins used by his forebears in
the eighteenth and nineteenth centuries, except that his were constructed
with transparent plexiglass heads rather than wood, sawdust and beeswax.
These were later used in his new London boutique in Conduit Street.

The latest transatlantic trend in static display design is the development
of conservationally correct, hollow mannequins, each shaped to the exact
measurements of the inner layer of the garment it will 'wear'. Headless,
armless and characterless, these are seen as resolving all the old difficulties
of inaccuracy and 'dressing up', when used alongside supporting period
and textual material.

Display and issue of period body stance

Period size, shape and body stance are further basic display problems for
the display designer-curator. Garments come in every shape and size. It is
not a given fact that Victorian women had seventeen-inch waists. Langley
Moore expended many words, as far back as 1949, trying to expose this
myth in her book *Women in Fashion*[14] even going as far as drawing a
seventeen-inch circle to show how tiny and unrealistic this was. In fact,
many dresses survive worn by large men and women, but these are rarely

displayed by censoring curators because they create a far less elegant image than slim-line figures.

Every garment put on display has to be fitted individually to its own display stand. This in turn has to be designed with a matching stance because every period and every culture has its own identifiable way of standing, walking or sitting. This forms an absolutely integral part of the 'look' of the time. If dress stands do not reflect this accurately the clothing will simply look 'wrong'.

Women in fashionable European society were expected always to be gracious, delicate and 'feminine' in their body stance and movement – and indeed on balance still are. Examples of the impact of clothing on body stance within our own memory span are easy to spot: for example, the effect of high-heeled shoes, which displace the natural angle of the spine, throw the shoulders forward and bottom outwards, unless the wearer makes conscious efforts to stand particularly straight. Models learn to walk with elegance in their catwalk stilettos, but few of us will forget Mrs Thatcher's famous walk, with head and shoulders forward and bottom out – probably engineered by her high heels. In the mid-eighteenth century, etiquette-conscious men walked with their calves turned out to display their elegant calves. In the 1920s it was not enough for a stylish woman to cut off her hair, lose a good few stones and wear a waistless shift. She also had to adopt a specific form of curved spinal slouch when standing although not when sitting, or the entire chic effect was ruined.

Dress stands and the history of museum display

There are two fundamental issues in the construction of dress display stands for museums – the first is that conservation considerations should be paramount and the second centres on the long-running design debate of 'realism versus stylisation'. The problems and costs of re-creating period body stance in plaster, plastic, wood or fibreglass can well be appreciated. Arms and legs must come off so that fragile clothing is not damaged as figures are dressed. Surfaces must be scrupulously clean, pollutant free and often require to be soft so that elements of clothing can be stitched into place.

Four basic types of dress mannequins have been used for the exhibition of period clothing – the artist's lay figure which was usually of wood with jointed body parts and movable fingers and head, the wax display figure, commercial exhibition and retail mannequins and, finally, the specially created museum mannequin. All four types have an interrelated display history centred around venues of popular entertainment, fashion retailing and museum exhibitions.

Of specific interest, as Bronner and Leach have shown, are the close links between commercial retailing display, international exhibition design and developments in museum displays in late nineteenth- and early twentieth-century Europe and the USA. George Brown Goode, for example, the supervisor of exhibitions for the Smithsonian Institution's museum display at *The Centennial Exhibition* in Philadelphia in 1876 was already borrowing from the latest commercial methods used in the showcases of the great department stores.[15] The display of both historic and contemporary clothing proved to be a major success at all these great public venues and this in turn encouraged the development of ever-more enticing display methods. The same fundamental design display debate of 'realism versus stylisation' was to be found in all these contexts.

Artists' lay figures

Aileen Ribeiro has researched the figures used by artists in their work. Some were dolls' size and a few of these have survived, such as the one belonging to Arthur Devis, which is in the Harris Museum and Art Gallery in Preston, together with its 'two Hussar costumes and other small items of dress'. Artists also used basic, full-sized figures, 'generally of wood or cork and sometimes with movable brass joints'. Ribeiro recounts the use of a lay figure in Reynolds's studio in 1772, for draping the Garter Robes used in the portrait of the Duke of Cumberland. 'Grand and elaborate costume of this kind necessitated far more time than the noble owners had at their disposal, and of course it had to be accurate.'[16] The lay figure stood in the Duke's place, helping the artist (whether Reynolds himself or a drapery painter is not known), to catch the texture, detail and light on the garments. These mannequins were simple figures designed for the use of artists with no intent to add allure in the manner of a fashion mannequin.

Commercial display mannequins

According to Riotor's study of 1900, *Le Mannequin*, commercial fashion-related dressmaker and shop display dummies have been manufactured since the eighteenth century. They were originally of willow. Riotor noted that by the middle of the nineteenth century the design of mannequins had responded

> to the vagaries of fashion, with high or low busts, long or short waists, with or without hips ... willow or wire dress dummies really came into their own. It was a period of body deformation – Eugenie was very short-

waisted, a shape copied widely. The mannequin manufacturer, Lavigne, sought out the advice of Mme. Conneau, the wife of the Emperor's doctor to learn the exact shape to be copied.

Between 1869 and 1900 the French firm of Stockman developed more than twenty different series of dressmaker-type forms following body shapes dictated by the great couture houses.[17] *Grabam and Co.* of Goodge Street, London, were selling dress stands in 1884, 'peculiarly adapted and so essentially necessary for making a dress stylishly'. With frames of strong wire complete with wooden ebonised poles, telescopic and revolving features, some had India rubber bodies and all could be personalised to the customer's exact body shape.[18] Shop windows became ever more crammed with ranked displays of these headless dressmaker-style manne-quins in the 1870–1900 period.

By the time of the International Health Exhibition in South Kensington in 1884 the fashionable feminine shape dictated hourglass torsos and extremely rigid, exaggerated bustles. This was when public debate about 'body deformation' was at its height, fuelled by the Dress Reform Movement. The journal, *The Queen*, covered the exhibition's display of historical clothing but it also commented on the displays of hygienic and rational dress and the range of contemporary fashions, which ran in style from contemporary waterproofs to the latest couture garments. The journal complained that 'Messrs. Worth furnish a text for hygienic sermons in the lay figure on which is displayed their handsome evening dress. The waist is certainly terribly suggestive of displaced and maltreated internal organs, and far from beautiful in shape.'[19]

By 1900, as middle-class consumption levels continued to escalate, the design of such display mannequins was swept into the competitive rivalry between couture salons and the grandest department stores of the great cities of Europe and the USA. The commercial effectiveness of glamorous and seductive retail display was well understood by then. In America, L. Frank Baum, author of *The Land of Oz*, 'articulated the new ideas on display urging merchants to rid their windows of clutter and crowding, to treat their goods aesthetically, to immerse them in colour in light, to place them in the foreground and single them out, and to make them come "alive"'.[20]

In Paris from 1900 and in the USA from 1915, fashion displays in retail windows grew more and more artistically ambitious and mannequin design had to develop to keep pace. Stockman's of Paris fitted their stands with wax heads, natural hair, enamel teeth, glass eyes and fully jointed bodies, although these were still stuffed with sawdust. By 1903 internal clockwork mechanisms could turn a stuffed torso mannequin around and around in the shop windows for three hours without having to be rewound.[21] Some Paris stores featured displays of fashionable everyday life, with mannequins 'dressed in leather to ride in a car, others in evening dress dance the American quadrille. Passers by are amused by these puppet gimmicks, but they stop and they buy.'[22] Leach identifies this quest for realism as an attempt 'to invest artificial and material things, whole urban spaces, with plasticity and life, breaking down the barriers between the animate and inanimate'.[23]

The demand for innovation in fashion displays at the great international exhibitions was a trigger for yet more 'animated' designs. At the Paris International Exhibition of 1900, a retrospective historical display of dress and accessories from the period of Louis XV to Napoleon III was shown on headless stands, [24] but this display was totally overshadowed by the sensational success of the display of fifty-two couture garments by the *Collectivité de la Couture*. The houses of Worth and Paquin who made use of the newest super-realistic wax models – 'an idea completely new for the day' – were judged the most successful of all. The Worth display included a lifelike scene of Court presentation and was such an overwhelming popular success that 'the police had to be called in to deal with the crowds which never diminished during the next six months'. In the competitive race between the great couture houses for maximum publicity, Mme Paquin went further, ordering 'a figure of herself in wax and thus the crowd could see her in a beautiful dress and sitting at her own silver toilette'.[25]

Paquin next amazed the international public in 1911 at the height of the vogue for revival of classical and oriental-inspired chiffon draperies. Her Turin International Exhibition display was set in her own *Pavilion Paquin*. From the outside it looked like a little Greek temple complete with pillars and classical friezes. The interior was furnished and arranged as if an elegant high society soirée was in full progress crowded with the most elegant of Parisiennes. The reporter for *Les Modes* asked 'who are these dancers frozen in mid step, whose aigrette feathers and veils tremble in the warm evening air, but whose fans rest still in immobile hands, whose mouths smile soundlessly, and whose eyes are fixed on far distant visions, as if hypnotised?' Nothing but wax mannequins was the answer but 'so real that one believes them to be alive'.[26]

These were no ordinary wax mannequins but the latest designs by Pierre Inman who was awarded a first prize at Turin for these beauteous, sexually confident creatures, articulated at waist and arms – hence the graceful dancing poses. He gave them names, just as the couturier Lucile had renamed her own live mannequins. Inman's *Annie, Lucile, Roberte, Elyane, Linette* all had perfect natural hair set into their wax scalps.[27] The success of Paquin's display was instant. Huge queues again formed to enter the pavilion and charges were imposed in the hope of reducing the overcrowding.[28]

The cultural impact of these fluidly limbed mannequins reached well beyond the purely commercial. Leach believes that glamorous mannequins such as these

> were perhaps the most radical display fixtures ever to appear in the store window. They helped transform the character of the public female image. Unlike the female statuary of the past, which personified such classical virtues as justice and truth, as well as the domestic virtues of purity and maternal nurture, these figures … invoked individual indulgence in luxury as often as they did traditional domestic behaviour.[29]

Wax models, however, were expensive and required constant repair. As lighting levels were turned up in the retail windows, the problem of melting also reared its head – at 95 degrees Fahrenheit meltdown point was reached. In 1922 Inmans solved this problem with *carnesine*, a plaster and gelatine base which withstood intense heat. The next improvement was a new wax finish, *cira dura*, and by 1933 'peach skin' models increased 'realism' still further.[30]

For a brief while as the fashion mood changed towards modernism, progressive retailers made a significant turn towards stylisation of design, triggered in 1922 by the Director of *Galeries Lafayette*. He was the first to commission young avant-garde sculptor-designers to work on fashion display figures. Yani Paris designed mannequins for this store with a 'gaunt, sinewy silhouette whilst the Modernist designer, René Herbst, who was deeply involved in the design of the Paris 1925 exhibition produced a very simple carved plank stand with detachable arms and head. Tag Gronberg has noted the interest shown in such *mannequin de l'étalage* at the Paris 1924 *Salon d'Automne* where Siégal and Inmans displayed their latest models. These mannequins even became icons of the modernity of the 1920s fashionable woman. Guillaume Janneau argued strongly in favour of radically modernist styling in his review of this exhibition.

> Yet another new art, that of mannequins; one tires of those frightful wax cadavers, disturbing facsimiles … Certain gilded mannequins have been condemned. Why this restriction to the possibilities of stylisation? Aren't these [figures] all the more arresting for their lack of verisimilitude?

Gronberg argues that 'the rhetoric of *publicité* invoked the non-figurative tendencies of avant-garde art in order to justify the erasure of the female face and to claim this eradication as modern'. Thus, she explains, stylisation was claimed as the means of 'shifting attention from female body to commodity so that the discourse of *publicité* proposed yet another "physiognomy" of the modern'.[31]

At the Paris International Exhibition of 1925, still further progress was made. Much comment was heard on the design of the mannequins in the *Pavilion de l'Elégance* where the great couturiers showed their designs. Whilst the House of Worth, by then starting its decline, displayed clothes on traditional, pale-skinned, wax figures with natural hair, the more avant-garde salons, such as *Jenny*, selected 'modernist' dummies with boldly sculptured, elongated, chignoned heads and gilded and metalised bodies. The simple fashion silhouette of the 1920s allowed Siégel and Stockman (awarded a gold medal) to cast these all in one piece from a mould of hollow papier mâché. Progressive designers 'abandoned realism and lacquered them uniformly in the same colour as the dress they were to wear in the exhibition: dark red, Tyrian pink and ebony. If they were in *lamé* fabric they were covered with gold and silver powder.'[32] Vionnet, seventy years before Alexander McQueen, demanded transparent mannequins for her display but no method could then be found to produce them.[33]

Autié described this debate as set around 'two irreconcilable mentalities',[34] the realism of the 'traditional' figures versus the stylisation of the new modernist mannequins. *Vogue* loved all these experiments and commented in August 1925 that 'a new art form has been born, the artist has succeeded in evoking the complex personality of the modern well-dressed woman'. All this proved too extreme for most commercial retailing and the trend only survived in major international exhibition displays.

For the design of the couture display in the 1937 Paris International Exhibition, stylisation again won the day. Paris couture clothes were exhibited 'set within a fantastic labyrinth' in a *Temple of Taste*, in the pale blue faience and white lacquered interior of the *Pavilion de la Parure*. Aggressively stylised mannequins, described as elongated, terracotta giants made of roughly finished plaster and oakum more than six feet tall, were commissioned from the young sculptor Couturier. With their arms uplifted in protective poses, they had no refined detail of face or hair (Figure 6). Couturier described them as 'intentionally devoid of any pleasantness, of the gentleness that usually goes with elegance'. This style was said to be effective for some of the more neoclassically draped, fluid evening styles, then much in vogue, but was quite unsuited to display tailored garments. 'I didn't expect such violent reactions', Couturier remembered later. 'There was an enormous scandal and a public demonstration.'[35] Elsa Schiaparelli hated them. 'In some respects they were hideous', she declared, and in protest simply pegged her creations out on a washing line, causing much free publicity for her salon.[36] The British fashion exhibition trailed lamentably behind in the style stakes and was derided by *Women's Wear Daily* for 'the rigid and old fashioned dummies used to display two tailored

6 Mannequins for the *Pavilion d'Elégance* at
the Paris International Exhibition of 1937

suits'. The newspaper noticed that these were 'soon replaced by ones with
more fitting silhouettes and plaster heads'.[37]

By the mid-1930s, however, commercial mannequin design had
switched back to the 'real' and to the 'animate' because increasingly the
period's figure-fitting fashion styles demanded more conventionally shaped
forms. Unlike the waistless 1920s shifts, the more curvaceous 1930s dresses
and suits could not be slipped on easily over the heads of simple stands,
so once again arms had to be removed and body curves replaced. In the
United States, where Hollywood movies exerted a strong popular influence
on fashion, mannequins were modelled to resemble famous movie stars
and 'New York socialites'. This proved to be a far-sighted trend which had
a massive impact in the post-war period on the design of commercial dress

stands. These remained heavily styled towards realism, aided from the 1950s and 1960s by the new technologies of plastic and fibreglass. Sarah Schneider writes that by then two major design advances were the development of figures made 'without the use of a rod and base' and Adel Rootstein's manufacture in 1966 of the Twiggy mannequin.[38] Rootstein built on this success with her Tussaud-style, lifelike figures based on a series of transatlantic fashion icons such as Twiggy, Sandy Shaw, Donyale Luna and Marie Helvin. Rootstein's intent to develop figures of mass popular appeal was no different from Siégel's copying of Empress Eugenie's figure in the 1860s or Mme Tussaud's policy of displaying effigies of the famous to public view.

At the start of the twenty-first century, debate within the fashion retailing world remains unresolved and design moods are still riven by the same 'two irreconcilable mentalities'. Many fashion retailers are now displaying simpler styles of clothing hung on horizontal poles – only a mildly updated version of Schiaparelli's 1937 washing line. Others still prefer articulated lifelike stands based on the bodies and faces of the fashion superstars of the 1990s. Schneider comments that 'in the Rootstein era, the highest form of realism has been considered the exact duplication of a human model'. The hunt for realism has reached such heights that in her retail advertising, Rootstein photographs the perfect supermodel alongside her perfect copy-mannequin as a challenge to the viewer. Which one is which? As Rootstein's Creative Director, Michael Southgate believes 'you must create a fantasy that makes the viewer want to be part of it'.[39] There is no doubt that Mme Paquin would agree with him.

Dedicated mannequins for the display of historical dress

The very same debate of realism versus stylisation has riven the costume museum world too, especially over the last fifty years. Dress stands created specifically for displaying historical or ethnographical dress have always been extremely expensive, far more costly than commercial stands because they have to be so varied in shape. Typical 1999 catalogue prices in London ran from £400 to £1000.[40] With this in mind, under-funded museums have long had to resort to showing period clothes on adapted commercial shop display mannequins although these are almost always unsatisfactory. As Anne Buck warned in 1958, 'costume should never be distorted to fit a series of mass-produced stands and the methods of the moment in shop displays'.[41] This realisation dates back to nineteenth- century costume exhibitions.

I Day dress with aesthetic
touches, worn by Maud Messel,
about 1905 (see p. 9)

II Evening dress, Elsa Schiaparelli, Paris, mid-1930s,
(left) shown with black mousseline dress, about 1935, worn
by the painter Gluck (right) in Surrealist-styled display designed
by Mike Jones and Nigel Cunningham in 1980 (see p. 15)

III Sample of brocaded silk, Lyons, France, about 1740–50 (see p. 25)

IV Debbie Cohen, student, University of Brighton, 1999 (see p. 81)

V Léon Girn, *Une Dentellière d'Espaly*, about 1889 (see p. 127)

VI Detail of dowry pillow embroidery, Kalotaszeg, Transylvania, probably mid-to-late nineteenth century (see p. 208)

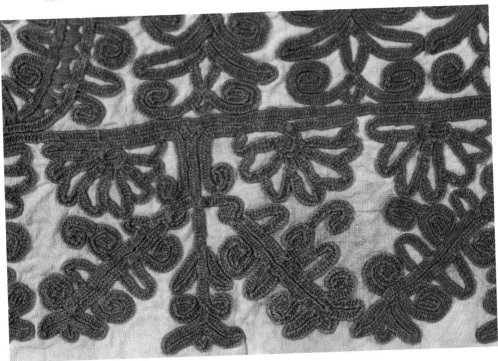

VII Contemporary reworking of 'traditional' Irish dance dress by Gail Flood, final degree collection, B.A. Hons Fashion, National College of Art and Design, Dublin, 1999 (see p. 223)

VIII *Akha Traders Selling Silver in the Night Market* in Chiang Mai, North Thailand, pen and water colour sketch by Dan Jones, 1999 (see p. 224)

Wax mannequins

The development of the wax display stands seen at the international exhibitions in Paris in 1900 and Turin in 1911 has a direct link to the display of historical and contemporary dress which can be dated as far back as the late seventeenth century.

Wax modelling as a fine art form reaches back into Europe in the mid-sixteenth century, particularly in Italy and France when Court society commissioned lifelike portraits, cameos and sculptured busts. Wax figures and body parts were sculpted too from the eighteenth century as part of medical/anatomical research. Full-sized wax models also appeared as funeral effigies laid on the top of coffins dressed splendidly in the departeds' own clothes, as witnessed in the famous effigies collection in Westminster Abbey. This practice went out of fashion in England after the 1660s, although still in 1805 after Nelson's death, Catherine Andras was commissioned by his family to model his effigy which was then dressed in his uniform, including the shoe buckles he was wearing when he died. She was paid £104.14.9. by the Abbey where the celebratory effigy was publicly exhibited.[42]

Courtly interest in the artistic skill of wax modelling had long blossomed. Louis XIV's official painter, Antoine Benoist, produced full-size, dressed models of many of the great of the English and French Courts in the late seventeenth century. A full-size mid-eighteenth-century wax figure of Peter the Great of Russia seated in his Court dress survives, made by Count Bartolmeo Carlo Rastrelli. The Tsar had acquired an interest in waxworks following his visit to Versailles. The wax modeller Johann Wahl made figures of Frederick III, King of Denmark, and his wife Queen Amalie in about 1740. All of these are dressed in the fashionable clothes and accessories of their period, complete with wigs and tinted faces.[43] At the other end of the size scale, in England, Henrietta Wade, one of a good few women wax artists, used wax to model nine-inch-high figures of Sarah and William Siddons, seated, wearing voguish Turkish dress. These figures date from the 1780s and, although very fragile, are now in the safekeeping of the Russell Coates Museum in Bournemouth.[44]

As soon as it became clear that the public much enjoyed viewing lifelike figures of famous and wealthy personages, the development and exhibition of lifesize, realist wax figures began to flourish. As early as 1688, dressed wax figures were already being exhibited to the general public when Benoist was given royal permission to exhibit his 'large wax puppets of the Court' in the fairs of provincial French towns.[45] Mrs Mary Salmon opened her *Moving Wax Works of the Royal Court of England* in the early eighteenth century. *The Spectator* commented on 2 April 1711 that this display was 'one of the curiosities of Fleet Street ... and delighted the sight seeing public' with its 140 figures 'as big as life'.[46] Evidence drawn from later developments indicates that Mrs Salmond's 'moving' displays would have been driven by inbuilt clockwork mechanisms.

Dr Curtius's famous *Cabinet de Cire* opened to the public in Paris in 1770.[47] It was he who trained the young Marie Grosholtz-Tussaud. The *Cabinet* remained open until 1802. All through the revolutionary upheavals in France it profited from the now well-recognised commercial combination of displaying figures of Royalty, politicians, actors and actresses and the famous and infamous to the viewing public. Marie had been a drawing instructor at Versailles and was well connected to the Court. Modelling was undertaken from life, or death in the case of the famous Royal masks taken by Tussaud after executions. A *Caverne des Grands Voleurs* opened in 1783. Marie Tussaud brought the collection to Britain in 1802, finally settling in London in 1835.

During the second half of the nineteenth century every major city in Europe opened its own waxworks and they continued thereafter to be a widely popular form of public entertainment, including elegant society exhibitions through to funfair freak and racist displays of the erotic and exotic Other. Many followed the Tussaud format and featured living, exotic and historical figures, dressed in 'accurate' clothes of their period. Alfred Reynolds opened just such a waxworks in the Freemasons Hall in Lime Street, Liverpool, which ran from 1854–1923.[48] Alexander Hartkopf's Wax Museum of Stockholm visited Paris in 1865, to much popular acclaim,[49] whilst the *Musée Grevin* opened in 1882 in Paris. At a charity 'Egyptian Bazaar' held at Kensington Town Hall in 1884, a whole Cairo street was re-created, typically with 'some capital waxworks, humorously described'.[50]

Mme Tussaud remains the most famous wax modeller of all because of the continuing commercial success of her company, her extraordinary personal history through the French Revolution and the long histories of many of the models that are still on display. Despite the vicissitudes of shipwreck in 1822, the burning down of the Tussaud building in Baker Street in 1925, and its wartime bombing in 1941, some of the moulds are still based on those of the late eighteenth century. Thus the model of *Sleeping Beauty* is reputed to be based on Curtius's model of Mme du Barry, last mistress of Louis XV. A driving determination to make the models as lifelike as possible led the Tussaud family to create a breathing mechanism for this figure. Tussaud family memory dates this back to 1837 when it was 'first installed by a Clerkenwell clockmaker'. By the turn of the century an electrical device was installed to drive the 'breathing' system.[51] Several figures with such clockwork breathing systems were on display in the Hartkopf exhibition of waxworks in the History Museum in Stockholm in 2000. These included his Swedish version of a 'breathing' *Sleeping Beauty*, with flowing blonde hair and her plump, prone, wax figure lightly veiled in pink chiffon. Mme Tussaud's public were kept constantly entertained by the addition of new and well-advertised figures. On 21 April 1860, an advertisement in the *Lady's Newspaper* proffered 'a full-length model of the late lamented Lord Macaulay, taken from a photograph by Maule and Polybank, for which he sat; also a model of S. A. the Imperial Prince Napoleon, in his uniform. Admission one shilling.'

The attraction of waxworks to Tussaud's largely middle-class public was the access it gave them to an extraordinary physical sense of the great and (in)famous. Dress was a major consideration in the creation of this fantasy with 'accuracy' greatly enhancing the magical processes. Contemporary figures were dressed either in their own clothes or in very careful copies of these. In 1928, Queen Mary gave the dress historian, Herbert Norris, who was then costume adviser to Tussaud's, permission 'to order a replica of one of her dresses from her own dressmaker' and 'sent a lady-in-waiting to demonstrate exactly how she wore her jewels'.[52]

Mme Tussaud was well aware that the sight of the gorgeous clothes of the wealthy, whether historic or contemporary, would be a great lure to a public who apart from small photographic and engraved reproductions otherwise had no access to such sights. One feature therefore of her 1846 season was a 'magnificent display of Court dresses of surpassing richness, comprising twenty-five ladies' and gentlemens' costumes intended to convey to the middle classes an idea of regal splendour, a most pleasing novelty and calculated to convey to young persons much necessary instruction'.[53] This display may well therefore have been the very first at which the general public (albeit restricted to the middle classes) had close access to examples of current Court dress. Some were shown by Tussaud's again in the 1851 Crystal Palace exhibition five years later. These were the first displays to blur the edges between commercial fashion retailing, popular entertainment and dress history, a blurring much under debate one hundred and fifty years later.

At Tussaud's, historic figures were either put into surviving period dress or into splendiferous reproductions. Mme Tussaud used original period dress, whenever she could lay her hands on it, to enhance the sense of 'authenticity'. In this way her waxworks became indirectly the earliest 'museum' of European dress history. The company owns to this day the coronation robes of George IV bought when his goods were sold off at auction in 1840. The purple velvet train (which lacks its original ermine lining) was worn in the procession from the Abbey to Westminster Hall. It is twenty-one feet long and embroidered with the Royal Coat of Arms. Tussaud's based the stand on Thomas Lawrence's over-flattering coronation

7 Wax figure of George IV wearing the original set of his coronation robes of 1821, shown at the Royal Pavilion in 1968

portrait of George IV, elegantly coiffed and with no hint of his fifty-two inch waistline.[54] The robes were removed from display in the 1860s due to pollution damage from London's foggy air, but many of these clothes, including the train, survived both the 1925 fire and the bombing in 1940 because they were safely rolled away in storage. When an inventory was taken in 1965 they were recovered, restored and put on temporary display in 1968 in the Round Saloon of the Royal Pavilion, Brighton, the King's favourite home (Figure 7) and again shown in the museum's 1971 exhibition *Follies and Fantasies* on a new version of the original model.[55]

Mme Tussaud's influence was also evident in what may have been the first major dress history exhibition in London. She provided wax mannequins for Lewis Wingfield's much-publicised display of historical dress held at the Albert Hall during the International Health Exhibition in London in 1884. Her wax mannequins displayed and re-created original clothing from the Norman Conquest to 1820.[56]

Museum costume display stands

Tussaud's mannequins aim to entertain, confuse and deceive the public through the strength of their animated realism. Where original period dress is not available, no waxwork director has qualms about reproducing costumes. Dress displays in museums are certainly also designed to entertain the public, but, rather than deception through reproduction, educational and conservation aims are their goals. These boundaries are clear in museum work where curatorial and display skills function within recognised professional parameters.

It is within this context that the museum display debate over realism versus stylisation is set. How can plastic models with artificial hair, faces and hands ever be 'authentic'? On the other hand, how can dress ever look meaningful unless it is displayed on lifelike, period-oriented manne-quins posed with the correct stance, hair and cosmetics? We find here therefore the very same two 'irreconcilable mentalities' already discussed within the context of commercial display.

The costume displays for Arthur Hazelius's Stockholm ethnographical museum, which opened in 1873 in Drottninggatan in Stockholm, set a high standard for others to follow. *The Illustrated London News* was fascinated by Hazelius's mannequins for the Swedish display of the Paris International Exhibition of 1878. These were based on earlier versions shown in Paris at the 1867 International Exhibition which were modelled from life by the famous Swedish sculptor C. A. Söderman. They had cast wax heads and hands, and faces with lifelike, blue, glass eyes made by a leading Swedish eye specialist.[57] Two wax heads (one male and one female) and three hands survive in the archives of the Nordiska Museet. They have hair wigs and were painted with fleshlike tones over their wax base. The museum's archives prove that these were used in displays by 1889 though no-one is yet sure of their original dates of manufacture. They do, however, verify the conviction of *The Illustrated London News* that 'the stands were so real, so alive, so intelligently done ... that ... very little more would have made them human'. The Dutch figures, based on Hazelius's methods, impressed too. 'The lifelike appearance of some of the figures, those especially that are standing in subdued light, is very striking.' The magazine, however, found the stands for the display of French peasant dress to be 'badly made' and 'waxen of face'.[58] By the early years of the twentieth century by far the most popular ethnological display in the USA was the Museum of Natural History's *Arctic Life* exhibition. Its success was based on the publicity and interest in the recent arctic expedition of Robert Peary. A photo of this display taken in 1908 shows lifelike mannequins of Eskimo figures dressed traditionally and bent industriously over various craft works, with sleds and canoes placed nearby.[59]

Whilst Scandinavian ethnographical exhibitions had already resolved their display problems through 'realism' by the 1870s, the exhibition of fashionable dress was to prove far more problematic. In France, at the Paris International Exhibition of 1900, the retrospective historical display of dress and accessories from the period of Louis XV to Napoleon III was shown on headless stands.[60] A few years later, when the French Costume Society held its first public exhibition in the *Musée des Arts Décoratifs* in 1908, the society determined on more realism. Costumed seventeenth- and eighteenth-century figures were placed in large glass cases, whilst some free-standing fashion figures were seated in period coaches driven by uniformed coachmen. The clothes, many from the couturier Doucet's famous collection, were rare and beautiful, but the mannequins caused problems. Maurice Leloir, the President of the Society, admitted in a review of the exhibition that 'some approved of the mannequins whilst others did not'. The difficulty of creating period-looking dress stands from articulated wooden, artists' mannequins fitted with papier mâché heads had in fact defeated the Society's best intentions to period accuracy.[61]

Photographs of displays of eighteenth-century dress in the Victoria and Albert Museum of around 1913 indicate a preference for the use of headless and armless figures in London (Figure 8).[62] Historical fashionable dress was also put on view in Bethnal Green, the East End of London annex of the Victoria and Albert Museum, which had opened in 1872 to bring education to the workers in the neighbourhood. One display included exhibits related to the locality's eighteenth-century Spitalfields silk industry. Dress stands were needed on which to show silk dresses and fortunately we know what they were like because at least two survive, dating probably from around 1900–20.[63] Unlike its headless sister display in the Victoria and Albert Museum, realism was clearly the goal. Built upon extremely heavy strutted wooden and padded bases, these stands had beautifully and realistically modelled plaster hands, arms, heads and shoulders, with carefully sculpted eighteenth-century hair-styles (Figure 9).

It was not until the growth of museums of costume in the post-Second World War period, however, that the design debate heated up. The very same discussion that had occupied the minds of commercial mannequin designers in the 1925 period reappeared once again. This time the 'realism versus stylisation' debate was sharply articulated by Britain's leading women dress historians. Langley Moore's policy was to use realist stands complete with heads and hair whilst Anne Buck at Platt Hall, Manchester, had a preference for headless stands, unless the heads were exceptionally carefully designed. Langley Moore asked in 1964

> should we aim at sheer realism? ... the cost of such models in large numbers would be absolutely prohibitive. Should we go to the other extreme and provide only those contrivances of metal tubing, transparent, or cut and curled paper which afford a shape for the garments without attempting to do more than faintly suggest human form? The objection here is that figures, however ingenious, have a temporary look and are liable to go rapidly out of date.[64]

left 8 Headless costume figures in the display of eighteenth-century dress at the Victoria and Albert Museum in about 1913   *right* 9 Original wood-framed, stuffed calico and plaster mannequin from Bethnal Green Museum, *c.* 1900–10

Langley Moore saw heads, hats and hair as essential to the success of displayed clothes. 'It is never quite effective to show such important items as [wig or hat] except in their proper relation to face or figure'. Nearly all the Langley Moore stands used at her Regency exhibitions at the Royal Pavilion, Brighton, in the mid-1950s (Figure 10) and later at the Museum of Costume in Bath, were therefore fitted with period-styled heads and arms, with styled wigs of real or simulated hair.

Exhibition catalogues show that over the last forty years most curators displaying international 'European' dress have adopted the Langley Moore neo-realism policy. The Costume Institute of the Metropolitan Museum of Art, New York, was using 'realistic' stands with papier mâché torsos, lifelike heads and wigs (but unfortunately rigid hands) by 1958.[65] The Costume Court at the Victoria and Albert Museum, rearranged in 1958, still favoured headless dressmaker-type stands. When, however, the Court was redesigned in the mid-1980s, the museum used beautifully crafted, specifically commissioned, resin dummies. These all had softly painted faces and skilfully styled off-white hair to indicate rather than replicate period feel. Some have found it hard to fight against the somewhat aging and ghostly mood imparted by the use of white-coloured hair and it is unlikely that this method will be used again under current renovation plans.

The *Musée de la Mode et du Costume* at the *Palais Galliera* also adopted

left **10** Period mannequin created by Doris Langley Moore in a dress of about 1818, postcard, *c.*1958   *middle* **11** Mannequin for the *Mariano Fortuny* exhibition, at Brighton Museum, 1980 *right* **12** Mannequin for a Royal Free Hospital nurse's uniform, 1918–22, which belonged to Ellen Foster; designed and made for the Brighton Museum Fashion Gallery in 1980

a 'realism' policy, but financial restrictions during its first thirty years of activity forced the curator, Madelaine Delpierre, to use Siégel commercial 1950s dummies for all too many years. The same ones appear constantly in catalogues from the first exhibition in 1956 through to the 1980s. They came complete with unfortunately lacquered smiles and 1950s *retroussée* noses which destroyed all attempts at period realism. In 1987 Guillaume Garnier's *Paris-Couture-Années Trentes* exhibition and catalogue established this museum's lasting reputation for the highest levels of professional practice. Using simple periodised stands alongside related photographs, magazines and thorough text, the museum's display methodology has since been copied by many other museums. For the 1990 *Robes du Soir* exhibition, which covered the 1850–1990 period, the problem of period look and stance was successfully dealt with by using a complete mix of mannequins. Dressmaker stands and realistically adapted commercial stands were shown alongside space-age-styled mannequins of the 1960s.

For financially starved museums, especially smaller ones, cost remains the major problem. Needing to create timeless, beyond-fashion figures for Brighton Museum's *Mariano Fortuny* exhibition in 1980 limited funds necessitated much invention. Heads were cast in plaster by the museum's design team from a Victorian marble garden statue and from the sculptured plaster faces on the two dummies rescued from Bethnal Green Museum (Figure 11). For the new fashion gallery, which opened in 1981, the neo-realist approach was adopted, and the plaster faces of the mannequins were gently painted with period features and wigs were set in period hair-styles. A seated figure of a nursing sister of 1920–21, dressed in the uniform of the Royal Free Hospital, London, is, for example, typical of the realism still sought in this display (Figure 12). Margaret Hall, exhibitions' designer at the British Museum, was also still supporting this 'realism' approach in 1987.

> The visitor confronted by the face of a model immediately seeks the eyes, as in day-to-day social contact. If these are lifeless or in any way odd, the whole effect of the costume will be marred and the illusion of the period shattered. Absolute realism is difficult to achieve and calls for extremes of modelling skills and good taste, both backed by substantial sums.[66]

When the new costume gallery opened at the Royal Ontario Museum in Toronto in 1989, as with the *Palais Galliera* displays, a policy of using mixed display stands was implemented. The curator, Alexandra Palmer, explained that for four sections dealing with draping, straight cutting, tailoring and making-to-shape within the design and manufacture of Western fashionable dress, headless dressmaker stands were the most suitable. However, for the fifth section on European Costume which concentrates more on style, 'fully articulated forms, complete with heads and stylized wigs made from gros-grain ribbons' were preferred.[67]

The exhibition *Becoming American Women: clothing and the Jewish immigrant experience, 1880–1920* organised by the Chicago Historical Society had to tackle the same classic display problem. Neither the body shapes nor the faces of conventional commercial stands were suitable. Since the theme of the exhibition dealt specifically with generational differences between the older women of the old East European world and their daughters in the New World of New York, fashionably styled mannequins were of no use because any hint of cutesy, trendy fashion faces would have unravelled the whole intention of the exhibition. The exhibition team took the brave route of making their own 'life casts' from the faces of contemporary Jewish women which were then modelled and used as the heads of the dress stands. Skin tone was an all-over pale colouring with free-style but neat pale wigs. The stand designer-maker Donna Shudel left face details unpainted. The intention, well achieved, was to 'capture the very heart of the exhibition' by avoiding any indication of conventionally elegant retail-styled faces and bodies.[68]

Anne Buck, however, has always been quite clear that all such efforts at realism are unwise. She wrote in 1958 that she preferred headless stands because 'unless the heads are in themselves aesthetically pleasing and in harmony with the dress and bear also that authentic but indefinable sense of period that the most meticulous accuracy cannot always capture, they will be obtrusive and jarring'. However, if 'sufficient money and the right artist' were available, she proposed formalised, impersonal head shapes which could be 'produced and used in some quantity' rather than 'the exhibiting practice of adding a stylized head, simply to show a coiffure in hemp or curls of paper, also stylized'.[69]

Forty years later, the display trend seems to be shifting back to Buck's view and an increasing museum consensus in both ethnographic and fashion displays now finally supports less artificially created 'realism' and far more stylisation. Whether this is driven by funding shortages or by clearly defined new professional philosophies is hard to determine. Simple headless, armless, display stands are shown with related, two-dimensional contextual information, such as period photographs and fashion plates. This method was very effectively used in the 1996 exhibition *Textiles of North Africa*, at the Museum of Mankind in London. Here the largely T-shaped garments were simply but effectively hung flat and extended to their full width on padded poles.

Urban, Western dress, however, presents more complex display problems because of its more constructed shapes. The Victoria and Albert Museum's 1994 *Street Style* exhibition of post-war subcultural clothing styles used thin, flat backed, stands, designed for the show by *Universal Ltd*. Amy de la Haye, the exhibition curator, explained that these were adapted with 'heads' made of abstract, metal shapes given a rusty-looking finish (Figure 13). These were designed to give correct body proportions, to hold headwear and to be both 'gender and race free'.[70] De la Haye also confirms that conventional shop mannequins proved unusable because subcultural style pits itself so forcibly against the ideals of beauty commercial mannequins are designed to represent.

In New York, the Costume Institute at the Metropolitan Museum of Art, under the curatorship of the late Richard Martin and Harold Korda, has also adopted a policy of using stylised dressmaker mannequins. Both their 1994 exhibition *Orientalism, Visions of the East In Western Dress* (which included exotic and gorgeous examples of European fashion from the mid-eighteenth century to the present day) and their 1996 *Haute Couture* show reverted to using nineteenth-century-looking display stands shaped to the desired stance. All were headless, though some were fitted with removable

13 The 'head' of a stylised
mannequin, for the
Street Style exhibition at
the Victoria and Albert
Museum, 1994

arms fixed with elegant articulated wooden hands. These had beautifully jointed wooden fingers, curiously like nineteenth-century artists' lay figures. The effect was most successful, avoiding entirely Hall's concerns over the magnetic attraction to the viewer of realistically modelled faces.

The generally agreed view at the beginning of 2001 is that dress is best displayed on headless, simple, stylised, but correctly proportioned stands, with detailed, supportive, illustrative period material close by showing exactly how the garment would have been worn.

Live models

Having living models wearing garments would seem quite straightforwardly to be the best and easiest way to show off clothing. This method places the garments back on the breathing, walking bodies they were originally designed for. Paris couturiers understood the advantages of this method from the 1850s. Visiting Paris in the 1890s, Lucile (Lady Duff Gordon) hated seeing couture clothes modelled on 'horrid lay figures – dreadful affairs of saw dust and wax faces'. The other alternative was live fashion models but

> there was no parade, oh, dear, no, nothing so frivolous. Remember they
> were fighting prejudice ... As a guarantee of the respectability of the estab-
> lishment, the director could be relied upon to choose only the plainest of
> girls to show off his creations ... there must be nothing ... that might
> suggest that [the model] was capable of any more emotion than the sawdust
> dummy she replaced.

Lucile rejected all of this and by 1907 invited her clients to genteel teas, where her 'glorious girls, with generous curves' paraded in the model gowns of her latest collections.[71]

Dress historians have also recognised the advantages of 'dressing up' models, especially for photographic purposes, a practice which can be dated back to the Victorian period and a middle- and upper-class passion for 'tableaux vivantes'. These re-created famous historical or mythological paintings or historical moments, using live models posed rigidly still wearing reproduction dress in suitable 'sets'. These were often photographi-cally recorded for heirloom photograph albums. The Hon. Lewis Wingfield was fond of these twenty years before his involvement with the historic costume exhibition at the *Healtheries* exhibition in London. He was photo-graphed by Victor Albert Pront in 1863 posing for a tableau, wearing a rather poor version of mid-sixteenth-century dress. He was posing here as *Rizzio* with Miss G. Moncrieffe as *Mary, Queen of Scots* for the entertainment of the Prince and Princess of Wales when they were visiting Mar Lodge in Scotland.[72]

'Living' exhibits in peasant and exotic clothing were a popular feature at the great nineteenth-century international exhibitions – the more 'exotic' the better. Human 'specimens' along with their entire families, animals and general accoutrements became a regular feature. They were shown within scenes of 'authentic village life' including dancing, singing, food preparation and tasting, and the 'live' manufacture of localised arts and crafts. All emphasised, directly and indirectly, the superior cultural and racial status of white, urban, European colonial rule. Thus 'peasants' from all over the world could be seen wearing their traditional dress and apparently quite naturally going about their daily business. At the 1884 *Healtheries* exhibition the 'Tartar Tent' featured Siberian horses, their at-tendants and families, including a young boy – 'a pretty picture in his long soft silk frock'.[73] One of the many sensations at the Paris International Exhibition of 1900 was the *Village Suisse*, with its cascade, old watermill and daily performance of goats and cattle being led up 'mountain slopes' by herdsmen and village maidens wearing peasant dress and blowing horns.

The *Art Journal* reported that 'the various types of figures especially among the men were quite a study in themselves, some of the older ones being unquestionably the genuine article, no amount of "get up" would produce such interesting results'.[74]

In the museum, rather than international exhibition setting, however, any kind of 'dressing up' in original clothing has long been seen to create many moral, conservation and 'accuracy' problems. Although widely used in illustrations for early to mid-twentieth-century dress history books, this is now the most despised display method of all. Buck warned nearly forty years ago that

> very rarely should consent be given to this use of museum specimens and of course never in any circumstances with rare and delicate objects … because dresses worn indiscriminately without sufficient preparation, reveal far less than a dress mounted in a museum.[75]

Buck and Langley Moore did together, however, set a pattern for dressing up living models for photographic purposes, possibly one regretted later. Buck used this method for her series of eight Platt Hall *Picture Books*, published between 1949 and 1963. Photographed in black and white, these were aimed at school children, students and serious visitors and were sold as educational aids at deliberately cheap prices. Langley Moore, with her strong contacts in the theatre, ballet and society circles, dressed famous actresses and society models (and their children) for her two books, *The Woman in Fashion* and *The Child in Fashion*. Finally, however, neither found this a satisfactory method and both warned of the dangers of damage disasters. Unfortunately their example was copied, and is still copied, by all too many local museums where 'dressing up' live models seems an easy and glamorous option for catalogue photographs. In 1987 the Costume Society of America, in order to try formally to discourage all aspects of this practice, passed a resolution 'encouraging the prohibition of wearing objects intended for preservation'.[76] Accepted international museum policy now no longer tolerates 'dressing up' for any purpose at all. It is therefore no surprise that the contemporary fashions modelled at the Victoria and Albert Museum's 1999 *Fashion in Motion* series were not samples from the museum's own collection.

Anne Buck concluded in 1958 that costume presentation in museums 'must always be imperfect'.[77] Perhaps, despite the new innovations of *Fashion in Motion*, the use of accompanying film and cleverly designed hollow mannequin display stands, dress curators will always hold that view. In 1990, fifty years after her first introduction to the problems, Buck summarised guidelines issued by the International Committee of Museums for costume collections. Opinions are now firm and clear. 'No object should remain on display for a long period ... No object should ever be worn as a means of display.' Buck concludes that

> The constant co-operation of curator, conservator, scientists and designer is needed to take advantage of research, tested by experience, so that making our collections available for public study and enjoyment does not mean their loss to future generations. The first aim and underlying principle of all who are responsible for any aspect of a museum's collection must be to preserve the integrity of each object in it.[78]

Reactions to artefact-focused approaches

As we have seen, the basic criticism levelled at artefact-based dress history by other historians is that all this attention to the object signifies a narrowness of approach. Many find the attention to detail found within the conservation and curatorial professions dulling. Fine and Leopold in their *The World of Consumption* of 1993 reject the concentration on 'every flounce, pleat, button and bow, worn by every class on every occasion'.

In this book (see also Chapter 3) they discuss the importance of clothing in the context of consumption, which they assess as an increasingly powerful economic and social force in the First World over the last one hundred years. They examine 'the Fashion System', 'Clothing: industrial or consumer revolution', 'Trickle-Down' theories and the 'Advertising of Clothing' over the 1860–1993 period, stressing that approaches to consumption should be 'based on the recognition of distinct systems of provision across commodities'. They explain the need for 'discussion of the private versus social (or individual versus collective) nature of consumption' which has to be 'sensitive to differences in the way objects are produced, distributed, consumed and interpreted as discussion that sets supply against demand'.[79]

The dress historian would argue that without very precise analysis of 'every flounce' where would the historian find the information that would enable recognition of these 'distinct systems of provisions'? How are coded cultural readings of 'the private versus social' nature of consumption to be made except through meticulous study of these details?

Few would argue that the internal debate within the field of dress history over its own artefact-centred approaches has been resolved. Self-criticism in recent years has already attacked the dearth of consumption analysis. It remains true that all too many artefact-centred studies still barely deal with this centrally important theme and omit to enter into any detailed debate on lifestyles, beliefs, work or personal interests of the wearers whose clothes are under discussion. The relationship between consumers and their clothes is thus almost never dealt with in exhibitions and rarely in publications. The Victoria and Albert Museum's *Street Style* was a significant landmark in this respect because the biographies of garments and wearers were so carefully documented.

It also remains true, with the notable exception of ethnographical exhibitions, that by far the greatest emphasis in publications and exhibitions still concentrates on the most glamorous levels of clothing production – the garments of the top 0.5 per cent wealthy of Europe and the USA. It is a scandal that there have been no major national exhibitions in Britain which have examined in any depth ready-to-wear clothing design, manufacture and style diffusion, let alone consumption. The pioneering exhibition, *Off the Peg: the Jewish contribution to the women's wholesale garment trade*, held in 1988 at the Museum of the Jewish East End in London, was a rare exception and yet mass-produced clothing has for over one hundred and fifty years been a major national industry and one that has had massive political, social and cultural ramifications.

The lack of interest shown here by museum dress curators has clearly played a major role in the creation and continued existence of this void. Ann Wise, Assistant Curator at Worthing Museum and Art Gallery in West Sussex, is an exception here. Conscious of the gap in British dress collections, over the last ten years she has set herself the task of collecting 'ordinary' ready-to-wear for women. As a consequence, this museum now has a large, well-documented and rare collection of such clothing dating from the 1930s onwards, including swimwear, nightdresses, corsetry and day wear, including rare examples of dress from companies such as *Marks and Spencers* and *Dolly Rocker*.

The economic/social historians Fine and Leopold do certainly recognise the social history value of artefact dress research, which has also long been understood by dress historians such as Avril Landsell. In 1973 she outlined the collecting policy of Weybridge Museum in Surrey where she was curator of costume. Even in the interwar period her museum had, along the same lines as a Scandinavian ethnographical museum, a policy of collecting 'clothes of the families of labourers and artisans, together with those of the women and children of the professional men – lawyers, doctors, city merchants – who travelled to town on the London/Southampton railway'. The policy of this museum ensured that clothing was not amassed in isolation but as a deliberate 'part of the larger collection that covers the whole history of one particular district; it is not a separate unrelated collection. The clothes, therefore, play their part in the unfolding of the local story, adding a new dimension to historic research.'[80]

Examples of 'good practice' in artefact-based dress history

There are now a growing number of examples of 'good practice' in artefact-based historical dress research. All of them combine the collecting of a specific, focused database of clothing, which is then examined in detail and set within its socio-cultural and historical context. In this way 'the flounces and pleats' of artefacts become properly fused into their broader cultural and economic setting. At its best, as the following examples of good practice will show, detailed examination of clothing can be and is being used to define and explain major historical and contemporary issues related, for example, to socio-cultural developments.

Because of the integration of clothing within the framework of ethno-graphical methodology, clothing artefacts have long been studied in this way by ethnographers. Peter Bogatyrev famously used this method in 1938 in his *Functions of Costume in Moravian Slovakia* (see Chapter 7). Andromaqi Gergji's account of *Aprons in Albanian Costume* during the late nineteenth-to mid-twentieth-century period makes a typically finely measured archae-ological and ethnographical use of objects of clothing. Based on examination of the cut and embroidery of a large collection of aprons, supported by oral history and archaeological research, Gergji is able to identify the ethnic origins related to thirteen different apron styles found within the twenty-seven regional township areas of the country. This in turn enables her to demonstrate which regions of Albania were deeply influenced by neighbouring cultures and which revealed distinctly separate Albanian cultural characteristics 'not found elsewhere'. She concludes that, far from developing in isolation, there are indications in these specific areas of prehistoric Albano-Illyrian cultural origins.[81] The strength of Gergji's case lies in its multidisciplinary approach, which overrides any nationalistic assumptions. Every piece of the ethnic puzzle is carefully put in place to create a whole picture.

The Hodson Shop dress collection, discussed in Chapter 1, also provides an excellent case study to highlight this same essential point. This very rare collection of nearly three thousand items survived from the stock of a small shop run from the front room of an unprepossessing, family house in a typical, two-storey, mid-nineteenth-century working-class, brick-built street, in the middle of a hard-working community. The shop was run by two sisters, Edith and Flora Hodson, in the small town of Willenhall, near Walsall in the West Midlands. Willenhall was home to a specialised lock-making industry, where workers were highly skilled but badly paid, especially the young women. At first glance the Hodson clothes would seem therefore to be an astonishingly rare example of the survival of clothing intended for sale to local working-class women and that the clothing must have been drawn from the very cheapest levels of ready-to-wear manufacture. Most dress histories are clear that such ready-to-wear styles trickled down, in Veblenesque style, from Paris couture into the ready-to-wear trade. This collection would seem to provide a perfect vehicle for confirmation of this process.

Amongst the collection are large amounts of surviving 1920s and 1930s underwear. The thick woollen combinations, plain cotton corsets and long-legged, pastel-toned, knitted rayon bloomers are all a far cry from the delicate garments featured even in middle-class fashion magazines of the period such as *Woman's Kingdom* or the more mass circulation *Mabs Magazine*. Surviving day dresses, hats and blouses are all simple and ready-made, and as their price tickets indicate, seem affordably priced. Typical late 1920s clothing prices in the shop ran from the cheapest 'tub' or washing frocks at 4/11d, through artificial silk summer dresses priced at around 6/11d–18/11d, to the most expensive which were rayon/wool mix jersey tops and skirts at 38/6d in pink or pale blue with striped trim (see Figure 3). [82] The latter were manufactured by N. Corah and Sons Ltd at their factory in Leicestershire and marketed under the trade name, *St Margaret's*. Research conducted by Emma Bryan at the University of Brighton in 1997–98 shows, however, that once these specific clothes are set into the reality of their period local setting rather than relying on theoretical or 'natural' assumptions, easily drawn conclusions about working-class clientele and 'trickle down' theories can be shown to be dangerously simplistic. [83]

What emerges is a far more interesting, if saddening, story. This shop in fact catered to an unexpectedly different social range of clients. Oral history conducted by Bryan, and Sheila Shreeve, the Honorary Curator, whose committed work has ensured the survival of this collection, revealed that most neighbourhood families working in the lock works thought the shop rather grand. The clothes sold were priced well above their financial possibilities and were also outside accepted peer group taste circles. Gladys Wakeman, born in 1901, and interviewed by the author when she was eighty-eight, lived in the same street before she was married. At the age of fourteen she was sent to work in a local factory and earned five shillings a week. She recalled that the shop's customers came mainly from the 'richer end of town' and that the shop 'was far too expensive for factory girls', who mostly made their dresses up from remnants or 'by buying on tick from a card'. The only purchases local women could afford from the shop were a few sewing notions and floral printed cotton overalls. Even these came in a range of qualities. Mrs Wakeman's mother declared that *Bell's* were the best value for money. [84]

Bryan concludes significantly that there is little evidence in the design of surviving Hodson garments of any direct influence from Parisian haute couture. 'Where emulation exists, it does so within cultural boundaries. It is not that working class women aspire to be like the upper classes, but that they have aspirations from within their own class.' She adds that

> histories which ignore the complexities of people's interactions with goods endorse outdated theoretical models such as Veblen's emulation theory ... Through analysis of surviving stock samples and the personal statements of the Hodson consumers, [we need] to acknowledge that goods carry specific cultural meanings, meanings which shift and alter depending upon the individual's experiences and interactions with those goods.[85]

Again, once the puzzle's pieces are put properly in place, a valid overall picture based on the reality of consumers' lives can be found.

Alexandra Palmer, the E. Vaughan Curator of Fashion/Costume at the Royal Ontario Museum, Toronto, is a dress historian who has studied the 'minute details' of couture dress worn by women in Toronto in the 1945–63 period. To this end, she has examined hundreds of couture dresses and suits in the collection of the Royal Ontario Museum, as well as garments in private collections in Toronto. Additional research was made into the archives of local department stores, press, through interview and through evaluation of couture archives in Toronto, London and Paris. The aims of Palmer's research were threefold: first, to identify consumers; second to identify the specific characteristics of British-based fashion taste in Toronto; and third, to explain the function and importance of these clothes set within the context of their related social milieux in Canada and Europe.

Close analysis of the garments exploded a series of established 'taken as read' assumptions. Primarily these women saw their couture clothes as a peer-group-required *social uniform* and indeed as a cultural requirement. Without these garments they felt that they would not have been able successfully to perform the social duties expected of them. Second, unlike the glamorous, ephemeral image attached to these clothes by fashion editors and designer biographies, Palmer proves conclusively that most English-Canadian couture consumers did not see their expensive dresses as passing luxuries at all but as long-term investments. By examining alterations to surviving dresses, and then comparing these to couture house archives, Palmer, like Janet Arnold before her, is also able to prove long-term usage. The 1950s archives of the London fashion house, *Lachasse*, for example, reveal that amongst Canadian clients, as others, 'couture was not bought as a disposable purchase. Rather it was considered so valuable that it was worth the effort to up-date with alterations and new buttons, and care by pressing. These records document couture that was worn for a period of three to five years or more.'[86]

Palmer's artefact research finally indicates that specific types of 'taste' alterations were made by retailers in Canada to Paris designs which they considered too showy for Toronto society. The department store *Holt and Renfrew* 'felt it necessary to alter design details such as the placement of pockets on a Balenciaga suit from the skirt to the jacket', to suit more conservative Canadian tastes.[87] Mrs Graham Morrow bought a Christian Dior dress from the autumn/winter 1951–52 collection through the same store. The original design was strapless but 'the dress had been altered by adding straps with the material cut from the hem of the skirt'. Mrs Morrow's daughter revealingly explained to Palmer that her mother wore the dress to evening weddings in Toronto and that she 'would not have considered it appropriate strapless'. A Balmain gown, from the autumn 1952 collection underwent even more drastic 'Canadianising' alterations. Mink bands on bodice and skirt, a central design feature, were removed by the purchaser because she considered them far 'too ostentatious'.[88]

Palmer's work provides a model of good practice because her methodology consistently places close artefact research and assessment within a carefully constructed framework of cultural and social analysis. The social historian Barbara Schreier also made deliberate and meticulously researched use of clothing artefacts in her 1994 exhibition *Becoming American Women: clothing and the Jewish immigrant experience, 1880–1920.* Examples of surviving late nineteenth-century clothing shown varied from a printed cotton headscarf, a fringed shawl and a Sabbath-best embroidered pinafore for a little girl, all three brought over from Russia. An example of an early twentieth-century, Orthodox *sheitel* wig was found and contrasted with examples of the Americanised fashions favoured by younger women. These included rose-bedecked hats, a swimming costume from the famous Chicago department store, *Marshall Field*, elegant suits, and day and wedding dresses from the 1910–15 period. All of these were styled to the dictates of Paris and 7th Avenue.

These artefacts were each carefully placed by Schreier within their precise biographical and cultural settings. Text, as with Palmer's research, was supported by a full range of photographs, period and oral history comments and surviving, related ephemera. Schreier explained in 1994 that the exhibition 'emphasises explicitly the experience of Eastern European Jewish women, epitomises the corrosive character of immigration and duality of identity that corrosion can create in those who suffer it'. The whole concept of the exhibition and its accompanying book is based on a sharp appreciation of first, 'the importance of dress as a sign of cultural mingling', second, as a force for the sustaining of cultural values and third as 'an identifiable symbol of a changing consciousness'.[89]

A final example of the valid use of artefact-based research, drawn from yet another academic field, is seen in the work of the French social anthropologist, Beatrix de Wita, who, like Palmer and Schreier, also uses clothing analysis to explain the cultural significance and social importance of taste cultures in her 1988 book on contemporary *French Bourgeois Culture*.[90] De Wita became personally interested in experimentally using ethnographical methodology to define the social and cultural driving forces set within bourgeois society, a group 'about which thousands upon thousands of pages have been written in the past, a group that has dominated and deeply influenced society as a whole'.[91] Her book caused a scandal in the Paris press because, rather than applying her ethnographical methodology to the more usually examined communities of peasantry in Africa, India or the French regions, she dared to apply it straightforwardly to the well-off, conventional, bourgeoisie living in the 16th arrondissement of Paris, the equivalent of Knightsbridge in London.

In the context of approaches used by Braudel, Bourdieu, Lévi-Strauss and Segalen and using interview, observation and family archives, de Wita examines issues of kinship, schooling, higher education, etiquette codes, social activities and selection and usage of goods. She concludes that even such a diffuse group as this can indeed be defined and recognised through its accumulation and usage of specific forms of 'trivia' because when these are added together they create a 'distinction' which 'enables [man] to mark out a sphere for himself in which he will live with himself and his fellows'.

De Wita's ethnographical interest in bourgeois dress rests on its role as an important 'distinguishing mark' from which wearers are able to decode peer group signals of both 'civilised' behaviour and belonging. 'Let us dwell for a moment on the example of bourgeois dress', she writes. 'Through it we can trace the formation and development of a true culture. The history of costume reveals how the bourgeoisie has repeatedly replaced the aristocracy's ostentatious distinguishing marks with marks that are more restrained, more discreet, though no less formidable in terms of symbolic effectiveness.'[92]

Analysis of what de Wita defines as the finely developed bourgeois sense of discretion is a key theme in her research. This is built around Cicero's term *mediocritas* – a state of being neither one thing nor the other, a happy medium and the rejection of every form of excess.[93] De Wita sees this mirrored in the 'classic' elements of contemporary clothing of young bourgeois women in Paris which 'conform to what a woman should present of herself. In this way they create an element of distinction, understood in the sense of separation.'

De Wita was not able to work from an existing museum collection of contemporary Paris bourgeois clothing because none such exists, so her garment research is based on interview, on observation and on photography of wearers. She concentrates on the daytime clothing of young unmarried and married women within this group. The basic day wear uniform consists of 'a tweed or flannel straight or pleated skirt, kilt, blouse, cardigan, cashmere or Shetland wool jumper, loden coat or jacket, moccasins or court shoes, scarf and a small shoulder bag', which 'do not change with fashion'. Other coded elements are discreet black velvet hair bows worn to hold back natural hair 'not waved, for example, or worn in too original a cut'. Discreet necklaces of fine artificial pearls and pastel colours are favoured. Bourgeois jeans are recognisable from other pairs: 'neither too tight, nor too baggy, nor too long, nor too short, bourgeois jeans are also recognisable by the fact that they allow a glimpse of socks and ankles, emphasising the neutralising elements represented by moccasins or courts'.

De Wita recognises the peer-group importance of sourcing these items from the etiquette-correct manufacturers (*Hermes* and *Pierre Cardin*, for example) – 'one knows where to buy them'. Finally, she is clear that the specific manner in which items are worn is also crucial, such as the *Hermes* silk scarf which is gently knotted with the ends tucked decorously inside the blouse, rather than flapping about in an uncontrolled way. She stresses, to give one example, the peer-group importance of the bourgeois engagement ring which she saw

> over and over again, adorning different hands. Sometimes it was a sapphire, sometimes an emerald; always surrounded by diamonds and set in white gold or platinum. Often the stone was a gift from a member of the family and the setting the choice of the fiancé. But beyond the resultant variations in details, what strikes the observer is the uniformity of this 'little thing' worn in all circumstances.

De Wita concludes that this sartorial process of *mediocritas* had to be carefully 'learned and handed down'; it calls 'for an education based on self control and presupposes almost a ritualisation of daily life'. Its specific bourgeois quality is its understated nuances, which are so peer-group clear that when young women marry and leave their central Paris homes for the suburbs, they can 'spot one another at the school gate or in the market and swiftly reconstitute their micro-milieu'.[94]

De Wita believes that clothing plays a vital role whereby

> the whole persona of the bourgeois, from appearance to voice modulations, is thus imbued with the values and cultural schemata of the group. And the thing by which these men and women set such store is experienced by them as belonging to humankind as such, to all 'civilised' beings.[95]

Conclusion

With these five examples of good practice in mind (all coincidentally written by women researchers), accusations of the pointlessness of over-attention to detail continue to rankle. Specialists basing research and exhibitions upon this type of close artefact study are curious that such criticisms are rarely levelled at fine art or architectural historians. Their detailed catalogue-style examination of paintings and buildings is applauded as exemplary scholarship, whilst a similar deconstruction of an eighteenth-century period dress by a specialist expert such as the late Janet Arnold can be dismissed as 'wholly descriptive'.

The academic barriers between curators of dress and textiles (who centre their work on object analysis) and the world of university research into social, economic and cultural history (see Chapter 3), although now heavily dented, do still remain in place. The exception here may be the field of ethnography (see Chapter 7). Yet dress history museum catalogues in recent years have demonstrated some first-rate levels of multidisciplinary and in-depth research. Three outstanding examples of this genre are Natalie Rothstein's *Catalogue of the Silk Designs of the 18th Century in the Collections in the Victoria and Albert Museum* of 1990, which assessed the design, making, consumption and supporting trade organisations within this London silk industry, Barbara Schreier's *Becoming American Women*, 1994, discussed above and Valerie Guillaume's first-rate research for her 1994 exhibition on the work of *Jacques Fath*. This courageously dealt for the first time in exhibition and catalogue form with the work of Paris couturiers throughout the Nazi Occupation of Paris.[96] Even so, there is still little interlinked and formalised academic activity between the two areas. As a consequence, curators of urban, Western European and American fashionable dress and textiles still remain largely excluded from academic circles, certainly in Britain. Sadly, these include university postgraduate, external examining processes. University administrators still declare that such curators do not hold the formally required paper qualifications. It is a very real loss to both students and university staff that this out-of-time situation still lingers on.

More saddening still is the view of Naomi Tarrant, Curator of Costume and Textiles at the National Museums of Scotland. Based on a lifetime of curatorial commitment she still believes that even 'in museums, costume is at present being marginalised'.[97] Confirmation of her view was proffered by the design historian Stephen Bayley in 1999 when interviewed in *The Independent* on 23 July, to mark the opening of his exhibition *Moving Objects: 30 years of car design* at the Royal College of Art, London. As if the peopled and dressed human world was entirely invisible, he commented that 'after architecture, cars are the things we see most of.' Thus museum costume curators can still find themselves marginalised both within their own profession and by the academic world too. In England a well-used museum term for dress curators is 'the frock girls' whilst in Norway an alternative version, but carrying the same dismissive connotations, is 'the buttoneers'.

Artefact-based dress history practice, as this chapter has shown, has its own disciplines which are no less rigorous than those demanded by academic institutions but they are clearly of a different nature. Professional skill and knowledge comes from library, archive and oral history research but above all from handling and examining dress in careful detail. Most dress curators have at one time mended, ironed, wrapped, folded, rolled and cleaned clothes and textiles in their charge and mounted them painstakingly in frames or on display stands. All this requires patient and gentle care. Much of this could fairly be described as traditional 'woman's work' and as collections built up in the post-war period, this work has indeed been largely undertaken by women specialists.

Tarrant believes that there has been little fundamental change of heart within museum establishments and within male-dominated academia. It is of significance, however, that as the new pragmatically driven, commercial pressures on museums require them all now to put on crowd-pleasing exhibitions, more and more are turning to dress displays, precisely because they do draw in the general public in large numbers. The *Street Style* show at the Victoria and Albert Museum of 1994 and the mouth-watering *Touches d'Exotisme* at the *Musée de la Mode at du Textiles* in Paris of 1998 are differing examples of this process. It is easy to be cynical about the blossoming of such exhibitions. However, through their success has come some level of professional museological recognition within museum hierarchies of the educational and cultural validity of displaying properly catalogued and analysed clothing, from whatever culture or period it derives.

Notes

1 *Les Modes, L'Exposition International de Turin: La Maison Paquin* (*Les Modes*, 128, August 1911), p. 8.

2 A. Buck, *Handbook for Museum Curators*, Part D, Section 3 (The Museums Association, London, 1958), p. 3.

3 L. Ellis Miller, *A Study of the Designers in the Lyon Silk Industry, 1712–1787* (Ph.D. dissertation, University of Brighton, vol. 1, 1988), pp. 81–82, quoting J. Godart, *L'Ouvrier en Soie* (1899), p. 389.

4 J. Arnold, A Court Mantua, of *c.* 1760 (*Costume*, VII, 1973), pp. 42–46.

5 L. Taylor, Dufy, the Lyons Silk Industry and the Role of Artists (*The Textile Society*

Newsletter, 2, Summer 1984), p. 8, quoting Colette, Soieries, *from le Voyage Egoiste* (unpublished, 1912–13; Quatre Saisons, Paris, 1928).

6 E. Saunders, *The Age of Worth, Couturier to Empress Eugenie* (Longmans, Green, London, 1954), p. 110, quoting le Petit Homme Rouge, *The Court of the Tuileries* (no publisher given, Paris, 1907), pp. 311–313.

7 R. Wilson, *Paris on Parade* (Bobbs Merrill, Indianapolis, 1925), p. 74.

8 A. Buck, ICOM Costume Committee Guidelines for Costume Collections (*Costume*, 24, 1990), p. 127.

9 Brighton Museum, *Mariano Fortuny (1871–1949)* (Brighton Museum and Art Gallery, Brighton, 1980), p. 7, quoting Marcel Proust, *Remembrance of Things Past*, vol. 1., trans. C. K. Scott Moncrieff (Chatto and Windus, London, 1960).

10 B. Chatwin, *What I am Doing Here, Encounters: Madelaine Vionnet* (Picador, London, 1990), p. 86.

11 Correspondence, 16 September 1996.

12 R. Martin and H. Korda, *Orientalism: visions of the East in Western dress* (The Metropolitan Museum of Art, New York, 1994), p. 87. The garment was donated by Emilie de Brigard.

13 http:www.vogue.co.uk, 19/05/99.

14 D. Langley Moore, *Women in Fashion* (Batsford, London, 1949).

15 W. Leach, Strategists of Display and the Production of Desire, pp. 99–132 and S. J. Bronner, Object Lesson – the work of ethnographical museums and collections, p. 223, both in S. J. Bronner, *Consuming Visions: accumulation and display of goods in America, 1880–1970* (Winterthur, Francis Du Pont Winterthur Museum, 1989).

16 A. Ribiero, *The Art of Dress: fashion in England and France, 1750–1820* (Yale University Press, New Haven, 1995), p. 9 and p. 292, quoting W. T. Whitley, *Artists and Their Friends in England, 1700–1799*, 2 vols (Medici Society, London, 1928).

17 L. Riotor, *Le Mannequin* (Bibliotèque Artistique et Litteraire, Paris, 1900), p. 70 and pp. 90–97.

18 *The Queen: the lady's newspaper*, 10 May 1884.

19 *The Queen, Ladies Dress at the International Health Exhibition, South Kensington* (London, 24 May 1884), p. 584, with thanks to Monica Brewis.

20 Leach, Strategists of Display, p. 107.

21 D. Autié, *Mannequins* (Academy, London, 1982), p. 43.

22 Riotor, *Le Mannequin*, p. 74.

23 Leach, Strategists of Display, p. 100.

24 Yvonne Deslandres, Un Temoin Bavard de la Mentalités des Sociétés, p. 270, in Union Centrale des Arts Décoratifs, *Le Livre des Expositions Universelles, 1851–1989* (Union Centrale des Arts Décoratifs, Paris, 1989).

25 A. Latour, *Kings of Fashion* (Weidenfeld and Nicolson, London, 1958), pp. 164–165.

26 *Les Modes*, August 1911, p. 8.

27 Autié, *Mannequins*, p. 51.

28 *Les Modes*, August 1911, pp. 7–10.

29 Leach, Strategists of Display, p. 113.

30 Autié, *Mannequins*, p. 65 and p. 74.

31 T. Gronberg, *Designs on Modernity: exhibiting the city in 1920s Paris* (Manchester University Press, Manchester, 1998), p. 86, quoting G. Janneau, Le Visage de la Rue Moderne (*Bulletin de la Vie Artistique*, 15 November 1924), p. 498 and p. 83.

32 Ibid. p. 86.

33 Deslandres, Un Temoin Bavard, p. 272.

34 Autié, *Mannequins*, p. 90 and p. 121.

35 Ibid. p. 147 and *Exposition Internationale, Le Guide Officiel* (Paris, mai–novembre 1937), p. 123.

36 E. Schiaparelli, *Shocking Life* (Dent, London, 1954), pp. 78–79.

37 *Musée de la Mode et Du Costume, Paris-Couture-Années Trentes* (Paris-Musées, Paris, 1987), p. 235.

38 S. K. Schneider, Body Design, Variable Realisms: the case of female fashion mannequins (*Design Issues*, 13, 3, Autumn 1997), p. 8 and p. 11.

39 Ibid. quoting H. Burggraf, *Mannequins: the retailer's silent salespeople* (no publisher given, n.d.), p. 18.

40 With thanks to Rebecca Quinton, Assistant Curator of Costume at Brighton Museum, for this information.

41 Buck, *Handbook for Museum Curators*, p. 21.

42 E. J. Pyke, *A Biographical Dictionary of Wax Modellers* (Clarendon Press, Oxford, 1973), p. 6.

43 A. Leslie and P. Chapman, *Madame Tussaud: waxworker extraordinary* (Hutchinson, London, 1978), p. 117.

44 Pyke, *Dictionary of Wax Modellers*, p. 41, with thanks to Shaun Garner, Curator of the Russell Coates Museum, Bournemouth.

45 Ibid. p. 105.

46 Ibid. p. 204.

47 Leslie and Chapman, *Madame Tussaud*, pp. 161–163.

48 Pyke, *Dictionary of Wax Modellers*, p. 119.

49 An exhibition of the surviving figures from *Hartkopf's Wax Museum* was on display in the History Museum, Stockholm, in the year 2000.

50 *The Queen*, 5 July 1884, p. 25.

51 Leslie and Chapman, *Madame Tussaud*, p. 20.

52 Ibid. p. 188.

53 Ibid. from a Tussaud poster of 1846.

54 This measurement was taken by the author from a pair of surviving breeches worn by George IV in the dress collection at the Royal Pavilion, Museums and Art Gallery, Brighton, no. C00.1238. With thanks to Jan Fielding.

55 Leslie and Chapman, *Madame Tussaud*, pp. 161–163 and Brighton Museum and Art Gallery, *Follies and Fantasies* (Brighton Museum and Art Gallery, Brighton, 1971), p. 33.

56 M. Ginsburg, Women's Dress before 1900, in N. Rothstein (ed.), *Four Hundred Years*

of Fashion, Victoria and Albert Museum (Victoria and Albert Museum, London, 1984), p. 13.

57 With thanks to Berit Eldvik, Curator of Costume, Nordiska Museet, Stockholm, for clarifying this; see also J. Berg, *Dräktdockor-Hazelius' och andras* (*Fataburen*, Noriska Museet, 1980), pp. 9–26.

58 The Illustrated Paris Universal Exhibition, From a Lady in Paris (*Illustrated London News*, 9, 6 July 1889), p. 101.

59 Bronner, Object Lesson, p. 224.

60 Union Centrale des Arts Décoratifs, *Le Livre des Expositions*, p. 270.

61 *Bulletin de la Société de l'Histoire du Costume*, vol. 1, April–July 1909, pp. 157–170.

62 L. Taylor, Doing the Laundry? A reassessment of object-based dress history (*Fashion Theory*, 4, December 1998), p. 340.

63 Of the original stands, given by Bethnal Green Museum to Brighton Museum in 1980, one (see Figure 9) retains its original cast plaster version of a fashionable 1780s hair-style. The 1750s plaster hair-style of the other was altered in 1980 by the design staff of Brighton Museum.

64 Bath Assembly Rooms and the Museum of Costume, *An Illustrated Souvenir* (1964), p. 5.

65 Buck, *Handbook for Museum Curators*, plate X.

66 M. Hall, *On Display: a design grammar for museums and exhibitions* (Lund Humphries, London, 1987), p. 157.

67 A. Palmer, The Royal Ontario Museum, Costume and Textile Gallery … measure for measure (*Costume*, The Journal of the Costume Society, 24, 1990), p. 113.

68 B. Schreier, *Becoming American Women: clothing and the Jewish immigrant experience, 1880–1920* (The Chicago Historical Society, Chicago, 1994), pp. x–xi.

69 Buck, *Handbook for Museum Curators*, p. 24.

70 Interview with Amy de la Haye, 6 August 1999.

71 Lady Duff Gordon, *Discretions and Indiscretions* (Jarrolds, London, 1932), p. 67 and p. 78.

72 S. Stevenson, *Van Dyck in Check Trousers: fancy dress in art and life, 1700–1900* (Scottish National Portrait Gallery and the Trustees of the National Portrait Gallery of Scotland, Edinburgh, 1978), p. 49.

73 *The Kensington and Hammersmith Reporter*, Our Ladies' Column, 23 August 1884.

74 *The Art Journal*, The Paris Exhibition of 1900 (London, 1900), p. 236.

75 Buck, *Handbook for Museum Curators*, p. 28.

76 Buck, ICOM Costume Committee Guidelines, p. 128.

77 Buck, *Handbook for Museum Curators*, p. 9.

78 Buck, ICOM Costume Committee Guidelines, pp. 126–128.

79 Fine and Leopold, *The World of Consumption* (Routledge, London, 1993), p. 94 and pp. 299–304.

80 A. Lansdell, Costume in a Local Museum – Weybridge, Surrey (*Costume*, VII, 1973), pp. 70–73.

81 A. Gergji, Aprons in Albanian Popular Costume (*Costume*, 20, 1986), pp. 45–62.

82 Sample items from the Hodson Shop Collection, Walsall Museum, include washing frock at 4/11d (HSW5); artificial silk summer dresses from around 6/11d–18/11d (HSW3); and rayon/wool jersey tops and skirts at 38/6d (HSW26).

83 E. Bryan, *From Haute Couture to Ready to Wear? An examination of the process of style diffusion within the British ready-to-wear industry, 1925–1930, with specific reference to the Hodson Shop Collection, Walsall Museum* (B.A. Design History dissertation, University of Brighton, 1998).

84 Interview by the author with Gladys Wakeman, Willenhall, 1988, in the course of researching for Part 3 of the 1989 BBC2 series 'Through the Looking Glass', produced by Suzanne Davies.

85 Bryan, *From Haute Couture to Ready to Wear?*, pp. 71–72.

86 A. Palmer, *The Myth and Reality of Haute Couture: consumption, social function and taste in Toronto, 1945–1963* (Ph.D. thesis, University of Brighton, 1994, vol. 1); see examples: Royal Ontario Museum no. 1986.765, p. 165; Appendix III, vol. 2, p. 10 and vol. 2, p. 20; fig. 5.7, pp. 16–20.

87 Ibid. vol. 2, p. 10.

88 Ibid. vol. 2, p. 20 and fig. 5.7, pp. 16–20.

89 Schreier, *Becoming American Women*, pp. xi, 2 and 5.

90 B. de Wita, *French Bourgeois Culture* (Editions de la Maison des Sciences de l'Homme and Cambridge University Press, Cambridge, 1994), originally published as Ni vue, ni connue: approche ethnographique de la culture bourgeoisie (Fondation de la Maison de Sciences de l'Homme, Paris, 1988).

91 Ibid. p. 141.

92 Ibid p. 57.

93 Ibid. pp. 64–65, quoting J.-C. Schmitt, Le geste, la cathédral et le roi (*L'Arc*, 72, 1978).

94 Ibid. pp. 64–70.

95 Ibid. pp. 141–142.

96 N. Rothstein, *Silks of the 18th Century in the Collection of the Victoria and Albert Museum* (Thames & Hudson, London, 1990); Schreier, *Becoming American Women*; and V. Guillaume, *Jacques Fath* (Paris Musées, Paris, 1994).

97 N. Tarrant, *The Development of Costume* (Routledge, London, 1994), p. 12.

3 ✧ Approaches based on social and economic history, material culture and cultural studies

Enthusiastic girls undertaking projects. (Negley Harte)[1]

Introduction: the great divide – the object versus the academy

A DEEP disjuncture has long existed between object-based dress history and the fields of social and economic history. Since the interwar period university departments have based their textile history research methodologies on primary source investigation of issues of production, technological determinism, work and trade organisation and on issues of entrepreneurship. Dress/textile history, which rarely addressed such themes, was seen to be inward looking, amateur, non-professional and basically a non-academic field. Typically, as we have seen in Chapter 2, Ben Fine and Ellen Leopold dismissed dress history in 1993 as in 'the wholly descriptive catalogue tradition'. Dress/textile historians, however, believed that because economic and social historians left out examination of the actuality of the fabrics produced, they were failing to address centrally important themes such as the significance of issues of the ephemerality of fashion, style change and related gendered consumption issues. Comments such as those by Fine and Leopold fuelled a strong feeling amongst dress historians that their professional expertise and indeed their entire methodological approach was rejected by 'academic' circles.

The fact that in Britain much of this academic criticism came from male staff in 'old' universities and was directed at a field still largely in the hands of women or gay men mostly in museum-based jobs or in 'new' universities, made the situation even more interesting and difficult. Such prejudice against object-based dress history was already evident in 1815 when Dr Samuel Rush Meyrick and Charles Hamilton-Smith wrote that costume history was burdened with 'the intemperate and hasty charge of carrying with it the inferiority of not being worthy of consideration of a man of letters'.[2] This attitude remained firmly in place for more than a hundred and seventy-five years.

One well-known and typical example of the economic history approach to textile history will serve here to encapsulate this whole debate, William Reddy's rigorous 1984 study *The Rise of Market Culture – the textile trade and French society, 1750–1900.* His study assesses the move from artisan to factory work in the cotton textile industries of northern France and amongst other themes discusses the significance of textiles within industrial transformation processes of the period. Reddy is clearly aware of the importance of issues of consumption and style. In tracing 'the breathtaking growth of the cotton industry under the Restoration' Reddy notes that this stemmed directly from the ending of the middle- and upper-class vogue for high quality calico fashion prints. This forced calico manufacturers to seek new markets amongst the less well-off. He comments that 'slight decreases in price brought large increases in consumption' which in turn led producers in the direction of new consumers. This process included 'supplying peasants and artisans with bright, pretty, abundant cloth whose price moved steadily downward'.[3]

There are ten illustrations in Reddy's book. Not one is of fabric and not one shows how these 'downward' price differences might have been achieved, probably with the help of simpler, less seasonally dictated designs. Reddy's interest clearly waned when it came to the artefacts of cloth. We never get to see how design change may well have made a major contribution to the success of this socially and economically important market shift. Thus evidence which an object-based textile historian would consider vital to Reddy's whole argument, and which is readily available in surviving textile sample books, is missing completely. What is also missing is any close examination of the consumption of these cheaper cottons, apart from a generalised opinion that 'peasants and artisans' may have bought them.

In this Reddy is no worse than other historians. Until about fifteen to ten years ago the specific artefact history of Western European feminine fashions and fashion fabrics was largely deemed to be unworthy of the attention of 'big' history, which in the field of economic textile history was largely taught by male academics. In Negley Harte and Ken Ponting's *Textile and Economic History* of 1973, for example, out of its fifteen chapters only two were written by women.[4] Following in the footsteps of Lilian Knowles and Julia Mann, they represent a distinguished minority of female economic history academics at British universities. Interestingly Joan Thirsk, Reader in Economic History and Fellow of St Hilda's College, Oxford, whose 1973 research dealt with aspects of the economic impact of style on the knitted stocking industry, attacked her male colleagues for according fashion such 'a lowly place' in academic research, a theme that has been repeated now for over twenty years.[5]

Professional journals

One way to look at these tensions is by contrasting two specialist British dress/textile history journals, *Costume* and *Textile History*. *Costume*, founded in 1967, is the journal of the British Costume Society, which has a membership of museum-based historians, private collectors, makers of costume (for film, television, theatre, re-enactment societies, etc.), school teachers, 'new' university-ex art/design college lecturers and people simply with an interest in period costume. Unusually, the journal aims to appeal both to expert and enthusiast. This reflects the non-elitist constitution of the Society as outlined in volume 4 of 1970. 'The objects of the Society are to promote, for the benefit of the public, education in dress throughout the ages and to encourage the preservation of historic examples and source material.' Over the years it had become a rather closed circle of experts and enthusiasts when compared to the Costume Society of America which has active student sections and gives prizes for student research achievement. Through the annual volumes of its journal, *Costume*, edited since its inception by Dr Ann Saunders, has built up a unique twenty-six year record of highly informative, specialist research, using primary artefact and archive sources. Members of the society and journal contributors were and are mostly women. In the 1970 journal, for example, there were seven articles by women and three by men whilst in 1993 eight articles were by women and one by a male historian.

Emphasis is always on 'object-based' research, basically analysis of surviving clothes with some debate on approaches to research. There has always been a determination to include European peasant and Oriental dress. Indeed close examination of volumes of *Costume* also shows it has always dealt with the full social range of clothing, from the aprons of Cullercoats' fisherwomen through to the garments of Royalty.[6] Close reading of *Costume* clarifies that this journal has always considered clothing to lie within the embrace of social history though it does not as a policy provide space for in-depth social history research *per se*. *Costume* only occasionally includes articles on ethnographical dress and deliberately rarely deals with theoretical debate. The inclusion in the 1997 edition of the text of a lecture on 'Street Style' given by Caroline Evans of Central/St Martin's College of Art and Design, London,[7] is a progressive move for this journal. Energetic moves from 1998 were set in place to encourage a younger membership. These have included study days on the work of new designers and on fashion journalism. The Society has a membership of just under two thousand and is run entirely on a voluntary basis.

Most textile history research in 'old' universities in Britain came out of departments of economic and social history. The Pasold Research Fund, supported by Eric Pasold, a successful textile manufacturer and knitting historian, gave financial support to the publication of specialist research, as it does today. The fund also supported the setting up of the journal *Textile History* in 1968, to encourage research into the history of textiles and their technological development, design and conservation. Stanley D. Chapman has edited this journal since it started and by 1983 Negley B. Harte, Senior Lecturer in Economic History at University College, London, had taken over as Director of the Pasold Fund. Contributors both to the work of the fund and the journal were for many years mostly male academics or museum curators.

The debate starts

With Negley Harte as a determined *agent provocateur*, the tensions between *Costume* and *Textile History* and the 'old and 'new' economic/social histories blew apart in 1976 when Harte launched his first attack on fellow economic historians. He accused them of failing to understand that

> the textile industries have played a critical role in the economic history of Europe. Given the nature of the climate, the demand for clothing has taken second place only to the demand for food as a fundamental factor in the economy of the continent for many centuries ... The production, the distribution and the consumption of textiles cannot therefore be ignored by any serious economic and social historian of Europe.[8]

In 1981 he demanded to know why social historians were still not looking at clothing. 'All manner of fascinating and critical aspects of social life in the past have been brought under scholarly study for the first time in a serious way, from witchcraft beliefs and literacy to sport, sex and other recreations ... yet it is odd that dress has not yet begun to be added into the social historian's lucky dip.'[9] In 1991 he repeated his point that 'economic historians ... have shied away from attempting to address their statistical questions to clothes themselves'.[10] It is clear, however, that Harte reserved his deepest ire for dress historians, declaring in 1977 that

> The history of costume as a field which evinces considerable popular interest is highly developed; as a scholarly subject it is backward ... The history of costume as conventionally perceived is wanting in at least two important respects ... Firstly clothing is generally quite inadequately related to wide matters of concern to the historian of social change and movements in the standard of living for example or to price levels, patterns of expenditure and consumption. Secondly, and more particularly, dress is studied almost entirely separately from textiles, from the textile trades and from the changing technology of textile production. Until such dimensions have been added, costume history is in danger of aspiring no higher than to antiquarian status

– a position that is itself by no means reached – it has to be added, by a good many existing publications in the field.[11]

In 1981, he renewed the offensive. 'Clothing and fashion has been left to a peculiar breed of historians, cut off from the old economic history and the new social history alike, an inward-looking breed with links with that other peculiar breed of historians of art, rather than historians more generally.'[12] His final barb was launched in 1991 when he described the dress history field as 'a prolonged picnic attended by hordes of school children and enthusiastic girls on textile or design courses undertaking "projects"'.[13]

However, behind all this public invective, Harte was actively campaigning to improve rigour of research and to pull both sides together. He organised two innovative interdisciplinary conferences, the first in 1985, *The Pasold Conference on the Economic and Social History of Dress*, in London and the second, *Social Aspects of Clothing* at Tilburg in the Netherlands in 1992. These threw 'old' and 'new' university and museum curators from Europe together for the first time. In 1982, the editorial board of *Textile History* changed the journal's title to *The Journal of Textile and Costume History and Conservation* to indicate their new broader interests. Looking back over twenty-six years of publications it is clear that *Textile History* has successfully broadened its interests to include analysis of clothing artefacts and ethnographical approaches. The spring 1999 issue, for example, edited by Ruth Barnes of the Ashmolean Museum, Oxford, was entirely devoted to new research on South East Asian textiles. The autumn 1999 issue included new research by Rachel Worth on technology and design at *Marks and Spencers* and book reviews which not only covered expected themes such as research into the cotton mills of Oldham but also folk art in Bali.

In the dress history world, too, progressive forces were at the same time also arguing for change. In 1984, Jane Tozer (then joint Costume Curator at the Gallery of English Costume at Platt Hall, Manchester with Sarah Levitt) made an appeal to Costume Society members for a broader and more analytical method of interpreting dress.

> For curators, interpretation means the lucid and effective presentation of the materials of art and social history ... We should seek to relate dress to its historical, artistic, social and economic context. Both the social and economic content, and the aesthetic and cultural background, are important in the eclectic, empathetic approach; it is unfortunate if these disciplines seem at times to be opposing camps. The standard texts of the future will come from a synthesis of these views.[14]

In the world of higher education, tensions were rife from the 1960s. It was taken for granted that there were (and are) virtually no 'old' university-based dress historians, but even in art and design colleges in Britain where fashion and textile design was very successfully taught from the 1950s, there were also almost no dress historians.[15] What few there were, struggling against the masculine and art historical domination of 'Complementary Studies' teaching,[16] followed the methodologies put forward in *Costume*.

Positive developments in the academic world since the 1980s: material culture and history of consumption approaches

The late 1980s and early 1990s witnessed seminal methodological developments on both sides of the Atlantic. In the USA fresh approaches to consumption history and material culture answered many of Harte's anxieties, although at first few historians included clothing and textiles in their remit. Valerie Steele, Chief Curator of The Museum at the Fashion Institute of Technology in New York, acknowledges the impact of the work of Jules Prown from Yale University on her own work, citing articles in the influential American material culture journal, *The Winterthur Portfolio*. Prown in 1982 proposed a three-stage methodology for 'reading' objects, which moved from *description* to *deduction* to *speculation*, thereby 'framing hypotheses and questions which lead out from the object to external evidence for testing and resolution'.[17]

Two periods have excited the most interest amongst consumption historians. In Britain it has been the eighteenth century whilst in the USA the late nineteenth- to early twentieth-century period has attracted research into the development of mass-oriented commodity culture. Simon J. Bronner's editorship in 1989 of *Consuming Visions – accumulation and display of goods in America, 1880–1920*, was one key contribution with contributors drawn from history, folklore, museology, sociology, psychology, art, anthropology, semiotics, literature and American Studies departments. Out of ten contributors only one was a woman. Bronner noted then that consumption history was a relatively new field and that his book set out to examine how 'distinctive visions of a consumer culture were formed and accepted and how they have affected our society, our world view, and our lives'.[18] Chapters that have proved to be useful to dress historians include Jackson Lears's *Beyond Veblen: rethinking consumer culture in America*, and William Leach's contribution *Strategists of Display and the Production of Desire*. This argues that developments in department store window display across the USA at the dawn of the twentieth century encouraged consumers into a new commodity aesthetic which opened up the 'new commodity culture that challenged at its core the moral heritage of the nineteenth century'. Leach believes, for example, that the new dress mannequins (as discussed in Chapter 2) became a highly successful 'device to excite desire for goods'.[19] Related research, much of it by women, includes, for example, *Counter Cultures: saleswomen, managers and customers in American department stores*, by Susan Porter Benson of 1986 and Robert Shields's, *Life Style Shopping* of 1992.[20]

In Britain the groundbreaking study was *Consumption and the World of Goods* of 1993 by John Brewer, University College, Los Angeles, and Roy Porter, from the Wellcome Institute for the History of Medicine in London. This volume, which directly encompassed analysis of clothing and textiles, was premised with the belief that it was

> high time for 'big history' to address one of the special features of modern Western societies; not just industrialisation or economic growth, but the capacity to create and sustain a consumer economy, and the consumers to go with it. Modern Western economies have transformed the material world and thereby, it seems, stabilised the social and political.[21]

And thus the barriers were broken. From the early 1990s new inter-disciplinary methodologies were developed by both male and female researchers using ethnographic, material culture and consumption-based approaches. John Benson, Professor of History at the University of Wolver-hampton, defended the new field in 1994 confirming its specific ability to examine social, economic and cultural shifts and developments through 'the individual and/or family selection, purchase, ownership and use of goods and services'.[22]

Ben Fine, an economist, and Ellen Leopold, an economic adviser on architectural issues, used assessment of clothing and food in their 1993 research which discussed consumption as such a powerful force over the last hundred years that it has become embedded 'in our thinking, our practices and our theory ... thrust into a position of prominence in a way that is historically unprecedented'. Their argument that analysis of the processes of consumption through which specific artefacts are designed, produced, retailed, distributed, purchased and used can 'explain the mores and practices of society' is now widely accepted. It is of interest to note that consumption historians, emerging out of the fields of social history, sociology, psychology and cultural history, consist of a far more equitable gender balance. Sharing Harte's views, they reject 'old' economic history approaches as too inflexible, with Benson preferring a 'social-cum-cultural approach' which 'has the advantage, it seems, of coming closer to the complexity of reality'.

In seeking to understand this 'reality' Fine and Leopold recognised too that 'old' approaches made 'little contribution to an understanding of the processes of fashion' leaving 'unexplained the causes of rapid turnover in product and the proliferation of styles'.[23] What has been fascinating for many dress historians who have long understood the connections between consumption and the 'mores and practices of society' as manifested through fashion, has been to watch as these newly converted investigators finally deal with the issues of fashion and style change (in its broadest sense). In 1991 D. E. Allen, an economic textile historian, struggling to understand 'fashion as a social process', still felt able to write that 'the frivolous image that fashion unfortunately wears is doubtless in large part to blame'[24] for the little interest shown in it by the academy.

Nevertheless, a new academic field blossomed out of this convergence of research interests and the problem was then laid out for resolution. Until we know what goods were purchased by whom, what motivated choice, how long consumers used artefacts in the home and what consumers felt/feel about their goods, we know little about the real issues of consumption. If we fail to answer these basic questions, how is it possible to unravel key issues of the relationships between demand–production–consumption? Here clothing became an obvious source of research because it was/is consumed across all levels of society. As Harte had stated in 1981, 'what is needed is for economic and social historians no longer to so neglect the subject, even those interested in the production and distribution of textiles. Clothing after all took up a quarter of the national income at the time.'[25]

Dress studies within consumption history

John Styles, Head of Postgraduate Studies at the Victoria and Albert Museum, is convinced that 'the growth of interest in consumption has moved dress towards the centre of historians' concerns ... With it has come an explosion of work in the history of that most personal and expressive form of consumption, dress.'[26] Styles cites Daniel Roche's *The Culture of Clothing: dress and fashion in the Ancien Regime* of 1994[27] as of very real methodological importance with its carefully probed, cross-class archival analysis. Styles, in his own investigation, *Manufacturing, Consumption and Design in Eighteenth-Century England*, used period press and an unusual range of archives which moved beyond probate inventories of clothing to examine criminal depositions listing items of stolen dress in the north of England in the 1780s and 1790s. As a result he was able to make a fresh assessment of the consumption practices of both middling and labouring classes, which avoided the period prejudice that Neil McKendrick perhaps absorbed a little too easily.[28] Styles concluded that there was an extension of consumption 'of certain types of new consumer durables' amongst the labouring poor and was struck by 'their capacity to respond to accessible innovations' including the 'buying of cheap cotton clothing'.[29]

Material culture approaches

Now that economic and social historians have taken to looking at 'goods', precisely where the methodological boundaries now fall between consumption history and material culture has become something of a mystery. Where the boundaries now fall between material culture and anthropology, both of which use the consumption and interpretation of objects as a means of examining 'society' and 'culture', has also become confusing. Daniel Miller, an anthropologist at the University of London, acknowledged this in the introduction to his study *Acknowledging Consumption: a review of new studies* of 1995. He launched 'a polemic by Way of an Introduction: Consumption as the Vanguard of History'. The topic of consumption was not simply 'an additional accretion' to the old fields of study but 'a fundamental challenge to the basic premises that have sustained each discipline up to the present'. He suggests that it represents an 'across the board sea-change ... Such studies may not only cause us to rethink our conception of consumption but also point to the need for a radical re-thinking of areas of already acknowledged importance such as economics and politics.'[30] Miller relishes the all-encompassing social embrace of material culture, very well aware that 'however oppressed and apparently culturally impoverished, most people nevertheless access the creative potential of the unpromising material goods about them'.[31]

In 1993, Ann Smart Martin, Assistant Professor in the Winterthur Program in Early American Culture, also summarised helpfully material culture interests in consumption issues.

> Material objects matter because they are complex, symbolic bundles of social, cultural and individual meanings fused onto something we can touch, see and own. That very quality is the reason that social values can so quickly penetrate into and evaporate out of common objects.

By drawing together debate on makers, buyers and users Smart Martin suggests consumption research can help penetrate

> the meanings people give to objects, the whole process of acquisition, notions of taste, style, social competition, the emotional pleasure derived from material objects, and symbolic product values and indeed help us examine the shifts in intellectual feelings about the core relationships between humans, goods and society.[32]

If ever there was an answer to Fine and Leopold's condemnation of artefact research which details every 'flounce, pleat, button or bow' of dress, it lies here in Smart Martin's words. These new approaches, boosted by the work of Grant McCracken, Igor Kopytoff and others, are currently becoming a positive framework within 'new' dress history approaches. McCracken's *Culture and Consumption: new approaches to the symbolic character of consumption* of 1988 proposed that artefacts have 'three locations of meaning' centred around processes whereby 'advertising and the fashion system move meaning from the culturally constituted world to consumer goods, while consumer rituals move meaning from the consumer good to the consumer'.[33]

The anthropologist Igor Kopytoff proposes a not dissimilar route of transference of meaning in his 'biography of a thing'.

> What sociologically, are the biographical possibilities inherent in its 'status' and in the period and culture, and how are these possibilities realized? Where does the thing come from and who made it? What has its career been so far, and what do people consider to be an ideal career for such things? What are the recognized 'ages' or periods in the thing's 'life' and what are the cultural markers for them? How does the thing's use change with its age, and what happens to it when it reaches the end of its usefulness?[34]

Styles identifies the one embracing factor in all these approaches as 'the postmodern turn in the human sciences – a downplaying of long historical trajectories and deep causes, a focus on surface phenomena and on diversity, a concern with the personal, with the subjective and with identity'. Styles sums up the excitement for the dress historian of these developments. 'They render important the very characteristics of dress that previously made it intellectually suspect [to the academy] – its ephemerality, its superficiality, its variety.'[35] Styles made these points at the turning point, the international conference *Dress in History: studies and approaches* held in 1997 at the Gallery of Costume, Manchester, called by Anthea Jarvis, Keeper of Costume, to mark the museum's fiftieth anniversary and to celebrate Anne Buck's lifetime of invaluable, pioneering work across so many areas of dress history. Delegates included curators, conservators, costume makers, teachers from schools and 'new' and 'old' universities and private collectors. Anthea Jarvis, representing object-centred approaches, made it clear that she too felt that 'the language and methodologies of fifteen years ago are no longer adequate structures for modern approaches'.[36]

These debates, just as current in North America, are arousing interest in Scandinavia too. In September 2000 over one hundred museum dress history curators, collectors and teachers from Sweden, Norway and Denmark met at a conference titled *Dress, Body and Identity* to discuss future directions for the subject. The conference was called by Dr Bo Nilsson, Head of Research at the Nordiska Museet and by the Department of Ethnology of the Swedish Institute for Folk Life Research. Amongst the speakers were some from the Manchester conference of 1997, invited to continue the debates started there. Most delegates were once again women. Interestingly, many were young ethnographers with a keen interest in analysis of contemporary dress. This museum, unlike those in Britain, has since its original inception by Arthur Hazelius in 1873 collected and displayed both peasant and fashionable urban dress and artefacts under the same roof, which made it an apt setting for open-minded debate. As Dr Nilsson suggested in the conference publicity, this museum has anyway long been addressing issues of the 'social, symbolic and life history aspects' of dress, including fashionable dress. The conference sought to debate 'modern approaches' and in particular to debate how museum curators might enfold new theoretical approaches within their gallery displays. That of course is the key question for the future of the field and is one that may be resolved only through the reality of museum and other historical research and practice.

Examples of the application of good practice in the use of new approaches within dress history

In 1997, Beverly Lemire, Professor of History at the University of New Brunswick, Canada, published her investigation of the cheapest levels of ready-to-wear clothing manufacture and distribution in England in the eighteenth century when few dress historians, relying on information drawn from far more elegant surviving clothing, knew that such a large-scale industry even existed. Using a wide range of archives, her *Dress, Culture and Commerce: the English clothing trade before the factory, 1660–1800* concentrates on garments made in Britain mostly by badly paid women outworkers, for naval and military purposes. She also looked at archival records of systems for the manufacture and retailing of clothes ready-made for women, such as quilted petticoats and at the second-hand clothing supply system.[37] Her illustrations and acknowledgements make it clear that, in the spirit of the new approaches, she also sought the advice of Alexandra Palmer, the E. Vaughan Fashion Costume Curator at the Royal Ontario Museum, Toronto, in at least a token search for surviving garments that might relate to her research.

An absorbingly successful application of the new approaches to dress/textile history research is to be found within Amanda Vickery's *The Gentleman's Daughter: women's lives in Georgian England* of 1998, which builds on her earlier essay of 1993, 'Women and the World of Goods: a

Lancashire consumer and her possessions, 1751–81'. Vickery, a historian from the University of London, challenges many 'given' assumptions held hitherto by social historians, such as those cited by D. E. Allen, who believe that women's role as consumers of ephemeral fashion was of little economic or social significance. Vickery researched the life and possessions of Mrs Elizabeth Shackleton through examination of thirty-nine surviving diaries covering the 1762–81 period supported by a full range of related archive research.

Vickery's conclusions are far-reaching and of very real significance. She concludes that 'reassessment of consumption paves the way for the historical reclamation of the female consumer'. She also challenges the 'long-held [academic] disdain for the study of "fashion" and opens the door on one of women's most important historical roles, as managers or participants in household consumption strategies', which emphasises the personal rather than the institutional. Vickery is quite clear about the gendered significance of this statement within her academic field.

> The historical prejudices against the female consumer are legion … Women have been relentlessly derided for their petty materialism and love of ostentation. An allied tradition of socialist analysis imbued with a similar puritanism, has habitually contrasted the cultures of production and consumption: the former characterised as collective, male, creative and useful, the latter individualistic female, parasitic and pointless.

Vickery proves her points through combing late eighteenth-century archives and by a careful placing of Mrs Shackleton within her specific social milieu and taste setting. Born into a London linen draper's family, Shackleton married into the social elite of a worsted wool weaving area of the West Riding of Yorkshire, living in a manor house with a 'handful of servants'. She had three sons and was twice widowed. 'The daily management of consumption fell to her', states Vickery.[38]

Themes of appearance, behaviour, dress and style run all through Vickery's research as an enlightening and fascinating thread. She showed that Mrs Shackleton based her clothing style and sources of fashion information on style news gleaned from Pocket Books published in London, similar, as Vickery shows, to *The Ladies Most Elegant Pocket Book for the Year 1776*. Mrs Shackleton had even pasted similar fashion plates into her diaries. Other style sources were visits to shops in York and letters and gossip with friends and relatives in London. Vickery confirms, however, that 'Mrs Shackleton was not a slavish imitator of elite modes, nor a passive victim of the velocity of fashion', and that in her circles 'toning down of aristocratic designs was often preferred to "a great deal of shew"'.[39]

Vickery's proposal that women's use of goods within the household owed little to myths of 'petty materialism and love of ostentation' is clarified by the fact that although Mrs Shackleton was 'not financially constrained', her diaries show that the careful consumption of clothing received particular attention. It was mended, made over, retrimmed, redyed, converted into household items or cast off to servants. Favourite dresses turned up in a variety of new forms over the years. 'Made me a working bag of my old, favourite, pritty red and white linnen gown', she wrote in 1773. Three years later her diary reveals 'made a cover for the dressing drawers of my pritty red and white linnen gown'. Vickery found details of Mrs Shackleton's gifts of clothing pieces to her woman servants. In 1773 she gave her young servant, Nanny Nutter, 'a pair of black silk mitts for knitting a pair of stockings', only to write later, 'Nanny Nutter run away ... went to be chambermaid at Carr. An ungrateful lying girl.'

The survival of these rare diaries enables Vickery to produce cultural biographies of some of Mrs Shackleton's favourite 'things', in terms Kopytoff would enjoy, including details of a bracelet made up from the hair of all three of her sons and 'a new light brown fine cloth pincushion [made of] a piece of coat belonging to my own dear child Tom'. Vickery defines this as Mrs Shackleton's 'awareness of extra-material meaning'.[40] Vickery is certain that women like Mrs Shackleton denied access to the professions and to public office

> could not pass on the invisible mysteries of institutional power or profes-
> sional expertise to their descendants. A gentlewoman's skills were
> characteristically embodied in the 'unskilled' arena, the household. Small
> wonder if, in consequence, she turned to personal and household artefacts
> to create a world of meanings and ultimately to transmit her history.[41]

Vickery thus uses analysis of items of clothing and attitudes towards clothing as a fundamental tool of her analysis of Mrs Shackleton's processes of consumption and her cultural–talismanic relationship to her 'things'. Missing entirely are any portraits of Mrs Shackleton and her family, which have not been found, or any of the objects she wrote so caringly about, except for a piece of grey brocaded Spitalfields silk from Mrs Shackleton's wedding dress. This seems miraculously to have survived and was shown by Vickery in her television series on the lives of Georgian women shown on BBC2 in the spring of 2001. All the other 'things' remain like ghostly shadows just out of reach, hiding behind her text. And, yes, had the relationships between the fields of dress and consumption history been more confidently established, Vickery might have tried to find surviving examples similar to the 'elaborately patterned silks purchased from London in 1764'. Natalie Rothstein found samples of just such a fabric in a pattern book of silks woven in Spitalfields, London, by a firm called *Batchelor, Ham*

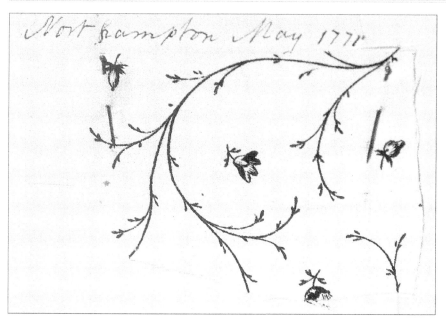

14 Detail of cotton print, 1771, Victoria and Albert Museum; no. T. 219.1973,
Dept of Textiles

and Perigal.[42] Examples of a 'prettie red and white linnen' of 1773 are easy
to find as this was not a rare fabric. Indeed Barbara Johnson, living in the
same period although in somewhat more socially elite circles on the fringes
of London high society, also bought a similar fabric when visiting North-
ampton in May of 1771, 'a purple and white copper-plate linnen' print for
a gown, 'seven yards, 3s.–2d a yard'. This has a delicate repeat sprig design
on a white ground (Figure 14). [43] It might also have been worthwhile looking
through the late eighteenth-century dresses in the costume collections at
York Museum or Platt Hall, Manchester, to see if any garments similar to
her 'old green' and 'new drab'[44] quilted callimanco petticoats exist. These
too are not unusual items. With these and other 'look-a-like' period examples
in place, Vickery's research would form the basis for a truly contemporary
museum exhibition which would go a long way to further her intent of
overturning major historical and gendered misconceptions and prejudices
surrounding women and consumption of 'fashion'.

Such innovative research is finally bringing Benson's 'complexity of
reality' closer and closer. Chapter 2 has already cited work by Schreier,
Palmer and de Wita as examples of strong use of interdisciplinary
approaches. Vickery offers a first-rate example of painstaking archive research interpreted through bold and innovative use of the new
methodologies – even without the object study in place. The blending of

object-based and material culture approaches may not have yet reached the point when material culture historians actually discuss examples of clothing in any depth, but we are getting very, very close.

Cultural studies approaches

Christopher Breward, Reader in Historical and Cultural Studies at the London College of Fashion, debated *Cultures, Identities: fashioning a cultural approach to dress* at the 1997 Manchester *Dress in History* conference, outlining the sweep of dress research stemming from new approaches within the fields of cultural history and cultural and media studies. He noted that these concentrate mostly on contemporary issues such as 'the study of representation and promotion, using social anthropology and semiotics as tools to define meaning'. To the list of new approaches already cited here, Breward adds textual analysis (through semiotic use of film and magazines), sociology, the role of ideology (hegemony, subcultures and pleasure) and the political question of identities (race, gender and sexuality). Finding the study of dress and fashion still to be 'marginal to wider design historical concerns', Breward prefers to use the term 'dress studies' over 'dress history'. Breward, like Styles, is convinced that assessment of 'clothing and fashion have finally become a vehicle for debates that now lie at the heart of visual and material culture studies'.[45]

Breward cites the theme of 'fashion and signification' as central to the way in which 'cultural studies offers a way of studying objects as systems rather than the simple product of authorship'. He cites semiology approaches by Ferdinand de Saussure and Roland Barthes as offering 'cultural signifying systems, allowing the scholar to examine the social specificity of representations and their meaning across different cultural practices'.[46] These include dress, behaviour and the construction of appearance. Caroline Evans discusses punk dress through just such use of dress as a set of signs whose meaning is changed

> through being jumbled up, re-ordered and re-contextualised next to other signs. So the suspenders and straps and chains of a punk woman's outfit do not mean S. and M. sex or 'prostitute' any more because they are juxtaposed with swastika, the alienating face make-up, and the hair standing unnaturally on end.[47]

Valerie Steele, Chief Curator of the Museum of the Fashion Institute of Technology in New York, also enjoyed applying the semiotic approaches of E. McClung Fleming to her work, building on his advice to 'go out of the object to understand what each sign means'.[48]

Sociologists, including Pierre Bourdieu and Fred Davis, also found analysis of clothing to be of significant use. In 1979 Bourdieu's pioneering study *Distinction: a social critique of the judgment of taste*, offered a general methodology for unravelling the complex sociological processes which lead to the development of personal taste and social attitudes to taste. Rejecting the notion of taste as 'a gift from nature', he asserts through careful empirical research that in reality 'scientific observation shows that cultural needs are the product of upbringing and education', and that tastes 'function as markers of class'. Bourdieu's assertion that taste is 'used as a weapon of exclusion by the dominant class ... or any group building barriers around itself'[49] can help the dress historian, for example, towards a far greater understanding of the creation, social function and consumption of aesthetic dress in the 1880s, punk dress in the late 1970s or even haute couture garments all through their existence.

Fred Davis, Emeritus Professor of Sociology at the University of California, San Diego, also made a major contribution to cultural studies methodologies in his *Fashion, Culture and Identity* of 1992. This examines clothing as a means of communicating non-verbal information that relates to the development of 'our social identity, as this is framed by cultural values bearing on gender, sexuality, social status, age, etc.'. Davis examined the cultural and social forces at work within fashion/dress at all levels of Western society, mostly in the twentieth century, including the actuality of the social and economic processes of fashion cycles, anti-fashion and minority dress. He argued finally that there are two fashion systems at play at the turn of the twentieth century, the globalised world of mass commodified international fashion and the 'veritable cacophony of local, sometimes exceedingly transient, dress tendencies and styles each attached, however loosely, to its own particularity, be it a subculture, an age grade, a political persuasion an ethnic identity, or whatever'.[50] Davis calls this a centre-to-periphery versus periphery-to-centre debate.

Feminist approaches

Amanda Vickery, Jane Gaines and Elizabeth Wilson have argued that much feminist consumption analysis of the 1970s all too easily accepted a male view that women's interest in dress was frivolous and that women had allowed themselves to become 'the gilding of the patriarchal cage' and on display for male pleasure.[51] Jane Gaines refers to this Second Wave of feminist politics and writing as a period which saw feminists as 'enemies of the stiletto heel and the beauty parlour ... as enemies of glamour'.[52] Elizabeth Wilson, Professor of Cultural Studies at the University of North London, was a pioneer in challenging such anti-fashion views in feminist terms. 'Strange that when so much else has changed there still exists such a strong hostility to fashion amongst so many radicals ... There must be some moral quality about dress that makes us abnormally sensitive to its relationship to our ethical system.'[53] Wilson had famously declared in her 1985 analysis of fashion, *Adorned with Dreams: fashion and modernity* that 'the most important thing about fashion is *not* that it oppresses women'.[54] Wilson proposes that feminists should accept 'fashion as a legitimate and highly aesthetic pleasure',[55] a view shared by Caroline Evans and Minna Thornton who wrote in 1989, that fashion 'is a field in which women have found pleasure in the elaboration of meaning – meaning which is there to be taken and used'.[56]

Kathy Peiss, too, in her account of the development of a mass cosmetics industry in America in the early twentieth century, whilst acknowledging that 'in one sense the cosmetics industry was to represent "woman" as a kind of merchandise or objectified spectacle', also saw the mass availability of cosmetics in a far more positive light, as a way 'to destabilise nineteenth century cultural hierarchies among women, open economic opportunities, and represent, however inadequately, new claims for cultural legitimacy'.[57] It is worth considering here, too, Vickery's view that in the eighteenth century, 'fashion had far more significance for a woman's relationship with other women than for her relationship with men'.[58]

Cultural studies interest in feminism, social marginalisation and subcultural dress

Caroline Evans and Minna Thornton used what they saw in 1989 as fashion's 'culturally marginalised status within the hierarchies of art and history' as inspiration for their study *Women and Fashion: a new look*. 'It is precisely as a culturally marginalised practice that fashion can utter those meanings which are both compelling and oblique.' Their focus was both sub- and counter-cultural dress and a new approach to 'reading' Paris couture designs. As Cultural Studies lecturers at Central/St Martin's School of Art and Design in London, they deliberately distanced themselves from the 'button and bow' approach, declaring that their book 'is explicitly analytical; it is, on the whole, about images and ideas in fashion, rather than about cut and fit'. They define their methodologies as 'coming out of post-structuralism and the specifically feminist appropriation of psycho-analytic theory', stressing that their book 'does not analyse fashion in terms of political issues, economics or sociology [but contributes to] studies of women's fashion which refer specifically to issues of *social* marginalisation, issues of race, class and sexuality'.[59]

Such use of clothing to examine 'deviant' or minority subcultures originated from the now widely recognised and pioneering sociology approaches of Stuart Hall and Dick Hebdige at the University of Birmingham's Centre for Contemporary Cultural Studies, founded by Richard Hoggart in 1964. From 1980 Angela McRobbie followed this through with specific assessment of the neglected place of young women within subcultures, through analysis, for example, of dress, dance and patterns of social behaviour, such as her *Feminism and Youth Culture: from Jackie to Just Seventeen* of 1991.[60] Caroline Evans regretted the absence of debate on consumption within the 'old' Birmingham approach. She wrote in 1997 that this was 'a kind of romanticized idea of authentic protest, outside of the commodity forum, which does not hold up to analysis'. As McRobbie had stated in 1994, consumption 'was always in fact a part of subcultural activity'.[61] The pleasure in constructing shifting patterns of personal appearance is one of the significant features of subcultural style. It 'consumes' change and ephemerality as it challenges the accepted tastes of 'conventional' society, typified by Debbie Cohen and her pink hair (Plate IV).

Carol Tulloch of the National Museum and Archives of Black History and Culture, has examined 'the impact that race and ethnicity have on dress and the methodological implications of this encounter'. Undertaking the first research into the dress of black women in Jamaica in the period 1880–1907, she found she had to create her own methodology, a complex fusion of cultural and post-colonial studies with sociology, history and dress history and material culture. Assessing Jamaica, then, as 'a multi-layered society of competing ethnicities', Tulloch developed a critique of 'the historical myths and perceptions of women's dress in the British colony of Jamaica'. She concluded that 'unquestionably, race is in the foreground of my work … informing the historiography, the rhetoric and the "material effect" of imperial discourse'. It became evident to Tulloch in the course of her research that

> Jamaican dress and its associated Jamaican aesthetic style formation did not begin in Britain as part of a black counter-cultural quake after the Second World War. Its roots stretched back to slavery by the intersection of races and ethnicities. I would like to see that dress history is informed by these matters as well.[62]

A new development in the 1990s, building on Farid Chenoune's innovative *Men's Fashions*[63] of 1993, has been the emergence of new critical examination of menswear. This differs from the subcultural focus of Dick Hebdige in that it looks at a far wider social range of male clothing. Christopher Breward, Frank Mort, John Tosh and Saun Cole[64] focus on the late nineteenth and twentieth centuries rather than on earlier periods. Their studies include investigation not only of style, retailing and consumption of men's clothing but also the cultural processes surrounding the construction of masculinity and, for the first time, analysis of gay culture and its impact on mainstream dressing.

Christopher Breward in his 1999 study, *The Hidden Consumer – masculinities, fashion and city life, 1860–1914*, issues a clear rebuke to the women-dominated world of dress history, which he rightly points out has shown all too little interest in men's clothing. Breward therefore 'challenges the understanding through which a large proportion of the consuming population have been written out of a history of modernity and urban life'. He dates this void back to C. W. Cunnington's founding work in the field of dress history in the mid-1950s 'which left men's concerns almost entirely out'.

Breward sets out to explode a series of firmly established dress history assumptions which propose that men took little interest in the style and consumption of clothing in the 1860–1914 period. He shows, on the contrary, that Victorian men, across the full range of middle-class society, in fact did take a deep interest in their clothing and that the concept that interest in the consumption of fashion was restricted to the world of women is entirely fallacious. Breward shows this with careful debate on the complexities of style and the urban consumption of men's clothing in that period. He sets this within debate focusing on patterns of class, retailing and the interest men took in purchasing and wearing clothing. Breward also examines conventional and counter-cultural images of masculinity, including aesthetic dressing and gay culture of the period.

Importantly, Breward also seeks to redress the balance of interest within the museum as well as the academic world. He stresses the fact that male clothing has been badly neglected in museum collections, with the implication that this neglect lies at the hands of women costume curators. Further he suggests that this neglect is seen as 'entirely appropriate … because it reflects the minimal time and attention assumed to have been lavished on sartorial matters by nineteenth century men'. This view is reinforced by the fact that in museum displays of elite costume, eighteenth-century, Western European men's clothing is given equal prominence to that of women, probably because it is just as gorgeous in form, colour and embroidery as that of women. Once the mid to late nineteenth-century period is reached, men's clothing in its dark tailored woollen cloth disappears almost entirely from display for the precise reasons given by Breward. Whilst it is a given fact that far less menswear has survived the passage of time than women's, Breward's view that 'men's concerns have been 'almost entirely left out' is all too obviously true.[65]

Other recent reassessments include a new look at the relationship between subcultural style and commercial, conventional fashionable dress. Both Angela McRobbie and Caroline Evans have assessed the new centrality of subcultural style to mainstream fashion. 'There is little doubt that it is the experimental "funhouse" of the British youth culture and club culture scene, in and around the art schools, in young graduates' studios and the small units, shops and stall-type outlets which they supply, that the creative work which influences major trends emerges'.[66] And so within this 'political economy' of fashion design, Veblen's emulation theories and Fred Davis's notions of fashion divisions collapse as 'peripheral' subcultural styles themselves become the 'centre'.

The style and cultural meanings of dress within the formation of lesbian identity have been debated by Katriona Rolley and Elizabeth Wilson. Rolley, through her postgraduate research into lesbian dress in Britain, used oral history, period literary sources and photography to reveal the deep levels of prejudice faced by lesbian women in the interwar period as a consequence of their choice in clothing.[67]

There is no doubt of the burst of energy that Cultural Studies approaches have injected into dress history/dress studies. This, however, raises specific new problems as it is seen to have contributed to a shift of interest away from garments to text and theory. In some ways this shift can be seen as a rerun of the old anti-artefact prejudices. This shift may indicate that within the field of Cultural Studies critical theory is also seen as far more academically weighty than object-based study of garments. To give just two examples of many, it is significant that Malcolm Barnard's *Fashion as Communication* of 1996 makes not one detailed or specific reference to object-based approaches. Whilst useful as a compendium of Cultural Studies approaches to 'fashion and clothing as ways of communicating class, gender, sexual and social identities', this lack of inclusion of any research on the actuality of clothing is a glaring ommission.[68] Object-based dress historians are absent entirely from his bibliography. Diana Crane, Professor of Sociology at the University of Pennsylvania, titled her study published in the year 2000, *Fashion and its Social Agendas – class, gender and identity in clothing*. Proposing more broad-minded interdisciplinary approaches than Barnard, she debates the differing worlds of mid to late nineteenth- and late twentieth-century Western, urban clothing consumption. She contrasts

> fashion and clothing choices in nineteenth century industrial societies, with their related 'class societies [in which] each class had a distinct culture which differentiated from other classes' with 'contemporary "fragmented societies" [where] distinctions are based on criteria that are meaningful to the numerous and diverse social groups in which they originate but not necessarily to members of other social groups'.

Crane here addresses issues of major social and cultural change through analysis of clothes and their 'meanings'. She is convinced, as are Fine and Leopold, Vickery, Breward and others cited in this chapter, that clothing is 'a strategic site for studying changes in the meanings of cultural goods in relation to changes in social structures, in the character of cultural organisations and in other forms of culture'.

Her focus ranges from analysis of the social life of working-class French families through dress, using case work published in France in 1862 by Frédéric Le Play, through to analysis of contemporary couture and avant-garde style, to global systems of fashion production and diffusion. Crane includes her own sociology research into contemporary women's responses to fashion photographs. Though rarely citing surviving clothing *per se*, she is evidently far less hostile to artefact-based approaches than Barnard. She details, for example (using the work of artefact-based dress historians), the subverted, specific use by women dress reformers of male ties, hats and tailored garments, using period photographs as her visual research base.

Crane concludes, confirming the strength of new academic approaches to the study of dress history, that 'tracing changes in the nature of fashion and in the criteria for clothing choices is one way of understanding the differences between the type of society that has been gradually disappearing and the one that is slowly emerging'. She suggests here, as have others cited in this chapter, that 'too often in studies of various forms of culture, consumption, meaning, space and production are considered separately. As a result, our understanding of how cultural forms influence and are influenced by their social contexts is greatly reduced.' Crane thus also throws her academic weight behind the new interdisciplinary approaches.[69]

These approaches have been greatly enhanced from 1997 when the innovative transatlantic dress history/dress studies journal *Fashion Theory* was launched in London and New York. Produced four times a year, this is edited by the American dress historian, Valerie Steele. The journal's editorial aims and scope are printed in each edition.

> The study of fashion has, until recently, suffered from a lack of critical analysis ... *Fashion Theory* takes as its starting point a definition of 'fashion' as the cultural construction of the embodied identity. It aims to provide an interdisciplinary forum for the rigorous analysis of cultural phenomena ranging from footbinding to fashion advertising.

This journal has already provided a new debating arena for progressive research of every kind through its courageous, if occasionally sensationalist, sweep of interests. It was this journal which published, to give just one example, the memorable article by Steven Zdatny which exposed one of the most commonly held dress history myths. This states that once young women were politically 'liberated' by being given the vote in the 1920s, this was reflected in the 'liberated' style of their short skirts and bobbed garçonne hair. Zdatny establishes through careful period research that indeed large numbers of women of all social classes (in France) did in fact cut off their long hair, often in defiance of their husbands' wishes. But, having established that notions of any real political and social equality were a myth, he is clear that 'spending money on a haircut and a perm did not amount to a revolution in the female condition'. In conclusion, however, rather than dismissing the debate out of hand, Zdatny suggests that 'a short hair cut *felt* like a kind of emancipation',[70] immersing many women into the new, post-war world of youthful modernity. Therein lies the complexity and fascination of the new interdisciplinary approaches to dress history.

Conclusion

The American dress historian Nancy Rexford touched the essence of the void between the academy and object-based historians when she commented in 1988 that 'serious academic scholarship, particularly in history, has invested very heavily in words, and the sensory aspect of the past is not always recognized as worthy of attention'.[71] Since then Benson's view that within 'big history' research, clothing study has become increasingly 'fashion-able'[72] is to be welcomed by all with an interest in dress history, as is the quality and challenge of the examples of new approaches given here.

Patricia Cunningham usefully warned that dress historians

> should not follow other approaches blindly, but rather let our own questions and materials lead us to new approaches. We must try out available models, but devise our own as well ... We should do whatever it takes to answer our research questions and, above all, when we think our questions take us *beyond artifacts*, we must shift, look back, and then reconsider the artifact. There is more there than we think.[73]

The most dynamic research in dress history has indeed now fused artefact-based and theoretical approaches. Where the 'valid' fine line is to be drawn between Prown's processes of 'leading out' from the object into theory, or working back from theory to object is the essence of future debate. But it is evident that the divisive walls within academia have been crumbling dramatically over the last ten years. Now, as the last remaining subject and gender-based prejudices are being mopped up, dress history/dress studies is being propelled into its new future by the high levels of interdisciplinary good practice emerging from both sides of the great dress history divide.

Notes

1 N. Harte, The Economics of Clothing in the Late Seventeenth Century (*Textile History*, 22, 1991), p. 277.

2 S. Rush Meyrick and C. Hamilton-Smith, *Costume of the Original Inhabitants of the British Islands from the Earliest Periods to the Sixth Century* (Thomas M' Lean, London, 1815), preface.

3 W. M. Reddy, *The Rise of Market Culture – the textile trade and French society, 1750–1900* (Cambridge University Press, Cambridge, 1984), p. 88 and p. 91.

4 N. Harte and K. Ponting (eds), *Textile and Economic History: essays in honour of Miss Julia de Lacy Mann* (Manchester University Press, Manchester, 1973).

5 J. Thirsk, The Fantastical Folly of Fashion: the English stocking knitting industry, 1500–1700, in Hart and Ponting (eds), *Textile and Economic History*, p. 50.

6 L. Hamer, The Cullercoats Fishwife (*Costume*, 18, 1984), pp. 66–73 and P. Wardle, Divers necessaries for his Majesty's use and service, seamstresses to the Stuart Kings (*Costume*, 31, 1997), pp. 16–27.

7 C. Evans, Street Style, Subculture and Subversion (*Costume*, 31, 1997), pp. 105–110.

8 N. Harte, book review (*Textile History*, 7, 1976), p. 198.

9 N. Harte, book review (*Textile History*, 12, 1981), p. 152.

10 Harte, The Economics of Clothing, p. 277.

11 N. Harte, book review (*Textile History*, 8, 1977), p. 183.

12 Harte, book review (*Textile History*, 12, 1981), p. 152.

13 Harte, The Economics of Clothing, p. 277.

14 J. Tozer, Cunnington's Interpretation of Dress (*Costume*, 20, 1986), p. 16.

15 L. Taylor, An Assessment of the Current State of Development of Doctoral Research into the History of, and Contemporary Practice of, Dress and Textile Design, *Proceedings of the Conference on Doctoral Education in Design* (University of Ohio and University of Chicago, Chicago, January 1999).

16 The author was one of these, employed by Muriel Pemberton, Head of Fashion at St Martin's School of Art, as a part-time dress history lecturer from the early 1970s.

17 V. Steele, A Museum of Costume is More Than a Clothes Bag (*Fashion Theory*, 2, 4, December 1998), p. 329, quoting J. Prown, Mind in Matter: an introduction to material culture theory and method (*Winterthur Portfolio*, 17, 1982), p. 7.

18 S. J. Bronner, *Consuming Visions: accumulation and display of goods in America, 1880–1920* (Norton, New York, 1989), p. 1.

19 W. Leach, Strategists of Display and the Production of Desire, in Bronner, *Consuming Visions*, p. 132.

20 S. Porter Benson, *Counter Cultures: saleswomen, managers and customers in American department stores* (Ph.D. thesis, University of Illinois, 1986) and R. Shields, *Life Style Shopping: the subject of consumption* (Routledge, London, 1992).

21 J. Brewer and R. Porter, *Consumption and the World of Goods* (Routledge, London, 1993), p. 1.

22 J. Benson, *The Rise of Consumer Society in Britain 1880–1980* (Longman, London, 1994), p. 1 and p. 5.

23 B. Fine and E. Leopold, *The World of Consumption* (Routledge, London, 1993), p. 9, p. 4 and p. 94.

24 D. E. Allen, Fashion as a Social Process (*Textile History*, 22, 2, 1991), p. 347.

25 Harte, book review (*Textile History* 12, 1981), p. 151.

26 J. Styles, Dress in History: reflections on a contested terrain (*Fashion Theory*, 2, 4, December 1998), p. 386.

27 D. Roche, *The Culture of Clothing: dress and fashion in the Ancien Regime* (Cambridge University Press, Cambridge, 1994).

28 J. Brewer, J. H. Plumb and N. McKendrick, *Birth of the Consumer Society: the commercialisation of 18th century Britain* (Hutchinson, London, 1983), see chapter 2 on the Consumption of Fashion.

29 J. Styles, Manufacturing, Consumption and Design in Eighteenth Century England, in Brewer and Porter, *Consumption and the World of Goods*, p. 538.

30 D. Miller, *Acknowledging Consumption: a review of new studies* (Routledge, London, 1995), p. 1.

31 A. Vickery, Women and the World of Goods: a Lancashire consumer and her possessions, 1751–81, in Brewer and Porter, *Consumption and the World of Goods*, p. 294, quoting D. Miller, Appropriating the State on the Council Estate (*Man*, n.s. xxiii, 1988), pp. 353–372.

32 A. Smart Martin, Makers, Buyers and Users – consumerism as a material culture framework (*Winterthur Portfolio*, 28, 2/4, Summer/Autumn 1993), pp. 142–143.

33 G. McCracken, *Culture and Consumption: new approaches to the symbolic character of consumption* (University of Indiana Press, Bloomington, 1988), p. 89.

34 I. Kopytoff, The Cultural Biography of Things: commoditization as process, in A. Appadurai, *The Social Life of Things: commodities in cultural perspective* (Cambridge University Press, Cambridge, 1986), pp. 66–67.

35 Styles, Dress in History, p. 387.

36 A. Jarvis, Letter from the Editor (*Fashion Theory*, 2, 4, December 1998), p. 300.

37 B. Lemire, *Dress, Culture and Commerce: the English clothing trade before the factory, 1660–1800* (Macmillan, Basingstoke, 1997), p. 4; see also idem, *Fashion's Favourite – the cotton trade and the consumer in Britain, 1660–1800* (Oxford University Press, Oxford, 1991).

38 Vickery, Women and the World of Goods, p. 278, p. 274 and p. 279.

39 A. Vickery, *The Gentleman's Daughter: women's lives in Georgian England* (Yale University Press, London, 1998), p. 180 and p. 178.

40 Vickery, Women and the World of Goods, p. 279, p. 282, p. 284 and p. 287.

41 Vickery, *The Gentleman's Daughter*, p. 194.

42 Vickery, *The Gentleman's Daughter*, p. 280 and N. Rothstein, *Silk Designs of the Eighteenth Century in the Collection of the Victoria and Albert Museum* (Thames & Hudson, London, 1990), p. 252 and plates 282–288, see Sample Pattern Book T. 375.1972.

43 N. Rothstein, *A Lady of Fashion: Barbara Johnson's album of styles and fabrics* (Thames & Hudson, London, 1987), p. 15 of the reproduction of the original album.

44 Vickery, *The Gentleman's Daughter*, p. 185.

45 C. Breward, Cultures, Identities: fashioning a cultural approach to dress (*Fashion Theory*, 2, 4, December 1998), p. 303 and p. 305.

46 Ibid.

47 C. Evans, Street Style, Subcultures and Subversion (*Costume*, 31, 1997), p. 107.

48 Steele, A Museum of Costume is More Than a Clothes Bag, p. 32, quoting E. McClung Fleming, Artifact Study: a proposed model (*Winterthur Portfolio*, 9, 1973), p. 161.

49 P. Bourdieu, *Distinction: a social critique of the judgement of taste* (Routledge, London, 1989; 1st edition, Minuit, Paris, 1979), pp. 1–2 and p. 12.

50 F. Davis, *Fashion, Culture and Identity* (University of Chicago Press, Chicago, 1992), p. 191 and p. 206.

51 Vickery, *The Gentleman's Daughter*, p. 274.

52 J. Gaines and C. Herzog, *Fabrications and the Female Body* (Routledge, London, 1990), p. 3.

53 E. Wilson, All the Rage, in Gaines and Herzog, *Fabrications and the Female Body*, p. 28.

54 J. Gaines, Fabricating the Female Body, in Gaines and Herzog, *Fabrications and the Female Body*, p. 7, quoting E. Wilson, *Adorned with Dreams: fashion and modernity* (Virago, London, 1985), p. 13.

55 Wilson, All the Rage, p. 33.

56 C. Evans and M. Thornton, *Women and Fashion: a new look* (Quartet, London, 1989), p. xv.

57 K. Peiss, Making Up, Making Over: cosmetics, consumer culture and women's identity, in V. de Grazia and E. Furlough, *The Sex of Things: gender and consumption in historical perspective* (University of California Press, Berkeley, 1996), p. 331.

58 Vickery, *The Gentleman's Daughter*, p. 183.

59 Evans and Thornton, *Women and Fashion*, p. xv.

60 A. McRobbie, *Feminism and Youth Culture: from Jackie to Just Seventeen* (Macmillan, Basingstoke, 1991).

61 Evans, Street Style, p. 8, quoting A. McRobbie, *Postmodernism and Popular Culture* (Routledge, London, 1994), p. 156.

62 C. Tulloch, 'Out of Many, One People': the relativity of dress, race and ethnicity to Jamaica, 1880–1907 (*Fashion Theory*, 2, 4, December 1998), p. 360, p. 364, p. 368 and p. 379.

63 F. Chenoune, *Mens' Fashions* (Flammarion, Paris, 1993).

64 C. Breward, *The Hidden Consumer: masculinities, fashion and city life, 1860–1914* (Manchester University Press, Manchester, 1999); T. Hitchcock and M. Cohen, *English Masculinities, 1660–1800* (Longmans, London, 1999); F. Mort, *Cultures and Consumption: masculinities and social space in the late 20th century* (Routledge, London, 1996); J. Tosh, *A Man's Place: masculinity and the middle class home in Victorian England* (Yale University Press, New Haven and London, 1999); S. Cole, *Don We Now Our Gay Apparel: gay men's dress in the twentieth century* (Bergs, Oxford, 2000).

65 Breward, *The Hidden Consumer*, p. 2 and pp. 10–11.

66 See A. McRobbie, Settling Accounts with Subculture (*Screen Education*, 39, Spring 1980), pp. 16–17 and idem, *British Fashion Design: rag trade or image industry* (Routledge, London, 1998), pp. 183–184.

67 K. Rolley, *The Female Dandy: the role of dress and appearance in the construction of lesbian identity in Britain, 1918–1938* (M. Phil. thesis, University of Middlesex, 1995); E. Wilson, The Post Modern Body, in E. Wilson and J. Ash, *Chic Thrills: a fashion reader* (Pandora, London, 1993), pp. 3–16.

68 M. Barnard, *Fashion As Communication* (Routledge, London, 1996), p. 1.

69 D. Crane, *Fashion and Its Social Agendas: class, gender and identity in clothing* (University of Chicago Press, Chicago, 2000), p. 2, p. 23, p. 236 and p. 238.

70 S. Zdatny, The Boyish Look and the Liberated Woman: the politics and aesthetics of women's hairstyles (*Fashion Theory*, 1, 4, December 1997), pp. 367–397.

71 N. Rexford, Studying Garments For Their Own Sake: mapping the world of costume scholarship (*Dress*, 14, 1988), p. 74.

72 Benson, *The Rise of Consumer Society*, p. 1.

73 P. Cunningham, Beyond Artifact and Object Chronology (*Dress*, 14, 1988), p. 79.

4 ✧ Approaches using literary sources

Where dress is used to express character and illuminate social attitudes and relationships, the novel can give more. It then shows dress in action within the novelist's world. (Anne Buck)[1]

DRESS historians have always drawn on literary sources to lend accuracy and historical 'feel' to their work. Novels, poetry, plays, newspapers, journals, autobiographies and diaries are all carefully trawled for the apt quotation. Joseph Strutt, the founder of British dress history, drew heavily on texts from the Bible, and from Ovid and Shakespeare onwards for his weighty volumes *The Complete View of the Manners, Customs, Arms, Habits etc. of the Inhabitants of England* (1774, 1775 and 1776). Nearly two hundred years later, two of the most famous mid-twentieth-century dress historians, C. W. Cunnington and James Laver made free use of literary sources. James Laver remembered C. W. Cunnington's enthusiasm for this research approach. After Cunnington retired from his medical practice he continued his researches 'going through every English novel he could find and noting the author's references to costume. He made this invaluable information freely available to other workers in the same field, including myself.'[2]

However, in 1976, as discussed in Chapter 3, the economic historian, Negley Harte, listed amongst his methodological objections to current fashion history practice that it drew far too readily from easy-access literary quotations. Doris Langley Moore had warned long before that 'the novelists of any period, enlightening as they are, tend to fall into the conventions of that period, which to a large extent they themselves create. Thus heroines in the Age of Sensibility faint on the smallest provocation, though in the diaries, letters and other literary records of the time there is surprisingly little of this swooning.'[3] Terry Lovell, researching 'the eighteenth-century discourse of imitation' warns of the dangers of attempting to make too close a fit between culturally available personas and categories of persons. It is perhaps only in fictional worlds and in ideology that characters always act in character. In their day-to-day existence … it may be that the identities of men and women were less unidimensional than those of their fictional exemplars.[4]

Can, therefore, such period literary comment be trusted as 'accurate' at all and why should dress historians use it when so many other sources exist?

Use of period novels, poetry and plays by the dress historian

One historian whom Harte excluded from his criticism was Anne Buck, who assessed the inherent problems of this approach in 1983.

> In letters and diaries, family and business accounts, published and unpublished, and a mass of printed ephemera … we may be able to discern influences other than fashion, influences which introduce their own sequences into the mainstream of change, modifying, resisting, or rejecting the current image. Why then should we turn to fiction when we have fact? … Assuming the novelist uses dress at all, a story set at the time of writing can with accurate observation and recording give factual and descriptive evidence. Where dress is used to express character and illuminate social attitudes and relationships, the novel can give more. It then shows dress in action within the novelist's world.[5]

Buck's term 'dress in action' is the key to understanding the significant and important advantages of this methodology. Her own work shows that analysis of the use of clothing by novelists can deepen our cultural understanding of the past through its coded signalling of gender, culture, politics and social stratum. Coming with her finely honed, hands-on 'object' expertise, Anne Buck's research thus specifically uses literary sources to pinpoint period socio-cultural issues rather than simply as aids to description. To give one example, in her article The Clothes of Thomasine Petre: 1555–1559, Buck uses text drawn from a little known mid-sixteenth-century play, referring to the specific rank-coded use of lavish gold, rather than white, 'billiment' hood decorations, as a means of positioning Thomasine very carefully within the new 'rising gentry' class of her period.[6]

Buck also draws examples from the works of Jane Austen, Elizabeth Gaskell, Anthony Trollope and George Eliot, explaining that Austen 'wrote of a society she knew intimately and she kept within it … a realist' whilst she saw Gaskell as 'an honest and perceptive writer'.[7] Buck stresses that text from such novels can help an understanding of the cultural meanings of the great range and variety of clothing, much of it not fashionable, which was worn throughout British society between 1825 and 1865. Having made clear that evidence from novels should always be used alongside the factual evidence of surviving garments and related archives, Buck also stresses their ability to give a feel for 'ways of life'[8] and those of men as much as women.

Rachel Worth, who has continued to develop some of Buck's methodologies, concentrates on the work of Gaskell precisely because the novelist uses clothing to help define the 'major themes' of her novels. Worth highlights Gaskell's sophisticated use of the 'unspoken assumptions' found within the codes of clothing to explain 'the complex language class' of her specific period.[9]

Novels can give perceptive and helpful accounts not just of the actuality of period dress, such as that of working people where so very little clothing has survived, but can also provide a special form of emotional insight into behaviour patterns which make up what John Harvey terms 'the complication of social life made visible'.[10] Worth, for example, is interested in the ways in which Elizabeth Gaskell used the complexities of Victorian clothing codes to expose the period's depths of social difference. She notes that Gaskell shows how lack of ownership of middle-class dress became a form of 'moral alienation' from bourgeois society. Worth picks out Gaskell's sensitive awareness to the use of cheap fustian cloth as an unspoken 'badge of identification' amongst poverty-stricken Manchester weavers, in contrast to the consumption of good quality, woollen, broadcloth by the mill owners.[11]

Novels can identify through subtle textural nuances how each stratum and member of society, male or female, rich or poor, young or old, enjoys, flaunts, defies or denies their social place through dress. In *Esther Walters*, George Moore gives an account of young servant girls forced into prostitution in late nineteenth-century London who try to enhance their sexual appeal and to deny their social place through wearing the second-hand finery of the middle classes. In doing so, however, they reveal only their desperate state because their 'finery' is so worn and battered. Moore describes them as 'poor and dissipated girls, dressed in vague clothes fixed with hazardous pins'. One wore a skirt of 'soiled mauve … a broken yellow plume hung out of a battered hat'. The other had a skirt of 'dim green and little was left of the cotton velours jacket but the cotton'.[12]

Ronald Paulson has used literary text to define and debate fundamental issues of cultural history too, one of his specific interests being to define 'the connection between emulation and consumption' in the first half of the eighteenth century. He concentrates on the period debate about 'the poor's dangerous emulation of their betters', but misses many opportunities for debate because at no point does he take any interest in the actuality of the clothing artefacts pictured by his painters and discussed by his writers, including Defoe and Richardson.[13]

John Harvey's book *Men in Black* takes precisely the opposite approach and is especially relevant here because, as a lecturer in English Literature at Emmanuel College, Cambridge, and a novelist himself,[14] he has come to an open-minded use of clothing in his cultural analysis with no prior specialism in dress history at all. In unravelling the use of black in sixteenth-to twentieth-century menswear, his study centres on why Victorian men dressed so consistently as if they were going to a funeral.

Harvey's use of 'the testimony of novelists' is extensive and moves beyond Worth's. 'Their famed skill is precisely in reading the inner meanings of externals', he explains. 'It is precisely novelists like Dickens, or Charlotte Brontë, who are at once most sentient and most exact in tracing people's dress, as in their words, their pushes of assertion and bids for control.'[15] He is not afraid to tackle these ideas in the boldest manner, writing, for example, of 'an idea running through both Dickens's and Charlotte Brontë's work that black dress may involve a form of black preaching, an unending sermon audible everywhere, while what is being preached is principally a social and political gospel'.[16] Anne Buck's term 'clothing in action' comes to mind when reading Harvey's assessment of the broad cultural signific-ances attached to clothing, significances which had largely been neglected in dress history and material culture studies until the 1980s. 'Styles of clothing', he writes, 'carry feelings and trusts, investments, faiths and formalised fears. Styles exert a social force, they enrol in armies – moral armies, political armies, gendered armies, social armies.'[17]

Harvey, uniquely for a literary critic, examines both clothes and a wide range of dress history research and approaches and such a rare interest deserves explanation. His route into this approach stems from his long-standing, 'pictorially-minded' interests, including analysis of the work of illustrators of Shakespeare and Dickens and mid-nineteenth-century paint-ings.[18] The text for *Men in Black* travels from Aeschylus's *Choephori*, through close discussion of Shakespearean, Dickens and Brontë texts and on through to Kafka's *The Trial*. Harvey fuses in discussion of period paintings, an interest derived from using slides when teaching courses on nineteenth-century Realism. He began to find the endless images of men in black and women in white a more interesting discussion point than the issues of Realism he was meant to be teaching.[19] The delight here is to find a highly skilled literary critic using clothing as a tool of cultural analysis with such obvious fascination.

Use of comment on dress from period press and journals

Quotes extracted from newspapers and magazines are another classic standby of the dress historian. The historian Neil McKendrick, whose work was discussed in Chapter 3, when warning of the dangers inherent in using fictional sources, noted that 'the prudent historian does well to pause before translating the proverbial wisdom of the poets, into the assumed behaviour of society'.[20] Yet he has no qualms about appropriating comments from period journals and travellers' tales uncritically himself. He uses both as key evidence in his debate on the important economic debate surrounding the rise in levels of consumption in Britain in the late eighteenth century. He centres much of this debate on clothing, seeing dress as 'the most public manifestation of the blurring of class divisions which was so much commented on'.[21] McKendrick marshals a fine array of period quotations which he uses to support the idea of fashion spreading like a fever to all social classes. He writes of

> not just the occasional visitor describing his admiring reactions to English fashion, but dozens expressing their astonishment, at not just a few burgesses' wives desirous of following fashion but virtually all the middle class, many of the tradesmen, mechanics and more prosperous working classes.[22]

He selected, amongst other sources, the view of Carl P. Moritz, a German traveller, who commented in 1782 that 'the poorest servant is careful to be in the fashion, particularly in their hats and bonnets, which they all wear'. In 1787 Sir John Hawkins was convinced too that 'a new fashion pervades the whole of this our island almost as instantaneously as a spark of the fire illuminates a mass of gunpowder'.[23] As Vickery points out, McKendrick completes this with his own view that 'it was this new consumer demand, the mill girl who wanted to look like a duchess ... which helped create the Industrial Revolution'.[24]

An aware reader will constantly come across similarly patronising period and post-period comment throughout the nineteenth and twentieth centuries. A Tory MP, Arthur A. Baumann, discussing possible remedies for the sweated tailoring system in 1888, noted 'a huge and constantly increasing class ... who have ... wide wants and narrow means. Luxury has soaked downwards and a raised standard of living among people with small incomes has created an enormous demand for cheap elegancies ... cheap clothes and cheap furniture', which Baumann saw as indicating 'democracy in dress. It is no longer possible, as it was even 30 years ago, to tell with tolerable accuracy what a man is by his dress.'[25]

Alison Settle, fashion journalist and writer, wrote of the same similar sartorial phenomenon in the pre-First World War period due to the vogue for 'the tailored costume worn by all social classes ... The lower classes wore copies in cheaper woollens so close on look that it became harder to tell the mistress from the maid or well-to-do stay-at-home lady from the career girl earning her living in an office'.[26]

This selection of period comment, spread over two hundred years, indicates that each period went through the same, often enraged, debate. In each case, the social structure of Britain was seen to be threatened, or at least confused, by the 'fact' that social place could no longer be identified as satisfactorily through clothes as it had been by the previous generation. Such commonly found opinion would seem to provide irrefutable period evidence of the democratisation of dress through the diffusion of high fashion styling. All of this would indicate that it was spiralling downwards through all social classes from the eighteenth century onwards. This in turn, as Settle implies, would suggest the development of a more equal society with a more democratic distribution of stylish goods.

However, on close inspection, neither these quotations nor the massive social flattening they imply could be described as factually correct. The heart of the problem lies in the uncritical use of period comment. Langley Moore noted in 1949 that some writers on dress 'will often prefer to be entertaining rather than accurate, quoting instances which are outstandingly exceptional as if they were the norm. They will take a joke in "Punch", a satirist's jibe, an anecdote about some daring celebrity as an accurate and factual picture.'[27] Zeldin noted in 1980 that 'historians still quote newspapers as expressions of public opinion no doubt because they can find no alternative source for discovering this'.[28] As Harte identified, the danger of such uncritical use is the creation of historical mythologies and ultimately of yet more revisionist dress and social history. Field hands, servants and mill girls in the eighteenth century did not in reality wear hats and dresses elegant enough to make them look like duchesses, or indeed even aspire to do this, as Vickery's work has made succinctly clear.

What such comments do interestingly reveal, however, are the deeply felt social anxieties and stresses of each period. These views exemplify ingrained social/gender fears and prejudices of their day, fears expressed by each generation that those they consider to be their social inferiors were increasingly able to replicate the style of the social class directly above them. This in turn is seen symbolically to threaten their security and the stability of society as a whole. What this highlights, to use Harvey's term, is society's 'formalised fears' rather than any reality of democratised clothing and appearance amongst the 'lower' social rankings. Period comment is all too easily prone to distortion, prejudice, exaggeration, social resentment and even jealousy. Vickery, specifically and correctly, condemns uncritical and unsupported use of quotations which accept 'ancient prejudices … passed off as actual behaviour'. She proposes instead Bourdieu's approach, in *Distinction* as presenting 'a system whereby each class is actively distinguishing itself from other classes in goods and lifestyle'[29] rather than attempting forms of envious emulative usurpation.

However, it also remains true that even when the 'lower orders' stuck to what others might consider socially appropriate products – those of an identifiably cheap, working character – their clothes and fabrics were and are still derided and patronised as 'common' by the rest of society, although what may seem 'common' to the elite will be 'novelty' or decency to the poorer client. James Thomson, a calico printer clarified this in his socially divisive account of the two branches of the mid-nineteenth-century British calico trade. He noted that 'the first, high in character, fewest in numbers and foremost in the race of competition [is identifiable by] the general merit and good taste of their designs. The second class is a numerous, motley ... mass of dissimilar and discordant elements ... associated with vulgar ignorance.'[30]

Precisely the same style of hostile comments, with the added ingredients of gender and anti-feminist prejudice, followed every nuance of the move-ment towards more practical and comfortable clothing for women during the 1850–1910 period. Fears in the public mind aroused by the debate on the emancipation of women, indelibly connected any forms of radical dress reform to social anxieties over women's rights. The same aggressive range of period comment appeared again and again. Mrs Eric Pritchard, the fashion writer for the *Lady's Realm*, typified conventional middle-class attitudes in her condemnation of progressive, practical clothing for women. In 1907, she defined 'feminine' dress as requiring 'delightful transparencies, wonderful laces ... daintiness'.[31] Five years earlier in her book *The Cult of Chiffon* she had attacked the 'athletic' woman. 'I am not sure she has not had a resurrection as a socialist woman. Anyhow, she is aggressive ... her ideas are limited to dead shades and washed out tints which somehow look muddy and only possess the virtue of matching the poor lady's complexion.'[32] Bourdieu defines this as cultural terrorism, 'symbolic violence through which the dominant groups endeavour to impose their own life-style ... flashes of self interested lucidity sparked off by class hatred and contempt'.[33]

What soon becomes clear is that by taking an alternative set of period comments it is possible to come up with a completely contrasting set of period socio-cultural views of the same decades, resulting in a final picture that is ultimately very different. The rural labourers' straw hats identified by McKendrick as 'fashionable picture hats' (a curiously 1950s term) turn into home-made straw hats when the dress historians Phyllis Cunnington and Catherine Lucas choose the period comments. They note the 1748 comment on the clothing of Home Counties countrywomen by P. Kalm: 'When they go out, they wear straw hats which they have made themselves from wheat straw and are pretty enough.'[34] As to the notion that 'fashion pervades the whole of this our island', Buck identifies profound differences

in both the actuality of clothes and attitudes towards clothes amongst the
working population. It was, for example, common practice for mistresses
to pass on or bequeathe their cast-off clothes and accessories to their
maids. In turn some of this was sold either in the second-hand clothing
shops or privately and some distributed to other female servants and much
altered. Buck quotes Mrs Ann Cook who wrote in 1760 that 'the mistress
noted at church on Sunday'

> the Maids all very neat at the Chapel ... all dressed in the gowns, handker-
> chiefs, aprons, ruffles and head suits that she had given her cook. A maid
> explained that the cook had divided out the spoils between the servants.
> They were only worn to church and put away immediately afterwards.[35]

Such sources are carefully recognised by Klein too in his work on Defoe's
texts. Klein discusses the writer's interest in people wearing the 'wrong
clothing for their social estate' in the eighteenth century, yet he is careful,
unlike McKendrick and Paulson, to point out that servants were supplied
with clothing by their employers, and that working people in the cities
had access to second-hand clothes.[36]

As to Baumann's 'luxury soaking downwards' at the end of the nineteenth century, a socialist description of only a few years later would
confound any talk of 'cheap elegancies'. Maud Pember Reeves, making a
social survey of a street in Lambeth with other Fabian women less than
twenty years later, found none at all. Their report of families where the
husband was in work concluded that trying to find sources of family
clothing budgets was

> frankly, a mystery ... The women seldom get new clothes: boots they are
> often entirely without. The men go to work and must be supplied, the
> children must be decent but the mother has no need to appear in the light
> of day. If very badly equipped, she can shop in the evening in the Walk,
> and no-one will notice under her jacket and rather long skirt, what she is
> wearing on her feet. Most of them have a hat, a jacket and a best skirt to
> wear in the street.[37]

As to the reality of Settle's maid looking just like her mistress, or
typists looking like duchesses in the 1920s, H. V. Morton was clearly aware
that this was a fictional myth, which he exposed in his stories of London
life of 1926. He expresses a socially contemptuous view of young, would-be
fashionable London typists with 'their chinchilla minds and coney incomes'.
He described the struggle they went through to look stylish, and especially
the problem of affording silk stockings. 'When you are trying to dress like
a duchess on seventy shillings a week, a ladder is a tragedy.'[38]

So which set of comments can be taken as 'true'? Where does this leave the confused researcher? What is clear is the danger of using such comment without a full range of other supporting sources – artefacts, paintings, photos, archival study, etc. Artefact-based dress/textile historians understand the subtleties of difference that lie within the actuality of clothing through the experience of handling period fabrics and all qualities of clothing. They can also spot give-away nuances of personal appearance, such as quality of hairdressing, make-up, accessories.

Dress historians are therefore less likely than others to make these 'can't tell the mistress from the maid' assumptions. However, in their eagerness to be properly artefactually accurate, dress historians may entirely miss another, broader, sociological overview also to be discerned from period comment. When their comments are examined in this alternative light, we see that McKendrick, Baumann and Settle share an approach that deserves more than easy dismissal. This view was clarified for this author during discussions with Elizabeth Wilson, when co-writing *Through the Looking Glass – a history of dress from 1860 to the present day* for the BBC in 1989. We debated the 'maid/duchess' issue and the related notions of the democratisation of dress within the specific context of issues of mass modernity in the 1920s. In trying to marry up our seemingly incompatible artefact-versus-sociological standpoints, in this specific case related to the wider diffusion of fashion in the 1920s, we concluded that an overview such as McKendrick's, which clearly does not stand upon any reality of the garments themselves, centres rather on

> the visual image created by the new styles. At this abstract level – the level at which fashion acts as a representation or symbol of this or that aspect of a social mood – the fashions … whether made up in precious crêpe-de-chine or cheap rayon, did suggest both the modernity and the democracy of urban society … despite the vast differences in the quality of the actual clothes, the myth [of democratisation of dress] had its own potency and may even have contributed to a subjective feeling of emancipation for women.[39]

This was the very same conclusion reached by Stephen Zdatny in 1997 in his analysis of the spread of the bobbed hair cut in France in the 1920s.[40] That fashion acts as a symbol of social mood in this way is precisely why McKendrick chose to use it in his debate on consumption developments in the late eighteenth century. This also validates Harvey's belief, worth stressing again here, that 'styles of clothing carry feelings and trusts, investments, faiths and formalised fears. Styles exert a social force, they enrol in armies – moral armies, political armies, gendered armies, social armies.'[41]

The use of autobiographies, diaries, letters and travel stories

Further well-trawled sources of period comment on dress are autobiographies, diaries, personal letters and travel stories. Exaggeration, political
bias, romanticism and invention are just as possible to find here as
elsewhere and no historian would accept these texts at face value, or
without additional evidence. They provide too many personal opportunities
to settle old scores, to distort and fantasise. They can also, however, provide
rare and valid glimpses into 'the complication of social life made visible'
and into the lost past of destroyed cultures.

Some writers are at least candid about their omissions. In 1936–37
Nadine Wolnar-Larsky wrote an account of her early married life within
the highest levels of Court society in St Petersburg in the period leading
up to and including the Russian Revolution. She declared her stance. 'All
that is written here is strictly true, as far as my personal knowledge goes'
– an encouraging thought, but then she adds that 'in order to avoid hurting
the feelings of those who are still alive, or the memories of some who
have died, certain facts are deliberately omitted'.[42]

However, Tim Breen, amongst many others, is prepared to use such
period accounts because they act as 'an intersection of intellectual and
social history'. For his interpretations of the mid-eighteenth-century consumer economy in America, he found such texts provided 'perceptions,
cultural readings – attempts by people of different backgrounds and
experience not only to interpret the 18th century consumer economy, but
also their place within it'.[43]

Period witness left to us by consumers writing about their own clothes
in the setting of their own 'place within society' is of value precisely because
it does reflect personal flaws, vanities and anxieties. Their responses to 'the
complication of social life made visible' echo down to us from the past
in few more vivid ways. The balance of these memories is weighted towards
the better off and the better educated, but fortunately not exclusively so.

Elizabeth Charlotte, the Duchess of Orléans, daughter-in-law of Louis
XIV, was 'a compulsive letter writer'. She left a vast amount of correspondence in German and French, detailing the complexity and exigencies of
French Royal etiquette. In 1701, soon after the death of her husband, the
heir to the French throne, she wrote to her aunt from St Cloud describing
the ritual of the first stage of a Royal widow's mourning. Her letter reveals
her clear self-awareness that her widow's role was that of a compliant icon
of Royal power to be clothed by courtiers who implemented upon her
body and all around her body every nuance of the requisite Court etiquette
– etiquette she did not even know.

I had to receive the ceremonial visit of the King and Queen of England wearing the strangest apparel: a white linen band across my forehead, above it a cap which tied under my chin like a veil, over the cap, *les cornettes*, and over them a piece of linen that was fastened to the shoulders like a mourning-coat, with a train seven ells long [and with] a girdle of black crêpe reaching to the ground in front and a train of ermine seven ells long. In this get-up, with the train arranged to show the ermine, I was placed on a black bed in an entirely blackened room. Even the parquet was covered in black and the windows hung with crêpe. A great candelabrum of twelve candles was lit … All my domestics, short and tall, were in long mourning-coats: forty or fifty ladies, all in crêpe, it was a ghastly sight.[44]

Jane Austen's personal correspondence, unlike 'the sparing references in dress in the novels', reveals a wealth of detail on dress, which Buck believes shows 'the limitations of the novelist's own everyday life and experience'. In 1799 Austen was recycling one of her dresses and wrote of trouble with a commercial professional dyer, who had clearly damaged her fabric with harsh dyes. 'How is your gown? Mine is all to peices [sic]. I think there must have been something wrong with the dye, for in places it divided with a touch. There was four shillings thrown away.'[45]

Two autobiographical examples of vastly differently socially located clothing references will serve here to demonstrate the value of this method. Nadine Wolnar-Larsky, whose father-in-law ran his household with great extravagance and luxury remembered that 'no-one who has not taken part in the life of St Petersbourg, in old days, can possibly imagine the gaiety, the charm, the happiness, the liberty of that marvellously free existence'. She was able to purchase anything she wanted in St Petersburg including

lovely dresses from Behr, Doeuillet, Doucet and Paquin, dozens of hats and more jewels than I could possibly wear became an ordinary part of one's life. The French model houses, the *maisons de couture*, held a show of their collections two or three times a year in one of the hotels in St Petersbourg … There were also some French dressmakers established in the town who provided and copied models from the best houses in Paris.[46]

At the opposite end of the European social scale of clothing consumers came Winifred Foley, the daughter of an impoverished coal mining family from the New Forest. When she reached her fourteenth birthday in 1928, she left home to work as a domestic servant in London, the only type of work open to her. Although now seen to be more fiction than fact, the account of the struggle that confronted her family when they had to provide her with a set of etiquette-correct, working clothes with absolutely no financial means to do so, was a familiar story. The problem was resolved, even if with haphazard results, through a last resort mix of barter, gifting and do-it-yourself. First, Winifred had to be provided with her own maid's uniform – a black dress and white cap and apron. 'Luckily Mam was able to make a swap. A young miner's wife, expecting her first baby, exchanged her maid's dress for Mam's treasured washstand jug and basin set.' Next Winifred had to have a respectable set of outdoor clothes for travelling and arrival at her employer's house. This desperate problem was resolved by the local teacher's donation of her own second-hand coat, hat and shoes, though all proved far too big. 'Miss Hale's head-hugging cloche ... came so far over my eyebrows that I had to lift it continually to see where I was going.' The brown coat, with fur collar and cuffs 'came down to the tips of my fingers and the hem nearly to my ankles. "Never mind" said Mam, "now you'll be gettin' your bellyful of good food, you'll soon be fillin' it, an' it'll last you for donkey's years".' As a final mark of her new urban maid's status, Winifred was given 'two properly hemmed handkerchiefs, the first I had ever owned. After a lifetime of using the inside of my skirt or sleeve, when no-one was looking, it seemed sacrilegious to use these dainty, ironed white squares for wiping my nose.'[47]

Accounts found within travellers' tales can provide vivid images of long past and eroded cultures, though again social and political prejudice has to be considered. Two diverse personal views of urban/political life in the Balkan states, both of which make use of sartorial references, can be found in the writings of Mrs Wills Gordon, a wealthy British woman travelling with her husband in the period just before the First World War, and the memories of Peter Thornton who filmed Balkan ritual village dancing in the 1935–36 period. Both visited Bucharest.

Mrs Gordon, whose text is riddled with overt anti-semitic and racist comment, was entranced by the luxury and refinement of cosmopolitan Bucharest and of the Royal Family. She wrote in eulogistic terms of the Royal Palace and Queen Marie, 'a cousin of both King George and Tzar Nicholas ... the Queen was dressed in a clinging gown of ivory crêpe de chine ... The poise of the head ... is admirable – regal, yet full of grace – the figure slender ... and the exquisite complexion – her English inheritance – one of pearl of peaches.' Mrs Gordon was also deeply impressed by the dazzling shops, restaurants, theatres and magnificent palaces, conjuring up a hard-to-imagine vision of pre-Ceaușescu conspicuous consumption in Bucharest.

> The streets are broad, well-paved and lined with gay shops, displaying all the Paris fashions ... here one sits dressed in demi-toilette ... [The] moving throng of carriages and streams of well-dressed people present at all hours is a lively scene ... one needs to have a good fat purse here, for it is one of the most expensive cities.[48]

Peter Thornton visited the same city in 1935, conscious of the country's move into Fascism[49] and yet fascinated by its thriving and ancient peasant culture. He leaves us with a rare account of the famous, national *Lunar Bucurestilor* exhibition, the remains of which form the National Ethnographical Museum's *Skansen* today. 'They had constructed a big village' where 'not only had they uprooted the very houses but the occupants with their children, hens, pigs and cows.' Here Thornton was happy enough to film peasant dress and displays of dancing by the transplanted villagers but his deep political unease makes itself clear as he writes of his consternation over the consequences of King Carol's policy of making 'the intelligentsia better acquainted with the peasants'. For one exhibition ceremony they were 'dressed up' in pseudo-village dress, marching 'around behind their band of exultant players, and each time they passed Prince Michael their right arms stiffened in the Fascist salute ... pseudo peasants in their machine embroidered shirts and skirts'.[50]

All these categories of text describing the purchase and consumption of period dress, if used with appropriate care, can serve to demonstrate both the past and present of Harvey's 'complication of social life made visible'. Examination of literary references to clothing can take us towards the heart of Harvey's 'inner meaning of externals' by identifying a whole range of characteristics and consequences of 'clothes in action' – our emotional responses to clothes, how fabrics move, sound, smell, how clothes feel on the body and their impact on the way their wearers move in them, for example.

Literary sources and emotional responses to clothing

One of the great voids of dress history has been its failure to examine emotional responses to clothing and appearance. Perhaps design/dress historians in their search for academic respectability have become over-nervous about departing from safely established academic methodologies, but in doing so they have missed a key approach to which others are increasingly turning. Ethnographers have long understood this relationship and a growing number of material culture researchers, such as Daniel Miller and Amanda Vickery, and sociologists such as Angela McRobbie, have now started to fill some of these voids.

Tim Breen has identified the cultural and historical importance of the 'private associations' we attach to goods. In discussing the eighteenth century, he notes that goods 'tell us stories about the creative possibilities of possession, about the process of self-fashioning ... about the personal joys and disappointments that we sense must also have been a product of that eighteenth century commercial world'.[51]

Material cultural researchers are, for example, thus coming to terms with the economic and cultural consequences of the fact that goods, including clothes, are usually used over periods of many years, whether out of love or necessity. The late dress historian, Janet Arnold, stressed this over many years.[52] Literary sources too can often movingly explain our personal reactions to clothes. The use of text from personal diaries, letters and autobiographies related to clothing making, selection, purchase and wearing thus offers another way through to an understanding of the cultural significance of clothing.

The Polish dissident novelist, Leopold Tyrmand, used the desperate emotional longing amongst the young for fashionable American clothes in post-war Poland, where such garments were both unobtainable and also officially frowned upon, as one of the central 'hooks' through which to expose the corrupt and collapsed state of the country in the late 1940s and early 1950s. His story in part deals with the attempted seduction of Martha, a respectable young Warsaw woman, by a young, black-marketeering, petty criminal, George.

Martha searches for a stylish but cheap blouse in the main second-hand clothes market in Warsaw where American clothing-aid parcels often, illegally, ended up. She 'went slowly along the alley ... her cheeks glowed with excitement as she came upon this richness'. She meets George, across a stall which is selling everything from 'taffeta ball gowns, to beach skirts and blouses, sweaters ... not to mention medicines and injections ... suddenly she leaned over a pile of underwear, seized the edge of something white and pulled out a superb bathing costume in white nylon' which, inevitably, she could not afford to buy. George

> smiled graciously, revealing two rows of massive, blackened silver teeth ... with a glint in his eye, like a hunter whose prey looks as if it is about to bolt. 'I can just imagine how you would look in it,' he said, stepping back and eyeing her expertly, 'you've got a figure like Rita Hayworth. Not so tall but your figure is heavenly. I bet you look marvellous with your clothes off.' He buys the coveted bathing costume for her. 'She's thawing' he thought.[53]

Amanda Vickery, through meticulous readings of period diaries, also assessed the cultural importance of emotional attachments to goods. We have seen how Vickery highlighted the talismanic associations that clothes held for her subject, Elizabeth Shackleton, the reasonably well-off widow of a wool merchant from North Yorkshire in the 1751–81 period. Others, however, had far less happy emotional attachments to their clothes. In his autobiography *I was One of the Unemployed*, Max Cohen, a skilled East End of London cabinet maker and one of the 'three million or so unemployed' in 1932,[54] often turned to the desperate, hated poverty of his clothing to try to explain to his readers the deep emotional, physical and psychological after-effects of lengthy periods of unemployment. At one point Cohen became the reluctant seller of what spare clothes he had. The second-hand clothes dealer examined them

> with sardonic indifference, and his indifference was wounding to me ... 'I'll give you a shilling for them,' he said. If someone had suddenly, without any possible reason or justification, come up to me and slapped me in the face, I could not have been more astounded ... I was tremendously indignant, and yet insulted and aggrieved, as one whose most intimate aspirations have been roughly handled, carelessly and indifferently thrown in the dust ... I went out of the shop crushed and overwhelmed with disappointment.[55]

Literary sources on the actuality of wearing clothes

The way men and women wore and wear their clothes on their bodies carries with it complex 'unspoken assumptions' of class, ethnicity and gender. The way European women and men sit, stand and even walk has changed constantly from decade to decade and class to class matching the demands of their under- and outerwear and peer-group etiquette codes. It is difficult to get close to this aspect of 'clothing in action', because no museum (and it is to be hoped, private collector) would see any serious purpose in dressing anyone up in original period clothing. The chances of serious, lasting damage would be far too high (see Chapter 2). However, when the BBC were filming an 1870s sequence for their series, *Through the Looking Glass* in 1989, an actress was fully dressed in original period costume, to suit an upper-middle-class consumer – complete with corset, split crutch drawers, camisole, petticoats, the correct *tournure*, the tied-back dress, tight boots and all accessories. She wore these for an entire day of filming and found moving about perfectly feasible, although consciously taking care to manage and control the movement of her bustle and train. Her breathing, however, became shallow. By the afternoon, she was feeling giddy and a little faint. The filming took place within the setting of Linley Sambourne house, using its complete 1870s–90s interior. In her full period dress, the actress used the late nineteenth-century lavatory, apparently with no problems at all, simply draping her flowing yardage and split crutch period drawers round the lavatory bowl. When Channel 4, for their year 2000 series *The 1900 House* dressed their 'lower-middle-class' housewife in her corset for the duration of the series, the real-life mother also eventually became breathless and felt unwell as she scrubbed the floors and struggled with the laundry. It may well be, however, that in this case the corset was made in an overly fashionable style for a purported lower-middle-class wearer. Surviving photographs tend to show that many lower-middle-class women were less tightly corseted than their wealthier sisters. Whatever the truth behind these differences and whilst making no pretence at all at historic accuracy, these little experiments tend to support the view that shallow breathing engendered by the pressure of corsets may indeed have impacted seriously on the routine physical functioning of women's bodies, as indeed the dress reformers claimed.

If 'dressing up' gives only imprecise evidence, fortunately literary sources can breathe body movement back into the dead bundles of clothes that survive in dark cupboards in museums. As memory fades, fleeting, period-related sartorial male and female body gestures survive in the pages of novels and autobiographies, often recorded far more graphically and perceptively than in a still photo or even a painted canvas. Thus period and gender-coded movements can be identified through examination of texts dealing with clothes in movement. How, for example, did well-off Victorian women in the 1850s and 1860s ever manage to genteelly control their huge skirts when they walked, when also enveloped in vast shawls and laced into corsets that prevented any flexibility of rib cage and waist? The grandest dresses were so elaborate and wide that 'in certain toilettes as much as six or seven hundred yards of ruched tulle or goffered ribbon are placed'.[56]

Mme Carette, who attended the French Second Empire Court during this period, remembered that

> to walk with so immense a paraphernalia around one was not very easy ... to be able to sit so as not to cause the rebellious springs to fly open required a miracle of precision. To ascend a carriage without rumpling such light textures, when the evening toilettes were made of tulle and lace, required a great deal of time, much quietness on the part of the horses and much patience on the part of husbands and fathers, whose compliance was put to an enormous test as they were to remain motionless in the midst of the *nuages fragiles*.[57]

Nancy Mitford gives a sharp little summary of the specific etiquette-correct sitting posture and dress of the late 1920s in *Love In A Cold Climate*. She describes a *femme mondaine* who

> was to the other smart women of her day as the star is to the chorus ... her bony little silken legs crossed and uncovered to above the knee, perched rather than sat on the edge of the sofa. She wore a plain beige *kasha* dress which must certainly have been made in Paris and certainly designed for the Anglo-Saxon market.[58]

Two examples of gendered gestures in the dress of women from Africa show similarly coded body movements. The explorer, Richard Burton, visited the Yoruba area of West Nigeria in the 1860s and noted that the women wore simple indigo blue skirts or wrappers fixed in front with a knot. Continually coming loose, the knots were constantly being re-tied with what he called 'a slippery hitch'.[59] This is a vividly emotive description of a specific clothing-related hand and arm movement made many times throughout the course of the day by rural Yoruba women then (and indeed now) and is one which conjures up an entire image of Yoruba life through one turn of the wrist.

Elspeth Huxley, travelling the Gambia in the early 1950s, noted the beauty of the clothes and body movements of Wolof women.

> They are tall and dress to enhance their height wearing head-ties of brilliant stripes and patterns fastened with bows and loose knots of gay insousiance. As they glide along the dusty streets in sandals they look like flowers on the move ... Ears and arms are hung with golden ornaments ... As the women walk, the gold glistens against their firm, peach-like skins. They look healthy, provocative, wanton and proud.[60]

Novels, diaries and letters can also tell us what clothing and fabrics felt as well as looked like on the body in a way we would otherwise only have to guess at. Two accounts of the 1900–05 period provide us with precisely this eye-view. Nadine Wolnar-Larsky remembered the Tsar's Fancy Dress Ball at the Hermitage Palace in the spring of 1903. All the guests

15 Princess Wolnar-Larsky wears her Fabergé *kokoshnik* at the Tsar's Winter Ball, St Petersburg, 1903

were dressed, and famously photographed, in reproductions of Russian Court dress styles of the 1600–50 period. 'It wasn't only my own jewels that I wore that night but also the Larsky family jewels', she remembered. Her own traditional style *kokoshnik* head-dress and deep *barma* collar were designed by Diaghilev and made up by Fabergé, who 'for three evenings before the ball ... sent his son to sew the stones into position ... The weight of those two heavily jewelled articles was indescribable. At first when trying them on, I could not wear them at all ... but after a little practice, one got more used to the *kokoshnik*' (Figure 15). The wealthy American Ambassador, Mr McCormack, told her that 'in his wildest dreams, he never could have imagined such a sight; the jewels alone were a revelation'.[61]

Gwen Raverat gave a rebellious young woman's view of wearing 1900–10 clothes. 'After the torture of stays came the torture of hats, the enormous over trimmed hats, which were fixed to an armature of one's puffed out hair by long and murderous pins. On the top of an open bus, in a wind, their mighty sails flapped agonisingly at their anchorage and pulled out one's hair by the handful.'[62]

Literary sources and the period socio-political coding of clothing

Analysis of 'clothes in action' through period text can usefully identify unspoken yet absolutely indicative social rifts and stresses. In *Mary Barton*, published in 1848, Gaskell used description of the way Manchester factory girls wore their woollen shawls as a route into explaining their social identity. She explained that they wore their shawls over their heads and pinned under their chins in an entirely idiosyncratic manner that no 'lady' of the period in her etiquette-correct, poke bonnet would ever dream of doing. The girls

> wore the usual out-of-doors dress of that particular class of maidens; namely a shawl, which at mid-day or in fine weather was allowed to be merely a shawl, but towards evening or if the day were chilly became a sort of Spanish mantilla or Scotch plaid and was brought over the head and hung loosely down, or was pinned under the chin in no unpicturesque manner.[63]

In the early 1900s a woman's social rank could be diagnosed by the manner in which she held up the hem of her skirt when she walked. Shaw's *Pygmalion* of 1912 is based precisely on challenging and overturning publicly recognised indicators of social class – language, dress and social manners. He could well have used Princess Daisy of Pless as his etiquette adviser. A famous English debutante, who married into the German aristocracy in the last decades of the nineteenth century, she fervently believed that the sensitivities of the correct etiquettes of dress still defined a truly refined woman. In July 1908 at Wildungen, she even criticised the Empress of Germany for wearing an unsuitable 'chiffon dress with a long train and a large ugly hat covered in feathers' on a sailing expedition instead of 'a smart plain yachting frock'. The next year, unexpectedly invited by Edward VII and Queen Alexandra to attend the Season's races at Ascot, Daisy's diary entry written on 20 May 1909, at Fürstenstein, reflects her anxieties. 'I really can't get Ascot dresses in Breslau.'[64]

Those 'in the know', both male and female, knew how to sit, stand and move and precisely what to wear and when. Those who were not of Princess Daisy's class, or those who flouted socially correct gestures out of ignorance, or deliberately, became subject to 'moral exclusion' processes. A postcard of 1912 shows an ugly maid with dishevelled hair and clothes, cleaning the floor and commenting to her elegant mistress 'Five pounds would make me a lady' (Figure 16).[65] The clear message being sent by the text on this novelty card is that nothing whatsoever could make this gawky, hideous creature (probably depicted by a male actor) into a 'lady'.

Many writers have chosen to define the politics as well as the social class of their characters through coded descriptions of clothing. Grant Allen

" *Yes, Miss, it's clothes as does it !*
Why, five pounds would make me
a lady."

16 Popular postcard, undated – about 1912, 'Yes, Miss, it's clothes as does it! Why, five pounds would make me a lady.'

used these codes to highlight the differences between male supporters of Socialist and Tory politics in his novel *The Woman Who Did* of 1895. His politically progressive heroine, Herminia Barton, lived in Bohemian circles in London, amongst whom were 'the little group of advanced London socialists who called themselves the Fabians'. Her daughter, however, develops a 'retrograde direction' after visiting a friend, the niece of a Viscount, at a Dorset country house. Here she discovers 'real men ... not the pale abstractions of cultured humanity who attended the Fabian society meetings ... and wore soft felt hats and limp, woollen collars'. In Dorset she discovered that real men were 'clad in tweed suits and fine linen'.[66]

Colin McInnes used clothing descriptions all through his novel *Absolute Beginners*, published in 1959, to codify the political–subcultural placing of his characters. His traditional jazz club girl, who haunted smoke-filled, scruffy dives, frequented by subversive singers wore 'long hair, untidy with long fringes, maybe jeans and a big floppy sweater, maybe bright-coloured, never-floralled, never pretty dress ... smudged-looking was the objective'.[67] This reference to untidy appearance as an essential feature of this period's renegade dress is used also by Margaret Drabble, writing at the same time as McInnes but about young Oxbridge circles. She describes Gill, a young would-be woman painter ('a great one for home-made dresses made of hessian and painted by herself in large bold flowers') unusually elegantly dressed for a society wedding. She was wearing a *'Young Jaeger* outfit ... Her hair was up too, very carefully, in a nice yellow dome'. However, Gill failed to keep up her would-be smart image even for the duration of the afternoon. As the reception progressed 'her hair had begun to escape from its pins, shaken out of its elaborate back-combed beehive ... she looked more like herself'.[68]

Physical attributes of fabrics, as analysed in literary text

The physicality of clothes – their smell, sound in movement and tactile qualities – has rarely been assessed in dress/textile histories although these characteristics are central considerations within the processes of design, manufacture and consumption. It is fascinating but not unexpected to find through literary sources that issues of comfort and practicality became secondary yet again to issues of fashionability and etiquette correctness. As Margaret Atwood put it, 'we remember through smells, as dogs do'[69] and indeed novelists and diarists do also record their memories through the smell of clothing. The use of Victorian mourning crape provides some useful examples.

Despite the fact that better-off Victorian widows and female mourners spent so much of their lives wearing black mourning crape veils and trimmings, the fabric was, as anyone who has handled it can verify, a most scratchy, itchy, unpleasant fabric to wear. It was also very impractical. It faded quickly and was difficult to sew because it would stretch and lose its shape. It also spotted in the rain and faded when packed away. Mourning crape was in fact a manufacturer's dream – a cheap de-lustered, waste silk, stiffened up with gum. Furthermore, it was fabric which the etiquette of death required bourgeois women to wear, and wear often. It was sold at expensive prices and at great profit to the manufacturers – especially in Britain, for Courtaulds.[70]

After the death of David Copperfield's mother and baby brother, the boy visits an undertaker's to be measured for his new mourning clothes. Dickens describes 'the close and stifling little shop' of *Omer, Draper, Tailor, Haberdasher and Funeral Furnisher*. 'There was a good fire in the room and a breathless smell of warm black crape. I did not know what the smell was then, but I do now.'[71] The smell related to the specific black dye – a mix of copperas, logwood and valonia – used on mourning crape, before the advent of synthetic dyes.[72] When subjected to the warmth and body heat in a crowded room it gave off this particular odour which Dickens describes as 'breathless'.

Ada Leverson, novelist and friend of Oscar Wilde, recalled through olfactory memory a moment at the height of his fame and success. She described the heady atmosphere of the first night of *The Importance of Being Ernest* in the middle of a severe snowstorm on St Valentine's day 1894.

> Outside, a frost, inside, the very breath of success; perfumed atmosphere of gaiety, fashion and, apparently, everlasting popularity ... Perfumed: for had not the word gone forth from Oscar that the lily-of-the-valley was to be the flower of the evening, as a souvenir of an absent friend? Flowers meant so much in those days, and nearly all the pretty women wore sprays of lilies against their large puffed sleeves, while rows and rows of young elegants had buttonholes of the delicate bloom.[73]

The fashionably popular *lamé* fabric of the interwar period seems to have left its idiosyncratic odour fixed forever in the minds and noses of writers of the period. Any dress historian who has handled these fabrics today is perfectly familiar with its sharp, acidic smell, but it is fascinating to discover that this is not only the result of the passage of seventy years. The popular novelist Nancy Mitford makes several references to the odour. One of her 1930s heroines declares 'silver *lamé* – it smells like a bird cage when it gets hot but I love it'.[74]

Max Cohen, gaining work after nearly two years of deprivation and malnutrition was able to abandon the stench of poverty along with his ragged clothes.

I remember how I undressed, and the removal of the ragged, out-at-elbow jacket, the often-repaired, shabby shirt, the torn and badly patched trousers, the shapeless, down-at-heel shoes – clothes that I had worn so long and so often that they were loathsome to me by their mere monotony; clothes that I had worn so long and so often that they were impregnated with my body-sweat – the removal of these was as the removal of a soiled and dirty bandage.[75]

Clothing even has its own sounds. The rustle of crisp silk petticoats in the early 1900s was an indication of *glacé* silk linings rather than cheap cotton ones and also a much-remembered symbol of Edwardian femininity. James Laver fondly recalled that as his mother lifted her skirts out of the mud as she walked, 'there was the rustle of innumerable silk petticoats underneath'.[76]

Conclusion

Margaret Atwood shows exactly how a sharp literary eye-view on period dress can uniquely assess cultural tensions, in this case contemporary ones. In *Cat's Eye*, set in late 1980s Toronto, her middle-aged, artist-heroine faces up uncertainly to meeting a representative of the confidently up-and-coming, rival, younger, post-modernist, feminist generation.

She's a painter ... She's in a miniskirt and tight leggings and flat clumpy black shoes with laces, her hair shaved up the back the way my brother's used to be – a late forties, square-boy cut. She is post everything. She is what will come after post. She is what will come after me.[77]

Notes

1 A. Buck, Clothes In Fact and Fiction, 1825–1865 (*Costume*, 17, 1983), p. 89.

2 J. Laver, Obituary for C. W. Cunnington (*Costume*, 9, 1975), p. 75.

3 D. Langley Moore, *The Woman in Fashion* (B. T. Batsford, London, 1949), p. 16.

4 T. Lovell, Subjective Powers? Consumption, the Reading Public, and Domestic Woman in Early Eighteenth-Century England, in A. Bermingham and J. Brewer (eds), *The Consumption of Culture, 1600–1800* (Routledge, London, 1995), p. 43 and p. 30.

5 Buck, Clothes In Fact and Fiction, p. 90 and p. 89.

6 A. Buck, The Clothes of Thomasine Petre: 1555–1559 (*Costume*, 24, 1990), p. 22, quoting N. Udall, *Ralph Roister-Doister*, Act II, Scene 3, in F. S. Boas (ed.), *Five Pre-Shakespeare Comedies* (Oxford University Press, Oxford, 1934).

7 Buck, Clothes In Fact and Fiction, p. 89.

8 Ibid. p. 90.

9 R. Worth, Elizabeth Gaskell: clothes and class identity (*Costume*, 32, 1998), p. 53.

10 J. Harvey, *Men in Black* (Reaktion, London, 1995), p. 17.

11 Worth, *Elizabeth Gaskell*, p. 55.

12 G. Moore, *Esther Walters* (reprint Dent, London, 1983, first pub. 1895), p. 165.

13 R. Paulson, Emulative Consumption and Literacy: the harlot, Moll Flanders and Mrs Slipslop, in Bermingham and Brewer, *The Consumption of Culture*, pp. 383–400.

14 See J. Harvey, *The Plate Shop* (Collins, London, 1979); idem, *Coup d'Etat* (Collins, London, 1985) and idem, *The Legend of Captain Space* (Collins, London, 1990).

15 Harvey, *Men in Black*, p. 19 and p. 193.

16 Ibid. p. 20.

17 Ibid. p. 19.

18 See J. Harvey, *Victorian Novelists and their Illustrators* (Sidgwick and Jackson, London, 1970).

19 Interview with the author, July 1996.

20 N. McKendrick, The Commercialisation of Fashion, in N. McKendrick, J. Brewer and J. H. Plumb, *The Birth of the Consumer Society: the commercialisation of eighteenth-century England* (Europa, London, 1982), p. 39.

21 Ibid. p. 53.

22 Ibid. p. 41.

23 Ibid. p. 60, quoting R. Nettel, *Travels of Carl P. Moritz in England: journeys of a German in England in 1782* (no publisher given, London, reprint 1965), pp. 33–34 and p. 99, quoting Sir John Hawkins, *The Life of Samuel Johnson* (J. Buckland, London, 1787), p. 262.

24 A. Vickery, Women and the World of Goods: a Lancashire consumer and her possessions, 1751–81, in J. Brewer and R. Porter, *Consumption and the World of Goods* (Routledge, London, 1993), p. 277.

25 L. P. Gartner, *Jewish Immigration into England, 1870–1914* (Allen Unwin, London, 1960), p. 81, quoting A. A. Baumann, MP, Possible Remedies for the Sweating System (*National Review* XII, 69, November 1888), pp. 289–307.

26 A. Settle, *English Fashion* (Collins, London, 1938), p. 44.

27 D. Langley Moore, *Women In Fashion* (Batsford, London, 1949), p. 16.

28 T. Zeldin, *France, 1848–1945: taste and corruption* (Oxford University Press, Oxford, 1980), pp. 221–222.

29 Vickery, Women and the World of Goods, p. 278, quoting N. McKendrick (ed.), *Historical Perspectives: studies in English thought and society in honour of J. H. Plumb* (Europa, London, 1974), p. 200 and p. 209.

30 *Journal of Design* (19 September 1850, III), p. 68.

31 Mrs Eric Pritchard, The Cream of London and Paris Fashions (*Lady's Realm*, XXII, July 1907), p. 24.

32 Mrs E. Pritchard, *The Cult of Chiffon* (Grant Richards, London, 1907), pp. 27–28.

33 P. Bourdieu, *Distinction: a social critique of the judgement of taste* (Routledge, London, reprint, 1989), p. 551.

34 P. Cunnington and C. Lucas, *Occupational Costume in England* (Adam and Charles Black, London, 1967), p. 46, quoting P. Kalm, *An Account of His Visit to England on his way to America in 1748*, trans. J. Lucas (Macmillan, New York, 1892).

35 A. Buck, *Dress in Eighteenth Century England* (Batsford, London, 1979), p. 113, quoting

A. Cook, *Ann Cook and Friend*, ed. R. Burnet (Oxford University Press, London, 1936), pp. 42–43.

36 L. E. Klein, Politeness for Plebes: consumption and social identity, in early eighteenth-century England, in Bermingham and Brewer, *The Consumption of Culture*, p. 374.

37 M. Pember Reeves, *Round About A Pound A Week* (Virago, London, 1979 reprint of 1913 original), p. 64.

38 H. V. Morton, Miss Jones in Bagdad, in idem, *The Spell of London* (Methuen, London, 1926), pp. 92–95.

39 E. Wilson and L. Taylor, *Through the Looking Glass: a history of dress from 1860 to the present day* (BBC Books, London, 1989), p. 89.

40 S. Zdatny, The Boyish Look and the Liberated Woman: the politics and aesthetics of women's hairstyles (*Fashion Theory*, 1, 4, December 1997), p. 387.

41 Wilson and Taylor, *Through the Looking Glass*, p. 19.

42 N. Wolnar-Larsky, *The Russia That I Loved* (Elsie MacSwinney, Haywards Heath, 1937), p. 8.

43 T. H. Breen, The Meaning of Things: interpreting the consumer economy in the 18th century, in Brewer and Porter, *Consumption and the World of Goods*, p. 254.

44 M. Kroll, *Letters from Liselotte* (Victor Gollancz, London, 1970), p. 99.

45 A. Buck, The Costume of Jane Austen and her Characters, *Costume Society Conference – Spring, 1970, the So-Called Age of Elegance* (Victoria and Albert Museum, London, 1971), p. 42 and p. 40, quoting Dr R. W. Chapman (ed.), *Jane Austen's Letters to her sister Cassandra and Others* (Clarendon Press, Oxford, 2nd edition, 1952), p. 215.

46 Wolnar-Larsky, *The Russia That I Loved*, p. 8 and pp. 89–90.

47 W. Foley, *A Child in the Forest* (Futurs, London, 1978), pp. 147–148.

48 Mrs W. Gordon, *A Woman in the Balkans* (Thomas Nelson, London, n.d.), pp. 183–184 and pp. 138–139.

49 F. Elwyn-Jones, *Hitler's Drive to the East* (Dutton, London, 1937), pp. 60–78.

50 P. Thornton, *Dead Puppets Dance* (Collins, London, 1937), pp. 286–287.

51 Breen, The Meaning of Things, p. 251.

52 J. Arnold, *A Handbook of Costume* (Macmillan, London, 1973), pp. 132–146.

53 L. Tyrmand, *Zly* (Michael Joseph, London, 1958, first published by Czytelnik, Warsaw, 1957), pp. 256–262, with thanks to David Crowley for this reference.

54 M. Cohen, *I was One of the Unemployed* (Victor Gollanz, 1945, reprint EP Publishing, 1978), foreword by Sir William Beveridge, p. v.

55 Ibid. pp. 43–44.

56 E. Saunders, *The Age of Worth* (Longmans, London, 1954), p. 118, quoting the *Illustrated London News*, 1864.

57 N. Waugh, *The Cut of Women's Clothes, 1600–1930* (Faber and Faber, London, 1968), p. 218, quoting Mme Carette, *My Mistress, the Empress Eugenie*.

58 N. Mitford, *Love in A Cold Climate* (Hamish Hamilton, London, 1949), p. 45 and p. 61.

59 R. F. Burton, *Abeokuta and the Cameroon Mountains – an exploration*, vol. 1 (Tinsley Bros, London, 1863).

60 E. Huxley, *Four Guineas: a journey through West Africa* (The Reprint Society, London, 1955), pp. 14–15.

61 Wolnar-Larsky, *The Russia That I Loved*, pp. 98–99.

62 G. Raverat, *Period Piece: a Cambridge childhood* (Faber and Faber, London, reprint 1984), p. 259.

63 Buck, Clothes in Fact and Fiction, pp. 101–102.

64 D. Chapman-Huston (ed.), *The Private Diaries of Daisy, Princess of Pless, 1873–1914* (John Murray, London, 1950), p. 195 and p. 217.

65 With thanks to Deborah Barker for this card.

66 A. Grant, *The Woman Who Did* (John Law, London, 1895), p. 172 and p. 210.

67 C. MacInnes, *Absolute Beginners* (Allison and Busby, London, reprint 1980, first pub. 1959), p. 63.

68 M. Drabble, *A Summer Bird-Cage* (Penguin, London, 1967), p. 36 and p. 44.

69 M. Atwood, *Cat's Eye* (Virago, London, 1990), p. 417, with thanks to Alexandra Palmer.

70 L. Taylor, *Mourning Dress – a costume and social history* (George Allen and Unwin, London, 1983), pp. 202–223 and Appendix 1, A Selection of Popular Mourning Fabrics, pp. 288–301.

71 C. Dickens, *David Copperfield* (Oxford University Press, Oxford, reprint 1987, first pub. 1849–50), p. 125.

72 Taylor, *Mourning Dress*, p. 219, quoting D. C. Coleman, *Courtaulds: an economic and social history*, vol. 2 (Oxford University Press, Oxford, 1969), pp. 73–89.

73 V. Wyndham, *The Sphinx and Her Circle* (Andre Deutsch, London, 1963), p. 109, quoting A. Leverson, The Importance of Being Oscar, from *Letters to the Sphinx from Oscar Wilde* (Duckworth, London, 1930).

74 Mitford, *Love in A Cold Climate*, p. 35.

75 Ibid. p. 237.

76 J. Laver, *Taste and Fashion* (George G. Harrap, London, 1945 edition), p. 199.

77 Atwood, *Cat's Eye*, p. 417.

5 ✧ Approaches using visual analysis: paintings, drawings and cartoons[1]

A portrait 'represents the joint contributions of artist, sitter and costume; in this context clothes can reveal character, both heroic and mundane, and all the frailties of human nature including vanity and pretension'. (Aileen Ribeiro)[2]

DRESS historians use a great range of visual sources as analytical tools in their work, centring on paintings, prints, drawings, redrawn illustrations, fashion plates and cartoons. All provide information on style, quality of fabrics and garments, cut, hair-styles, body stance, accessories and exactly how these were worn. They can reveal subtleties of sartorial gender and age coding, social aspirations and national, regional and local differences. In every case all these images have to be individually assessed through the lens of their own periods and the lens of the artists. No painting or drawing is free from the personal preferences and prejudices of its creator nor free from the etiquettes, politics and prejudices of its day. It can be positively misleading to accept visual sources at face value because the relationships between images and their cultural meanings are so multi-layered and complex.

Use of paintings

Paintings have always been an obvious dress history source. Through the brush of a skilful painter, the rich, glittering texture and detail of Tudor Court dress survives today whilst the originals have long rotted away or remain only as partial fragments. Through the perfectly rendered detail on the clothes of the women in Watteau and Ingres portraits, we can see how a woman managed to sit in her loose-backed *sacque* robe or how a long cashmere shawl was draped negligently around the body of a wealthy woman. Portraits also tell us how the commissioning sitters wished to be portrayed for eternity and how the artists added their own personal 'hand' to the work.

Since the Second World War, the methodology of interpreting clothing through paintings has become an increasingly skilled process. The first post-war British example was the series *Costume of the Western World*, of 1951, edited by James Laver, a six-part series covering periods from the Tudors to Louis XIII. Each volume was edited by an international period specialist with text based largely on descriptive interpretation. Brian Reade, Assistant Keeper in the Department of Illustration at the Victoria and Albert Museum contributed the volume, *The Dominance of Spain, 1550–1660*. Using portraits by Antonia Mor, Moroni and Velázquez, supported by engravings by de Bruyn and Vecellio, he was able to pinpoint a series of significant sartorial innovations. He comments that the narrow sleeve of Anne of Austria's gown from a dated 1570 portrait by Mor, now in the Kunsthistoriches Museum, Vienna, 'was still composed of two similarly cut pieces of cloth sewn together, this leaving the seams plainly visible'.[3] He chose a painting by Theotocopuli, dated to around 1600, which shows a pair of early, armless spectacles, worn by an elderly lady in a wimple. Reade comments that they were 'introduced to Spain from Italy half-way through the sixteenth century'.[4]

This methodology took a massive leap forward in 1965 when Stella Mary Newton persuaded the Courtauld Institute of the History of Art in London, to found the first postgraduate dress history course in Britain. The ostensible excuse was to train specialists to help date valuable paintings. The art/dress historian, Margaret Maynard, one of Newton's students, confirms that 'she believed that artists were not able to fool us by their invention of clothes, that the dress historian, who knew about the past, could show up these idiosyncrasies and discrepancies through very careful observation. This is almost the opposite to the cultural construct notion of imagery.'[5] Newton had provided dress historical evidence which helped her husband, the art historian Eric Newton, date seven Tintoretto paintings for his research in the early 1950s.[6] Stella Mary Newton, who was also an art historian, had trained as a couturier in Mayfair fashion houses and worked successfully in theatre costume design. She well understood both the actuality of dress and the cultural and social ramifications of the meanings of dress. Her 1974 study *Health, Art and Reason*,[7] is an excellent example of the wider cultural themes she introduced on to her course. This study was an examination of aesthetic and reform dress in England in the 1870–1914 period and contained analysis of garments through cartoons, painting and period literary and press sources, though not through surviving artefacts. It was the first serious *exposé* of what could now be termed early English counter-cultural dressing. Newton identified styles, consumers and the political and cultural messages delivered through this style of minority dressing. Her text remains valid and fresh today, more than twenty-five years later.

Newton was always clear that interpretations of paintings required supportive period textual analysis in order to draw out the full weight of hidden social nuances. Thus, her 1988 examination of early sixteenth-century Venetian dress uses the diaries of Marin Sanudo, a member of one of the oldest Venetian patrician families who had an 'almost obsessive interest in the dress worn by his male contemporaries'. Newton uses Sanudo's text to penetrate the complexities of the city's social hierarchy. She is able to show that Venice's sumptuary law system 'was subtle and complicated enough to allow of considerable deviousness and self-expression within what had at first appeared to be successfully administered discipline'.[8] She still relies heavily on paintings and her knowledge is so sharp that she is able to identify precise style development in the cut of sleeves of early sixteenth-century Venetian women, when few pieces of fabric or garment have survived the passage of time. Thus she was able to resolve the disputed dating for a painting by Vecchio. Experts argued over 1508 or 1513 as its date of origin. Based on dress styles in contemporary works by Carpaccio and Dürer, Newton firmly stated that '1513 would definitely be too late and 1508 possibly a year too early'.[9]

Aileen Ribeiro took over the Courtauld course after Newton's retirement and has since developed Newton's dress history approaches through her own area of specialism, which covers the seventeenth- to mid-nineteenth-century periods. Thus the aim of Ribeiro's 1995 study, *The Art of Dress*, is to dissect the ways in which a portrait 'represents the joint contributions of artist, sitter and costume; in this context clothes can reveal character, both heroic and mundane, and all the frailties of human nature including vanity and pretension'.[10] Ribeiro, and others who take this approach such as Marie Simon and Krystyna Matyjaszkiewicz, show how highly nuanced sartorial messages about class, nationality, sexuality and social ambition are now being 'read' through the clothing depicted in paintings and specifically through portraiture.

The role of the painter, notes Ribeiro, was to develop a 'fusion of character, likeness and costume', with a dose of inevitable flattery.

> The portrait was both public, in the sense of being subject to the conventions of society, and private, in the sense of being painted for the intimate contemplation of family and loved ones. It was of its time and yet timeless in its claims on posterity; it could represent reality in dress or it could express fantasy.

Ribeiro adds here an important warning: 'A portrait is not merely a mechanical image, it is a likeness of the sitter and his or her character seen through the temperament of the artist, whose views reflect the opinions of contemporary critics writing about art and dress.'[11]

Aesthetic conventions, portraiture and dress

Unravelling the meanings of clothes in paintings is complicated by the various aesthetic sartorial conventions used by artists from period to period. Academic stipulations decreed, especially in late seventeenth- and eighteenth-century Europe, that sitters, especially women, should not always wear fashions of the day for their portraits. These were seen as too ephemeral and lacking the required gravitas and refined aesthetic qualities needed for heirloom portraits. Fashionable dress was replaced by a range of romantic, fanciful garments with sitters wearing neoclassical or exotic draperies. Some wear complete fantasy garments whilst others only have small touches of the fanciful – a Renaissance collar or curiously puffed sleeves, for example.

Ribeiro has studied these styles extensively, especially eighteenth-century masquerade dress,[12] and notes that 'boundaries of fashion and fancy dress overlap' and that it is 'important not to be too insistent on a compartmentalised view of history; in many respects fashion and fancy dress (that is, dress of, or conditioned by, the past) are closely linked and sometimes interchangeable'.[13] The dress historian needs to be aware, for example, that re-creations of 'Van Dyck' dress of the 1630s, with its plain sheeny satins and large lace collars, were frequently used in society portraiture by the 1770s. Sometimes only a light touch of Van Dyck styling was added to otherwise conventional clothing. Two complete 'Van Dyck'-styled men's suits, dating from the 1770s, in pale apple-green silk satin embroidered in cream-coloured silk thread, however, survive, in the collection at Ipswich Museum, to verify that whole garments were made up for sitters to wear, further complicating the issues of conventions (Figure 17).[14]

Christopher Breward also deals with artistic convention in eighteenth-century painting, stressing that 'fashionability' lay in intermixing 'idyllic pastoral values with a more urbane observation of polite metropolitan etiquette codes'. English pastoral preferences ran from Renaissance touches through to Van Dyck styles, whereas in France, classical antiquity was the stronger influence. Thus Breward notes as a typical British example that in Kneller's portrait of about 1710 of Anne, Countess of Sutherland (now in the National Portrait Gallery), she wears only a simple, white satin, decolletée, classical open morning robe and that 'details and accessories have been kept to a minimum by the artist in a bid to lend the requisite pastoral values'. This robe replaces the decorative and fitted mantua gown she would have worn for formal occasions. Breward adds that by the middle of the eighteenth century 'visual references to Greek and Roman nymphs were intermingled with suggestions of an exotic orient, intensified by growing colonial and imperialist tendencies amongst the English elite'.

17 Van Dyck-styled silk jacket and knee breeches, about 1770

So, *Turquerie* styles too became a vogue which should 'be read as a construction rather than a literal recording of consumption choices ... there are parallels to be made with the expansion of Empire and a fashionable taste for the oriental'.[15]

In this period the dress historian has next to beware of the moment when dress styles moved from painterly convention into actual garments. For example, the draperies featured in David's historical classical paintings of the 1770s–80s were appropriated into 'fashion' and by 1795 were seen covering the bodies of the most elite of style setters of post-revolutionary Paris. In many ways the dresses looked similar but their social and cultural meanings had changed entirely as the demands of 'fashion' replaced those of 'art'. The overall 'negligence' within David's paintings was transferred into the new modes but contemporary etiquette codes ensured that loose drapery was replaced with neatly fitted, high-waisted bodices and that little sleeves covered the naked upper arms seen in the paintings. Two David portraits which significantly show this movement out of art into the world of the Paris dressmakers include the 1799 portrait of Madame de Verninac, aged 19, the wife of the Prefect of the Rhone. Her loose, sleeveless, white, draped gown *à l'antique* is partly hidden by an ochre-coloured shawl, featuring bold Greek palmette motifs. One year later David painted Madame Récamier reclining in a long-trained white muslin dress, but now her shoulders and upper arms are carefully covered by little sleeves and her high-waisted bodice fits closely over her bosom. To the dress historian, these shifting subtleties from 'artistic' to avant-garde fashionable elitism in the 1790–1800 period are of the utmost significance. To use John Harvey's words they clarify that 'meaning in dress is made of movement in history'.[16]

Another misconception that could be drawn from British portraits of gentry and rich merchant-class women during the 1740–75 period was that they could not afford, or did not like, large-patterned, coloured silk brocades. So many portraits by Hogarth, Devis, Nollekins, Gainsborough, Hudson, Ramsay and Highmore feature women either in plain-coloured, lustred silks or self-coloured damasks that it seems fair enough to draw this conclusion. In fact, surviving clothes and fabrics reveal that this is not the case either in Britain or America. Natalie Rothstein's meticulous research on the history of the manufacture, design and consumption of English Spitalfields silk indicates that wealthy British consumers did favour coloured, large-patterned silk brocades. To confirm this Rothstein matches up the silk in Hudson's 1752 portrait of thirteen-year-old Esther Hamner with surviving paper designs of the identical silk designed by the Spitalfields' designer, Anna Maria Garthwaite.[17] This brocade features scattered floral bouquets, in the brightest of colours on a toffee-coloured ground, so splendidly large that just one reached from the length of Esther's fingertip to her elbow. Rothstein's investigation into the dress of Barbara Johnson shows that Johnson, too, who socialised on the edges of high society London in the mid–late eighteenth century, also purchased these brocaded silks. In 1753 she pinned samples of white grounded red, green and blue flowered silks into her scrap album, adding the words 'two flower'd silks coats, 12s. a yard'. In 1775 she pinned in another example 'a brown and white striped and flower'd silk lutestring negligee – 9s. a yard'. In comparison her block printed 'linnen' for 'short sacks' of 1754 cost 2s./4d. a yard.[18]

The reason for the lack of such gorgeously rich fabrics in so many portraits of this period lies therefore not with the taste of the wearers but within period artistic convention. As Ribeiro notes advice given to painters in 1725 reminded them that 'Lace, Embroidery, Gold and Jewels must be sparingly employe'd. Nor are the flower'd Silks so much us'd by the best Masters as Plain; nor are these so much as Stuffs or fine Cloth.'[19] Margeretta Lovell has shown that in 1763 the American painter, John Singleton Copley, liked a fashionable, plain blue dress so much that he used it in three portraits of well-off women from Massachusetts, that of Mrs Benjamin

Pickman, the newly married daughter of a Salem ship owner, Mary Turner Sargent, also newly married and a near neighbour of Mary Pickman and Mrs James Warren from Boston. This sack-backed gown of 'imported satin-weave silk' featured matching 'serpentine ruched trimmed robings'. Lovell wonders if this expensive dress ever even existed or was created specifically by Copley as an elegant studio prop. However, having read family letters, the local press of the period and related biographies, she concluded that the dress was probably first bought by James Warren for his wife Mercy, who became 'well known in the next decade as a blue-stocking poet, dramatist, historian and political activist'. The rich lace seen in her portrait was kept in her family at least until the late nineteenth century. Lovell proves that Mercy's brothers were friends and business acquaintances of the Pickman–Sargent families and suggests that the use of the same dress underscores 'a friendship between two Salem neighbours of the same age cohort whose families and whose husbands' families had associated with and intermarried with one another for decades'. Lovell proposes that the dress, stripped of its costly lace, 'was passed on to the younger women who retrimmed it but more modestly' with the same lace-edged gauze ruffles that can be seen in both their portraits. Through the use of the same dress in this trio of portraits Lovell argues that Copley accomplishes 'a masterful synthesis of disparate kinds of texts, different categories of knowledge: observed visual facts, enacted social prescriptions, evaded aesthetic difficulties, and the very localized supra-linguistic exchange between six families'. She concluded that 'the project centrally involved the unseen husbands as well as the very present women in this intricate and successful collaboration of brothers, husbands, wives, mantuamaker, and artists, yet each painting makes a complete whole "with no seam or joint appearing"'.[20]

Common to these three portraits was the plainness of the blue silk. This visual code was repeated through the mid/late eighteenth century so that plain pink, pale blue and soft yellow silks appear over and over again in period portraits, whereas surviving clothes and sample books, such as that of Barbara Johnson, indicate that for 'best' formal dress, coloured silk brocades were in fact in use in these wealthy circles. The dress historian has therefore somehow to navigate her or his path through all these artistic and social codes before any 'safe' interpretations of the clothing in portraiture can even be offered.

Social convention, dress and portraiture

Aesthetic period conventions also mask social ones and impact with equal force upon both setting and clothing in portraits. Marie Simon has demonstrated how the nuances of dressing were used by portraitists to reflect fine social nuances within the highest echelons of Parisian society in the 1850 period. By contrasting two portraits by Ingres, Simon shows that their subtle clothing codes were a mirror image of specific social tensions which, according to Simon, lay between the French aristocracy 'who acquired the gift of dressing well by birth' and the bourgeoisie, who had to buy their way into high society. Simon is convinced that such portraits reveal 'differences of blood'. Thus she compares Ingres's 1853 portrait of Princess de Broglie with that of his Baronne James de Rothschild of 1844–48. Both women wear plain satin evening dresses. The princess's is in pale blue whilst the baroness wears deep pink. Both dresses have exactly the same off-the-shoulder, lace-trimmed *'bertha'* neckline. Both women wear necklaces, bracelets and feathers in their hair, which is identically parted and smoothed over their ears.

To the viewer today the two elegant women would seem obviously to move in the same wealthy social circles, but Simon argues that the Baronne gives away her *arriviste* roots through the superfluous ruffles on her hemline which underline her dress's 'relative frivolity ... while giving it a certain ponderousness'. Further, Simon notes that the Baronne's jewellery is 'more complicated' and her ostrich feather trimmed hat is 'almost in bad taste and certainly incongruous'.[21] Simon reminds us that correct period etiquette ruled that hats were not to be worn with evening dress. The princess, by contrast, has not put a sartorial foot wrong in Simon's eyes. A critic of the time who examined the portrait in 1855 commented that it revealed the Princess de Broglie to be 'refined, delicate, elegant to her fingertips ... a marvellous incarnation of nobility'. Knowing her etiquette 'by birth' she selected a far more refined coiffure trimming of delicate, pearl-spattered, maribou feathers which fall delicately over the back of her hair. For Simon, this delicacy of style reflects the convention amongst women of the aristocracy that 'good taste required them to show some moderation with regard to fashion'.[22]

Simon suggests here that Ingres was absolutely aware of these etiquette-directed sartorial indicators of social hierarchy and that he deliberately incorporated them into his portraits. She implies that the *arriviste* Baronne (who, however, ran one of the great society salons in Paris) was ignorant of these subtleties. Simon avoids mentioning that both women would have purchased their clothes from the same range of elite dressmaker/fashion houses in Paris where every detail of correct sartorial etiquette would have been perfectly understood. This discussion remains unresolved but nevertheless Simon has usefully highlighted the difficulties of interpreting dress through portraits of even the most fashionable women.

Fine art as a research source for the clothing of the urban and rural poor

Images showing the dress of the poor are also highly variable in their dealings with notions of 'realism'. These vary according to the interests and passions of painters and illustrators. In the 1870–1914 period, however, paintings of the poor provide some of the few coloured and detailed images we have of their clothing. This work offers hope of finding at least some semblance of 'accurate' images of this vast percentage of the population whose clothing has very largely not survived the passage of time. Most painters of urban poverty were committed to showing the 'reality' of the lives of urban working-class families as they struggled to earn a living in the slums of industrial cities. The work of Luke Fildes will serve here as just one example of art depicting the travails of the 'urban poor' intended to raise public awareness about their plight. Filde's huge *Applicants for Admission to a Casual Ward*, of 1874, bought by Royal Holloway College, shows a long queue of wretched, defeated people of all ages, including many children, waiting in the winter darkness under the high wall of a police station to get free tickets for a night's shelter in a workhouse. Their clothing is meticulously painted. All wear more or less worn out, ragged second-/third-hand clothes, except for the young widow with her children who wears the conventional middle-class black weeds decreed by Victorian society. These lift her socially, although evidently not financially, above the other destitutes surrounding her, whose ragged amalgamations of clothing pay no deference to the clothing codes of 'respectable' society.

The painter's son remembered that 'all the characters were out of real life, whom the artist had discovered in his nightly wanderings around the London streets, most of them sunk into utter misery'. Fildes invited some to the studio of his Haverstock Hill house, where he painted 'the Big Boozer' in his battered top hat. The Boozer 'had always to be quarantined by being made to stand on sheets of brown paper, sprinkled with Keatings powder'.[23] The widower and sick child, who later died, also posed in Fildes's studio.

Rural poor

Artists' images of the rural poor were far more picturesque because the clothes of European peasantry offered artists bold forms and striking mixes of colour and texture unseen in the cities. The reliability of these images, however, is again often open to question. Premised on utopian belief in the essential 'purity' of peasant culture, artists sought out villages 'uncontaminated' by modernisation and cheap consumer goods where ready-to-wear clothes had not yet replaced the 'authentic' dress of the villagers. Such communities were not hard to find and by the 1870s *plein air* painters from all over Europe were drawing their inspiration from the French Barbizon school of the 1860s and the work of painters such as Jules Bastien-Lepage.

Adherents of this movement settled, usually for the summer months only, in isolated villages where peasant dress was still worn. In 1882 Carl Larsson 'joined the foremost Nordic artists' colony in France' at Grez-sur-Loing, near the forest of Fontainebleau, working alongside Japanese, English, American and Norwegian artists.[24] Another international group, including Jan Toorup, Piet Mondrian, Denis Galloway, Ferdinand Hart Nibbrig and Sárika, Monica and Ada Goth from Budapest, painted in the sandy strands and villages of Domberg and Veere in Zeeland, on the Dutch island of Walcheren, in the 1900–30 period. Here regional dress for women featured stiffened white linen bonnets worn with spectacular spiralled gold ornaments.[25] In Sweden, painters settled in the 'unspoiled' region of Dalarna, where wooden farm houses still contained early nineteenth-century wall paintings of *The Wise and Foolish Virgins* and were full of carved and painted local furniture.[26] In the Hungary of the Austro-Hungarian Empire in the 1900–10 period, the English artists Marianne and Adrian Stokes[27] combed the countryside for the most visually stimulating and most isolated peasant communities. Adrian Stokes's account of their travels explains very precisely the fascination of such communities to painters.

The Stokes's travels started out in the big cities such as Kolozsvár (now Cluj-Napoca), the capital of Transylvania. Here they noticed that most 'people one meets are dressed like those in London or Paris and quite in the latest mode'. Thus their search for the most utopian landscape and the most gorgeous dress of the rural 'Other' led them to far more remote areas, such as the Tatra mountains bordering on to Poland, and to Eastern Transylvania and down to the Serbian borders.

In the hot summer months they sought the coolness of the Tatras. Hearing of its remoteness and wildness they visited Zsdjar, a Calvinist village in what is now Slovakia, close to the Polish border. At first they saw only an impoverished community of 'grey-roofed log-houses ... set far back from the road ... beyond that steep pine-covered slopes rose up again to bare dark mountains'. By chance, however, they came across a church procession of the entire village wearing their Sunday dress. This was exactly what they had been searching for. 'Had we been in China, or Tibet nothing more surprising could have appeared' in the dank landscape, Stokes commented later. With his painterly eye-view of the scene, he wrote that the colours of Zsdjar dress reminded him strongly of the work of the two Scottish painters, Hornel and Henry (who in their turn had been influenced by travel to Japan): 'The effect [the dress] produced was quite startling. Only once have I been affected in the same way, and that was in the days of the Grosvenor Gallery by a decorative painting by Hornel and Henry, composed of strange bold shapes of emerald green, gold, vermilion and white, with a scanty allowance of secondary colours to relieve them.'

A strikingly similar colour range suffuses Stokes's description of the dress of this Slovak village.

> On their heads the women of Zsdjar wore handkerchiefs, red, orange or green; gold and silver embroidery in broad bands sparkled on their bodices; their sleeves were of the whitest linen, embroidered with pale crimson at the shoulders; their skirts were scarlet and their aprons black or green ... Nothing was shabby not a thing torn or untidy in the whole crowd we passed.

Marianne was enchanted and the couple declared this dress to be the most becoming dress they had seen in Hungary. Marianne Stokes determined to live and paint in the village and this was achieved, though not without considerable difficulty. Stokes's account of their trials in organising their two months' stay would have been shared by other *plein air* artists all over Europe and Tsarist Russia. The couple, with the help of an interpreter, arranged to rent a room in the rather miserable local inn, a room which they had to furnish themselves. The priest hired furniture for them from the local town, including 'a handsome large washstand with heavy marble top ... and a stuffed sofa with a curling back'. Here they lived in some discomfort, sleeping on straw mattresses. Fortunately they had brought their own indiarubber baths with them.

Marianne arranged to paint 'in a small Catholic Church, where service was held but once a fortnight by a visiting priest'. She was able to socialise with the women she painted far more easily than her husband, who either 'painted from our windows or went further afield' seeking peace to paint in the woods and hills. 'Sometimes', Adrian Stokes wrote, 'we were short of food and had it not been that the Priest gave me permission to fish in the stream, we might have suffered from actual hunger.'

The fascination, despite the discomfort, was the villagers themselves, except for the few Jewish shop and inn keepers. Adrian Stokes constantly and always referred to them negatively and stereotypically as 'untidy Jews entirely devoted to money-making' or as wearing 'wet black coats and locks, sadly out of curl' or as 'unattractive-looking Jews in long black *kaftans*'. These they did not paint. Marianne produced a series of small portraits, mostly close-ups of women, children and babies, attending church, selling goods in the market and walking in the village, including

The Belle of Zsdjar and *The School Master's Wife*. Building on the tempera technique and style with which she had already established a strong reputation in London, she has left behind a detailed, profoundly moving and specific record of Hungarian/Slovak/Romanian dress of the 1900–09 period, with its indigo blue print and Turkey red cotton prints and specific village caps and embroidery styles. Adrian painted delicate landscapes of villages, forest glades and distanced hills, describing the Tatra Slovak mountains in painterly terms. 'Against the sunset', he wrote, 'the mountains became a warm plum colour, plane behind planes of purpley green.'

The couple made several long working visits to Hungary, always avoiding it in the winter. At no point did they seem to make contact (as did Walter Crane at the same period) with Hungarian artists and arts/crafts designers who were then so actively seeking out and working in similar villages. Some were making detailed ethnographical records of dress. In contrast to this, the Stokes's obsession with the landscape and dress of the Hungarian peasantry was driven by the same personal visual passion that took so many urban painters out into the countryside. Despite the dozens of paintings they produced, Adrian Stokes wrote that 'we are quite aware that we have only touched on the fringes of limitless fields of interest for artists and others'.[28]

Indeed, other artists and writers were interested in Hungary in this same period. In about 1908, the painter W. Pascoe and the writer W. M. Foster Bovill also visited Kolozsvár. Here Pascoe avoided the smart set described by Stokes, and painted a study of *Farm Folk Returning from the Morning Market in Kolozsvar* (Figure 18). Travelling down to Croatia, Foster Bovill's text emphasises the very same visual lure of the peasantry and their dress to 'outsider' visitors. Of an unmarried girl from Croatia he wrote

> perhaps it was her sweet face which caught my attention. Her hair was parted in the middle and well brushed down with a scarlet rose resting just at the back of her right ear ... But her jacket! We in our sombre Western dress know little of the joy of pigment these poor peasant folk feel. It was gorgeous ... a deep collar was composed of four embroidered rows of colour. There were also shoulder knots, simple and effective. And the back, it was a wall-paper design, while the border had no fewer than eleven different rows of embroidery and combinations of colour.[29]

Everywhere the intent was the same, to paint the peasantry and their dress as the artists thought they actually were, following Bastien-Lepage's doctrine of 'complete fidelity to visual facts'.[30] In all these communities the local population of sea-men, foresters, farmers and their families were still living in traditional vernacular homes and wearing 'authentic' peasant dress. Artists painted lacemakers, fish sellers, wood choppers, labourers

18 W. Pascoe, gouache illustration,
*Farm Folk Returning from the
Morning Market in Kolozsvar,* 1908

all seemingly going about their daily routines. Léon Giron's *Une Dentelliére
d'Espaly*, exhibited at the 1889 *Salon des Indépendants* in Paris, shows a
young married woman from this Haute Loire region of France, in her
regional dress making bobbin lace. She wears a bright red shawl, a lace
cap with large blue silk bows and the most splendid jewellery which
formed an essential part of her dowry – two gold necklaces, one with an
enamelled panel, a gold *St Esprit* pendant with a cross and a large pair of
matching earrings. An elaborate chatelaine is hung over the back of her
chair.[31] Clearly highly sentimentalised, it was nevertheless conceivable for
lacemaking to be performed whilst wearing such clothing (Plate V).

Some of the peasant communities, such as that of the Slovak Highlands,
where the Stokes's stayed, or the farming villages of Transylvania, were
still culturally stable, if impoverished, and still independent from urban
life. Other rural communities were collapsing under the weight of social
change and poverty, as were those in Tsarist Russia. Here artists and
designers such as Ivan Bilibin[32] and Wassily Kandinsky made collecting
and sketching journeys to catch the actuality and spirit of peasant culture
of the far-flung regions of the Russian Empire. Kandinsky undertook
ethnographic research (which he later wrote up as an ethnographic paper)
in north-eastern Vologda, amongst the Zyrian communities around Ust
Syolsk (Syktyvkar) for six weeks of the summer of 1889. Peg Weiss found
that he sketched Zyrian dress in detail, that he was 'fascinated by the

juxtaposition of pagan and Christian belief systems' and that in his 1913
Memoirs of the Zyrian People he wrote that the Zyrians 'captivated him with
their contrasting appearance "now grey or yellow-grey from head to toes",
now with "white faces, red-painted cheeks, black hair," clad in colour-
fully variegated costumes "like brightly-coloured living paintings on two
legs"'. The young Kandinsky, who took to wearing Zyrian dress to keep
out the night cold, described going into the painted interior of Zyrian
wooden homes as if entering 'a painting ... a miracle' and became
profoundly interested in Zyrian shamanism.[33]

In Scotland, where life for rural labourers and their families was
extremely hard too, the 'Glasgow boys', including James Guthrie, George
Henry, James Paterson, Joseph Caw and Edward Walton, lived and
painted at Brig O'Turk in the Trossachs, at Cockburnspath in the east coast
Border region and in the Dumfriesshire village of Moniaive. Roger Billcliffe
believes that in Scotland sympathetic paintings of the rural poor went
'beyond the mere recording of ... daily tasks, becoming icons of the plight
of the rural classes'.[34]

With their concentration on realism, the clothes shown in this genre
of ruralist painting seem to offer the dress historian rare period images of
both European regional, peasant dress and British country clothing. When
George Clausen was studying at the Academy in Antwerp in the late 1870s
he paid a summer holiday visit to the island of Marken in the Zyder Zee.
He attended Mass in the fishing village of Volendam and as a critic for
Studio magazine, explained 'alive to the paintable possibilities of the scene,
and although it was somewhat of an ambitious effort he accomplished it
successfully and awoke, as it were, one morning to find himself famous'.[35]
Clausen moved on to join the international gathering of painters in Brittany,
with Stanhope Forbes joining him at Quimperlé. Kenneth McConkey
believes Clausen's 1882 painting, *Breton Girl Carrying a Jar* (now in the
collection of the Victoria and Albert Museum), showing a young peasant
girl in stout turned-up toed wooden clogs, an indigo dress, bibbed pinafore
and white cap, reveals an 'evident sense of simple reality, honestly recorded.
Or so we are obliged to think.'[36] Clausen moved in 1881 to Chilwick
Green because there he could find 'people doing simple things under good
conditions of lighting ... nothing made easy for you: you had to dig out
what you wanted'.[37] His *Shepherdess* of 1885 (now in the Walker Art Gallery,
Liverpool) again shows a young farm girl, this time in a brown dress,
white bibbed pinafore and oversized tackety boots, standing beneath a
blossoming tree in spring, with lambs close by, yet boldly painted and
managing to avoid earlier forms of the sweetened, Victorian sentimentality.

Stanhope Forbes joined the painters Langley and Goch at the Cornish
fishing town of Newlyn in 1884 in his search for rural honesty. He wrote

that 'art was somehow improved or was more authentic if it was conceived in uncomfortable surroundings'.[38] He painted views of village streets, the inside of homes and the surrounding countryside, always with an emphasis on the people living and working there. His most famous painting, *A Fish for Sale on a Cornish Beach*, of 1885 shows the daily work of the Newlyn fishing community as the catch was unloaded and sold off on the beach at low tide. The foreground is dominated by images of two women whose clothes are painted in the most careful detail. One wears a battered straw hat and striped shawl, the other a large headscarf. Both wear full length pinafores, one evidently of sacking, long skirts and battered boots. Colours are shades of browns and dull blues. Forbes abhorred the introduction even of touches of urban fashion into the dress of Newlyn women, such as crinolettes and the 1880s urban hair-style with a fashionable fringe across the forehead. He declared that his work was 'a visual record documenting scenes and customs'.[39]

Plein air artists sketched from life on the beach and in fields and mountains but many also used photographs and reworked figures in the safety and shelter of their studios. So how reliable are these images of rural and urban working people? Do they in fact show clothes as they were? Can they be relied upon as a viable dress history source? If Fildes's intent, for example, was to use clothes to highlight the depth of misery of the poor of London, did he exaggerate their poverty-stricken appearance to suit his own needs? Did he fetishise the poverty of his sitters through what the ethnographer James Faris, in another context, calls the 'consumption of the subaltern ... most commonly expressed in ... sympathy for and a celebration or revelation of the integrity of local expressions; or a critique of the exploitation commonly dictating the lives of peoples. This nevertheless turns the representation into fetish.'[40]

Fildes's subdued and dark images have not been dismissed as sentimental or romanticised. There is no evidence that Fildes gave extra-raggy clothes to his sitters in the same way, for example, that Curtis gave 'authentic' dress to the Navajo to wear in photographs (see Chapter 6). There is no doubt, however, of the 'subaltern' status of Fildes's models, or, for that matter, those of any of the *plein air* painters. McConkey penetrates the heart of this debate suggesting that 'naturalism by definition ... was about conveying the idea of the truth by means of the false'.[41] Thus, for example, at its most questionable, the little Scottish cowgirl so convincingly painted by George Henry in 1885 leaning against a tree, with a switch in her hand and her cows in the adjacent field, 'may in fact have been the younger sister' of Henry's friend, the painter Edward Hornel, put into a plain brown dress and archetypal sacking apron.[42] The Danish genre painter Julius Exner, who died in 1910, worked for a long time on the

Danish island of Amager, where a small, conservative Dutch community had settled in the sixteenth century and which 'still retained their old fashioned dress, their particular architecture and furniture, their weaving techniques and traditional festivals – all quite distinct from their Danish neighbours',[43] in the last decades of the nineteenth century. All that would indicate a very genuine sense of realism and authenticity in Exner's work, but his imagery is complicated by the fact that in 1879 Bernhard Olsen placed an Amager living room bought from the farm of Jan Wibrant on display in an Art and Industry exhibition in Copenhagen. In 1885 this room was featured again in Olsen's new *Dansk Folkemuseum* as a background to a display of a wedding scene where carved wooden models were dressed in original Amager clothing. According to museum specialists, Adriaan A. M. de Jong and Mette Skougaard, the Amager room was used in the background of at least three of Exner's paintings. Furthermore Exner also 'owned a collection of native folk costume in which he dressed his models'.[44] So where does that leave 'authenticity'?

However, not everyone dressed their sitters up this way. There is no evidence to suggest that Marianne Stokes did this, for example. Comparing dress in Newlyn to the Breton peasant clothes he had just been painting in Quimperlé, Brittany, Stanhope Forbes commented that the Newlyn girls were 'quite pretty despite their ugly English costume'. He did, however, use photographic images as a tool towards his goal of realism, yet because of his ideological *plein air* commitment to 'unflinching realism' of method, he still painted what he saw.[45] With this wide range of different approaches to art, it would be unwise for the dress historian to take *plein air* images as any form of given 'truth' on their own. Juxtaposing them against surviving examples of clothing, photographic images and descriptive period texts would, however, help to confirm or deny the 'authenticity' of the clothing shown in all these paintings.

Individual clothing preferences of artists

This discussion already indicates that a painter's personal preferences exerted strong influence on the choice of clothing s/he chose to paint. Simon finds Impressionist period portraits valuable for the dress historian because by then artists had broken free from the formalised 'social conventions of the Salon' and were exploring in a modern manner what she terms 'intimist dress'. 'They very often painted close relations', she comments, often women reclining on sofas or benches. She finds 'a refreshing unselfconsciousness in such portraits by Manet, Degas, Monet, Renoir, Mary Cassatt and Berthe Morisot'.[46]

Krystyna Matyjaszkiewicz suggests, with some specific reservations, that

Tissot's work might provide useful images for the study of fashionable dress because both his parents were in the fashion trade. His 'meticulous rendition of fashionable toilettes is a rich mine of information for today's costume historian (if fraught with occasional pitfalls for the unwary)'. She sees Tissot as revelling in the same love of painting fashionable clothes as Ingres and Winterhalter, but points out that Tissot reused favourite garments over periods of two or three years. Thus the notion that his 1870s paintings reflected the most up-to-the-minute fashions may be flawed. Further, he loved to paint checks, stripes and checks, and dark ribbons of trimming on pale grounds 'aware of the graphic potential of patterns on clothes and the way in which folds and curves could be suggested through sharp breaks and alterations of pattern direction or edge trimming'.[47] In taking these as actuality, the dress historian could be encouraged to overemphasise the popularity of such highly patterned surfaces and contrasting colours. Surviving dress of the 1870s and 1880s in fact often reveals far more subdued colour contrasts. There was a widespread fashion in the late 1870s, for example, for using one colour only in an outfit, but made up from different fabrics, such as shiny satin contrasted with dull wool of exactly the same colour. None of this is reflected in Tissot's work.

A far more extreme example of an artist's clothing preferences lies in the work of Augustus John. If the clothes seen in his paintings of the 1906–30 period were taken as in any way 'typical', all English women would be seen as colourful gypsy lookalikes. In fact Augustus John was fascinated by and knowledgeable about Romany culture. He encouraged his second wife, Dorelia (who had already chosen to dress in artistic style before she met John) to wear colourful artistic garments. John's portraits of her show dirndl, floor-length skirts in Provençal prints, worn with loose box jackets, pinafores, white stockings, comfortable flat shoes and head-scarves or curious hats. Her 'Bohemian' style was copied by art student admirers. Following on from the anti-fashion, artistic style developed by Janey Morris and her circle in the late 1860s, all these women self-consciously rejected the fashions of the day.[48] John's paintings capture this timeless artistic style which Shore calls John's 'poetic dream world of beautiful women'.[49] John's Dorelia portraits are a world away from the elegant women in the portraits of those of Drian or Dufy of the same period.

Thus, in Ribeiro's words, dress shown in elite society portraits becomes 'words translated into style and movement – for they show us how people moved and had their being, and how they saw themselves as they really were or as they wished to be'.[50] But, in every case, the clothing in these paintings demands the most cautious of interpretations. Paintings of the urban working class and of European peasantry, on the other hand, show us artists' social realist or utopian visions coloured by their personal interpretations of urban poor or rural 'Other' clothing. Caution in interpretation is needed in all these paintings for it may well be that none show the actuality of clothing.

Use of drawn and redrawn illustrations

Period drawings, sketches and engravings provide additional sources for dress history study. Work by Dürer, Watteau, Hogarth, Ingres and Henry Lamb, for example, can reveal cut, fall of fabric and body movement with greater immediacy than an oil painting. Watteau's pencil sketches, for instance, provide rare detail for the dress historian on the ways in which garments were worn. Many of his chalk and pencil sketches detail very usefully how the draping looked when women stood or sat casually in their wide sack-backed dresses.

The engravings of Gustave Doré's *London – a pilgrimage* of 1872, with its text by Blanchard Jerrold, are another underused source of detail on clothing, this time of the poor. Doré became hypnotised by the packed throng of London poverty. His images may romantisise or fetishise, but he sketched so many careful images of street children playing in the gutters, wearing the same layers of torn and scabby over-size clothes, either shoeless or with ill-fitting, rotting boots and sleeves hanging over their hands, that the viewer becomes convinced that there must have been some sense of reality behind these images. His collaborator, Jerrold, described the East End drawn by Doré as filled with 'gaudy inns and public houses, the overhanging clothes, the mounds of vegetables and the piles of hardware, the confused heaps of fish, all cast about to catch the pence of bonnetless, dishevelled women, the heavy navvies and the shoeless children'.[51]

The use of drawings of costume redrawn at later periods is a quite different issue. Within the 'academic' and museum world of dress history there is now an accepted policy which firmly rejects the use of redrawn images and insists on reproduced original period images. Publishers of popular dress history, especially and unfortunately in books directed at children and students, love the use of the redrawn illustration because this avoids copyright fees, the technical difficulties of reproducing period photographs and because redrawings provide an overall 'house' style. Redrawn images have always been standard in dress history publications and this difficulty has always been present. In discussing the late eighteenth-century work of Strutt, Ribeiro warned that in his *Complete View of the Dress and Habits of the People of England* (1796 and 1799) inevitably, on a number of occasions, the visual sources have been mis-read ... Strutt's interpretation ... sometimes errs, as when for example he is unaware that some of the figures in the mediaeval manuscripts he copies, are themselves dressed in fanciful costume to represent historic characters.[52]

In this century, typical popular examples of redrawing would include Dion Clayton Calthrop's books on *English Costume*, published from 1907. He was clearly convinced of the merit of his own illustrations.

> I am compelled to speak of my own work because I believe in it and I feel that the series of paintings in these volumes are really a valuable addition to English history ... I would wish to be thought of as more friendly than the antiquarian and more truthful than the historian, and so have endeavoured to show, in addition to the body of the clothes, some little of their soul.[53]

Calthrop's books, divided into sections named after English kings and queens from William I to George V, were so popular that they were reprinted in full colour in 1913, 1917 and 1923. Each includes his own half tone, colour wash drawings. These certainly have personal charm and bold character but are inaccurate and highly sentimentalised. They include, for example, an imaginatively coloured version of a Hollar engraving from *Ornatus Muliebris Anglicanus* of 1640 and a soft-focus sketch of 'Victorian Dress' of somewhere in the 1860s, with rather curious puffed sleeves (Figure 19).[54]

Another classic example of the dangers of redrawing is to be found in R. Turner Wilcox's popular and very well-known *Dictionary of Costume*, originally published in America in 1969 and reprinted three times since, the last in 1986. This book uses loosely sketched drawings of surviving examples of dress as its central feature. Far from helping our understanding of period style, however, Diana de Marly believes that in this publication

> like all books where the authors draw their own versions of historical clothes the resulting inaccuracy and distortion is legion. The author's style was clearly formed in the 1930s and it cannot convey facial fashions as it uses the Thirties face for all periods ... She reduces the skirts and peascod belly of a doublet ... and the size of large sleeves and paniers ... One must query the re-publication of a work which needs a drastic revision, mammoth research and much alteration to bring it up to date.[55]

Concern about the validity of redrawing centres therefore on the inadvertent introduction of factual errors of cut, second, on the falsifica-tion of period style through sentimentalisation and third, on the addition of the artist's own sense of period resulting in fanciful images, as in Calthrop's work.

Occasionally this personalised artist's eye-view can be deliberately creative and have a period quality of its own, as in the books of three women graphic artists who were also, like Turner Wilcox, learning their trade in the interwar years, Barbara Jones,[56] Pearl Binder[57] and Kathleen Mann. All three set out to present simplified period images. None pretend museological 'accuracy' as did Calthrop and Turner Wilcox. Indeed Kathleen Mann's *European Peasant Dress* of 1931[58] is drawn and painted with a deliberately '1930s modern' periodisation of peasant clothing. Her intent was to inspire the design work of embroiderers and decorators. Mann's drawings could never be accepted as valid ethnographical illustrations but can certainly be enjoyed for their period 'feel' and vitality as her illustration of a Hungarian peasant couple shows.

There are two exceptions to the rejection of the redrawn image. Both are the work of highly skilled researchers/teachers who were specialists in the history of the cut of dress. The first was Nora Waugh, who taught at the Central School of Art in London, and the second, Janet Arnold, who died in 1999. Between them they made major contributions to our understanding of the style, cut and making up of fashionable European dress. This exception to the use of redrawn images is made because both were strongly aware of the dangers of letting 'inaccuracies' creep into their drawings.

Both Waugh and Arnold examined actual garments with the greatest of care, studying the exact cut of surviving examples of period clothing, providing flat cutting patterns.[59] Each one of these was supported by 'factual'

19 'Victorian dress', watercolour and ink drawing by Dion Clayton Calthorp, 1934

three-dimensional drawings of the garments, as if displayed on correctly shaped tailors' dummies shown without heads and accessories. One example of Waugh's research work was a set of sketches (Figure 20) she made in 1966 to help the Royal Scottish Museum, Edinburgh (now part of the National Museums of Scotland), resolve the problem of how the back of one of its choicest eighteenth-century dresses would have been worn. This dress is said to have been worn in the presence of Prince Charles Edward Stuart by Margaret Oliphant of Gask at the ball at Holyrood Palace after the Jacobite victory at the Battle of Prestonpans in 1745 (Figure 21). [60] It is made up in cream-coloured, finely ribbed silk, spectacularly embroidered with a gorgeously flowering, meandering branch in the brightest of coloured and gilt silks. It has, however, a sack-backed train nearly seven feet long and so curiously patched and shabby towards its hem that it must have been looped up and hidden from view in some specific way. Waugh sent drawings of similar dresses she had found in the collections of the Metropolitan Museum to try and help solve the problem over the cut of the back of this beautiful but curious dress. In fact the dress remains something of a mystery. Research undertaken in 1989 by Naomi Tarrant, Curator of Costume and Textiles at the National Museums of Scotland, in Edinburgh, and confirmed in 2001, indicates that an entire back panel is missing from the petticoat of the dress. The display efforts of the 1960s (see Figure 21) have therefore since been reconsidered.

M. Woodward was commissioned to create simple outline sketches for Waugh's books whilst Waugh added related period engravings, text and portraits to her cutting patterns. Over a lifetime of meticulously careful study, Arnold too established this approach as fundamental to object-based, dress history research. Her work will also be of lasting value to costume designers because it provides a vast range of cutting and making up details of dress across many centuries. Further it leaves us with accurate knowledge of the precise shape of European clothing that survives only in remnants, such as the Italian doublet of 1562, discussed in Chapter 2. Arnold's work was celebrated with a memorial research day, *Patterns of Fashion: Janet Arnold and the art of costume design*, held at the Victoria and Albert Museum in 1999. [61]

Use of fashion plates and fashion drawings

Another standard and over-used visual source in dress history is period fashion plates or drawings. Appearing from the middle of the eighteenth century, they are charming, clear, often dated and coloured and appear usefully at monthly intervals. They frequently came with useful descriptions of fabric, trimming and details as to where the clothing shown could be purchased. Beyond use in descriptive style analysis, their value to the dress historian can, however, be problematic. The first necessity is to check their 'authenticity', particularly in the case of loose ones. The value of coloured fashion plates as decorative commodities has increased steadily since the 1950s and as a consequence less ethical printsellers have arranged for the colouring of black and white plates and cartoons cut from journals. This increases their selling price but renders them unusable as 'historic' documents because the colours are bogus.

Fashion plates and drawings, just like paintings, need also to be cautiously used within dress history. They were, and are, after all, only idealised images of a seasonal, fashion image rather than any kind of stylistic or social reality. Doris Langley Moore, who collected fashion plates from the late 1920s, understood this perfectly. 'The Fashion plate is often merely propaganda for a new mode rather than a report of what is really being worn ... Fashion drawing', she stressed, 'is at times a highly stylised art and the belief that it is representational in more than a most limited sense is misleading. Those who specialise in fashion and whose business it is to make news of its allurements set before the public a mixture of facts and fantasies.'[62]

The use of plates of these elite fashion images as if they were a dress history reality is a common problem in dress history publications. This has perhaps arisen because women's magazines from the early nineteenth century onwards, such as Ackerman's famous *Repository of Arts and Manufactures*, did indeed feature Court dress and Court dress etiquette together with elite fashion images for the pleasure of their well-off middle-class readers (Figure 22). As Langley Moore comments, 'the writers describing the current modes pretended to take for granted that all their readers were rich and aristocratic, even when the advertisement pages plainly address a less lofty social stratum'. In fact the plates 'represented without the least modification, the topmost summit of the vogue at its most extravagant',[63] although as Christopher Breward comments the magazine readership fell across the full range of middle-class consumers and dressmakers.

Magazines aimed at the growing number of middle-class department store shoppers increased steadily through the nineteenth century, with their fashion plates still representing the elite of Parisian taste and style. Paris, as the recognised international source of seasonal fashion, was producing 81 fashion journals in 1881, 127 by 1901 and 166 by 1930.[64] *Le Petit Echo de la Mode*, bought by Huon de Penanster in 1879, was then selling 5000 copies. By 1893, numbers had increased to 100,000, rising to a million by 1923.[65] *La Mode Illustrée* (Figure 23) was owned by its printer, Firmin Didot, and edited for forty-two years by Emmeline Raymond, the

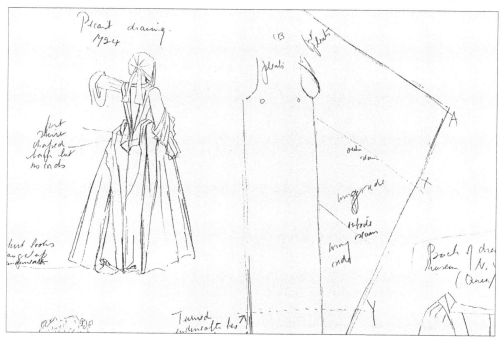

20 Research sketch by Nora Waugh, 1966

21 Silk dress of 1745, embroidered in coloured silk and gilt metal threads, with unusually long trained back, discovered in 1989 to have had an entire panel removed from the centre back of the petticoat

daughter of a Belgian officer in the Austrian army. By the turn of the century it was selling 100,000 copies a week. Its readership, according to Zeldin, was the middle and petty bourgeoisie of Paris and the French provinces. Breward, noting the expansion of fashion journals in the 1870s and 1880s, comments that the function of their fashion plates was by then far more than merely providing 'propaganda for a mode' to their readers. Beyond that their aim was 'to underpin, massage and reflect the modern experience of the reader',[66] by encouraging and celebrating increasing levels of fashion consumption. Thus some plates included images of women in department stores choosing elegant millinery or attending smart social functions.

As today, editorial policies were not as innocent and honestly inde-pendent as readers might have thought. Most fashion magazines had commercial tie-ups with specific fashion salons, even as early as the 1830s when the London-based journal *La Belle Assemblée* frequently illustrated garments available from Mrs Bell of St Paul's Churchyard, who was the wife of the proprietor John Bell, Gallery of Fine Arts, Southampton Street, in the Strand. In the late 1860s *La Mode Illustrée* had 'arrangements' with

Fashion plates *left* 22 *Ackerman's Repository of Arts and Manufactures,* 1 June 1820
right 23 *La Mode Illustrée,* 15 December 1889

left **24** Fashion plate, *La Mode Illustrée*, Paris, March 1870   *right* **25** Winter coats, *Mabs* magazine, October 1932

elite Parisian couturiers such as Mme Maury of Rue Vivier, Mme Fladry of Rue Richer and Mme Bréant-Castel of Rue du Quatre-Septembre, whose garments were frequently featured, to the exclusion of other rival fashion houses (Figure 24). These important commercial realities are rarely mentioned when fashion plate from these journals are used in dress history books today. Neither is the fact that the bourgeois readers of the 1840–1914 period recognised fashion plate images for what they were, the ideal rather than the real. It is the passage of time that has blurred this understanding and allowed some history publications to use fashion plates as representations of reality.

Through the production of new, cheaper, but still persuasive publications, the range of women's magazines widened to attract a far wider social readership from the late 1920s. As a consequence, in Europe and the USA, the women editors of journals such as *Woman's Weekly, Woman, Woman's Own, Women's Kingdom* and *Mabs Magazine* consciously changed the ideal images portrayed in their fashion drawings. Although the more up-market *Vogue* and *Harper's Bazaar* continued to offer the most elegant of fashion drawings by Willaumez, Bérard and Eric, *Woman's Weekly* showed far more down to earth, though still ideal, images of young married women. *Mabs* showed its styles on drawings of young women who looked more like young *ingenue* film stars or smart typists than elegant Parisiennes (Figure 25). This tactic was also used in mail order catalogues in the 1920s and 1930s, such as *Sears and Roebuck* in the USA and *Littlewoods* in Britain. Editors were aware by the 1930s that their younger readers and customers were more attuned to styles from Hollywood than the couture salons of Paris. These subtleties of fashion drawing helped boost the sales of these new magazines to a mass-oriented lower-middle-class market. The clothes, patterns, fashion advice and advertisements they contained also acknowledged the burgeoning development of a mass ready-to-wear and home dressmaking consumer. From the mid-1950s cheap mass magazines, such as *Jackie* and *Valentine*, were targeted at the next new market of fashion consumers, teenage girls. By the 1960s, these featured highly coloured and stylised illustrations of very young girls to attract their readers (Figure 26). Yet all too many dress histories have relied on *Vogue* and *Harper's* as the sole sources for their 'typical' period fashion images. All too few use illustrations from the mass-oriented journals cited here, although these reflect so well the significant consumer expansion of 'fashionable' dress in the 1920–60 period and thereafter.

The use of cartoons

Cartoons have long been a standby both for the popularist and 'academic' dress historian because of the broad range of political, social and cultural comment they offer through clothing analysis in witty and easily accessible form. However, little in-depth exploration has yet been undertaken to reveal the significant cultural meanings accessible through looking at clothing in cartoons. They remain an under-used and undervalued research source because they are much more than easy, witty sketches.

Although many cartoons involve exaggeration and overstatement, many also rely on levels of subtle social comment that both cartoonist and viewer enjoy unravelling. Bohun Lynch suggested that 'the critic was wrong who remarked that caricature is to the portrait what farce is to comedy, and that it chooses the monstrous instead of explaining the average. For that is exactly what good caricature can do and does.'[67] Cartoons can therefore offer to the dress historian 'average' images of supposedly typical period characters who were instantly recognisable to the contemporary reader.

Cartoonists use observation of clothing both to inflict wounds on their targets and to amuse their readers. Every nuance of posture, body shape and garment becomes grist to their social comment through their ability to catch or exaggerate the immediate, ephemeral moment. They are therefore useful as a gauge of period social reaction to dress rather than for their 'reliable' depiction of style. Dress has always been a favourite tool for the lampoon. From its start in 1841 *Punch* is peopled month by month with satirical and witty parody on the dress of both sexes and all ages and classes. Period gender attitudes can be probed usefully through the drawings.

The most successful cartoonists lampoon the circles they live amongst or close to, as did, for example, Thomas Rowlandson, George du Maurier, Phil May, Charles Dana Gibson and Osbert Lancaster. Rowlandson mercilessly lampooned high society London circles, living near them in Wardour Street, in Soho, from 1777–81. According to Lynch, Rowlandson 'had a wide knowledge of the world of Pleasure: he was a popular and genial personality ... a desperate gambler'.[68]

George du Maurier, too, moved in the same artistic and social circles of upper-middle-class London that he satirised with great success in *Punch* a hundred years later. His signature can be seen today in the visitors' book at the home of his fellow *Punch* cartoonist Edward Linley Sambourne at 18 Staffordshire Terrace in Kensington, just up the road from Lord Leighton's

left **26** Fashion drawing, *Jackie*, no. 389, 19 June 1971   *right* **27** 'Box o' lights, my Lord?', from Phil May's *Guttersnipes* (Leadenhall Press, London, 1896)

aesthetic home at Leighton House. Leonée Ormond's biography of du Maurier shows that he was 'in no way caught up in the whirlpool of fashionable life' and that, although he did attend society functions, 'his keen awareness of social nuance was backed by considerable intelligence'. For the amusement of his conventional middle-class readership, George du Maurier drew some savage images for *Punch* of the Aesthetes, of both sexes, whom he satirised mercilessly from 1873–82. Ormond comments that 'his distaste for affectation explains the bitterness with which he had attacked the "aesthetes", whom he pursued with an almost personal animosity'. Occasionally he drew a pretty aesthetic maiden, but mostly he seems to have despised what he saw as their cultural pretension, so he drew the women as thin, haggard and sour-faced, with drooping breasts and without the elegant shape induced by corseting, the very opposite of the fashionably feminine woman, with her unnaturally contrived curves. Du Maurier's drawings show that he clearly preferred these. He also clearly loathed the educated, bluestocking middle-class woman of the 1880s and 1890s. Ormond comments that 'his attitude to female emancipation, in any other field but love, remained hostile to the last … he assumed that the new woman must be either too hideous to get a husband, or infatuated with a passing fad'.[69] He consequently drew her always with raddled neck, masculine collar and tie, round glasses and a mannish stance. This same image was repeated by Phil May, who in 1896 drew the New Woman cyclist in her *zouaves* (cycling bloomers) and with such masculine features that in the cartoon a street seller urchin runs alongside her shouting 'Box o' lights, my Lord?' (Figure 27).

Most cartoonists develop such favourite stock characters often through the use of clothing imagery and often with great popular success. The simple elegance of dress and social directness of Charles Dana Gibson's 'Gibson Girl' cartoons of the dawn of the twentieth century may well even have had a lasting impact on the national character of fashion in the USA. His famous series 'the Widow and her Friends', which ran in *Life* magazine from October 1900 to July 1901, charted the social life of a beautiful widow, which contributed to the ever-growing elegance of mourning wear of the period (Figure 28). In the same way, the success of Phil May's 'guttersnipes' playing in the street and generally aggravating passing 'toffs', which he drew on visits to London's East End, became national stereotypical images of working-class street children.[70]

Osbert Lancaster both admired and gently mocked the heroine of his long-running *Daily Express* cartoons. From the late 1940s through to the 1960s he drew his 'Viscountess, Maudie Littlehampton' taking part in the collapsing circles of aristocratic high society London. He revelled in the outdated snobbism of this social elite through careful play on 'Maudie's'

28 Cartoon, Charles Dana Gibson, 'She is the subject of some hostile criticism'

ever etiquette-correct clothing. He showed her outshone in Paris by an elegante in French couture, and struggling to make her unwilling daughter Jennifer conform to the proper social conventions of a debutante as she 'came out' in 1957. There are tensions when Jennifer declares she wants to marry the son of an Italian *restauranteur* from Knightsbridge and more still when she meets bearded left-wing intellectuals. Lancaster's 1950s images leave us with his incisively sharp but not unsympathetic eye-view of the politics, gender, social and racist snobbisms of high society London circles of that period. He also understood perfectly well that aristocratic dominance of British establishment circles was disintegrating in front of his eyes.

All successful cartoon characters, such as Lancaster's, are the result of sharp observation of the nuances of social behaviour and appearance coupled with the imagination, satire and wit of the cartoonist. As Ormond wrote of du Maurier's work

> the emotions which gave [the cartoons] life – the social jockeying, the carefully delivered snub, the misery experienced by the nervous and the misfits, the gaffes committed by the *parvenu*, the status which birth conferred, to which all paid court, the advantage enjoyed by wit and beauty, the callousness and the superficiality which are the result of a rigidly organised and conventional society.[71]

A glance at cartoons, from Hogarth's onwards, shows a universal understanding amongst the artists of the cultural importance of clothing. They know their readers can 'read' their social comments instantly from the drawings. We still understand the mockery behind Daumier's 1857 *Charivari* cartoons of women in their hooped petticoats, such as one of 3 April which shows a woman taking flight with her hooped skirts blowing around her head. The caption reads: 'the dangers of wearing hoops at the time of the Equinox'. Another, of 9 September, features a park gardener sorrowing over his flattened flowers, wrecked by a woman passing by in her hoops: 'I would as soon have a hurricane in my garden as these accursed crinolines', he rages.[72]

Sometimes the sartorial target may be of such fleeting ephemerality that the meanings within some cartoons are now lost to us. One example can be seen in cartoons showing 'fast' young women in the late 1920s wearing 'rolled down' stockings. Barely recorded in dress history, this practice created a furore in its day because, when sitting, a little of naked thigh was revealed. Cartoons can thus permit the dress historian to recover lost styles and fashion practice. They can also allow us to regain a sense of the public shock some clothing caused in its day, which now may seem so tame and unsensational. It needs to be remembered that the consumption of cartoons through the eighteenth and nineteenth centuries was by a middle- and upper-class readership, the employers and the servant-owning classes. A series of stereotypical characters designed to amuse them filled the pages of *Punch* from the 1840s right through to the Second World War, such as pompous butlers, over-elegant maids and shop girls, cheeky cabbies, ignorant foreigners (especially black ones), country bumpkins and the buxom Cockney grandmother in her long skirt and apron. Ormond notes that du Maurier regularly satirised working people in this way. His 'arriet is usually round and small, with coarse features and no poise' but she noticed too that 'governesses and servant girls, when on duty, are ... characterised by good looks and upright carriage'.[73] Phil May's drawings of Cockney Girls in his famous Punch series in the 1890s leave us with a positive and far less patronising view of working-class girls than du Maurier's.[74]

The cartoonists' political views as well as their social attitudes need to be considered for right- or left-wing bias. Cartoons published in Russia, for example, under Stalinist censorship in the 1930s, featured standard anti-semitic figures of the evil capitalist Uncle Sam, with a frock coat, top hat and usually with a Jewish nose. Equally poisonous were Nazi anti-Jewish cartoons. In the 1990s, the British Prime Minister, John Major, was effectively and cruelly lampooned by the left-wing cartoonist, Steve Bell, for what Bell saw as his dangerous right-wing political ineffectiveness. This was identified by the creation of the character's famously large, droopy, sexless *Superman* over-underpants.

If dress historians have been laggard at realising this potential in cartoons, social historians have not. The Centre for the Study of Cartoons at the University of Canterbury, for example, contains 85,000 cartoons, and collections of the work of over sixty cartoonists from David Low to Steve Bell, with a database of over 25,000 images dating from 1904. The Centre is well aware of why cartoonists took such an interest in dress. Some postgraduate students from Canterbury have already focused research on specific cartoon topics, including the portrayal of suffragette women in cartoons.[75]

Towards a methodology for using cartoons within dress studies

It is astonishing how little careful and detailed analysis of cartoons has as yet been undertaken by dress historians. Alison Adburgham and Christina Walkeley are two who have at least collated cartoon images,[76] but few have attempted any close decoding of the cultural messages passed down to us in individual cartoons. A methodology needs to be established to help dress historians in this process. This would take as fundamental an understanding that unless period cartoons are set in their historical period context, they become meaningless. Thus a five-fold approach would be helpful. First, the cartoonist's personal, political and cultural interests need to be assessed. Second, the cultural and political stance of the publishing journal or newspaper has to be considered, as does, third, that of the readership. Next, the exact period context of the specific cartoon at the moment of publication needs to be assessed and finally specific cross-class period analysis would place the clothing shown in the cartoon within its proper dress historical context. In this way, a cartoon which reviled as 'pushy' the clothes of a smartly dressed department store salesgirl in the 1890s can be seen for what it was – a play on the anxious reactions of *Punch*'s middle-class women readers who felt increasingly socially threatened by the advent of cheaper stylish ready-to-wear costumes, which were allowing working-class young women in the great cities to dress smartly for the first time.

Conclusion

Cartoonists, like artists, to quote Ribeiro

> do what the dress historian does; they record, analyse and select or interpret clothing; they provide invaluable testimony to the culture, the manners, the *vision* of the times. *What* they depict and *why* is of crucial importance to anyone seriously interested in the study of dress.[77]

Careful research into the clothing in all the sources cited here can add profoundly to our understanding of the multi-layered functions of dress as a nuanced reflector of society's shifting attitudes towards issues of gender, race and class.

Notes

1 With sincere thanks to Margaret Maynard for advice on this chapter.

2 A. Ribeiro, *The Art of Dress: fashion in England and France, 1750–1820* (Yale University Press, New Haven, 1995), p. 236.

3 B. Reade, *The Dominance of Spain, 1550–1669* (George Harrap, London, 1952), p. 18 and plate 16.

4 Ibid. p. 21 and plate 34, *The Artist's Family* by Jorge Manuel Thetocopuli, Brn Athyn, Philadelphia.

5 Correspondence, May 1999.

6 D. de Marly, Bibliography of Stella Mary Newton's Publications (*Costume*, 21, 1987), p. 2.

7 S. M. Newton, *Health, Art and Reason: dress reformers of the nineteenth century* (John Murray, London, 1974).

8 S. M. Newton, *The Dress of the Venetians, 1495–1525* (Scholar Press, London, 1988), p. 1 and p. 8.

9 Ibid. p. 69.

10 Ribeiro, *The Art of Dress*, p. 236.

11 Ibid. pp. 6–7 and p. 14.

12 See A. Ribeiro, *The Dress Worn at Masquerades in England, 1730–1790 and Its Relation to Fancy Dress in Portraiture* (Batsford, London, 1984).

13 Ribeiro, *The Art of Dress*, p. 31.

14 See Ipswich Museum, no R.1945.12 a and b, pale green silk satin suit embroidered with cream-coloured silk thread in border feather design on centre front of jacket and on cuffs, about 1770.

15 C. Breward, *The Culture of Fashion: a new history of fashionable dress* (Manchester University Press, Manchester, 1995), pp. 115–116 and p. 120.

16 J. Harvey, *Men in Black* (Reaktion, London, 1995), p. 14.

17 N. Rothstein, *Silk Designs of the Eighteenth Century in the Collection of the Victoria and Albert Museum* (Thames & Hudson, London, 1990), p. 105 and plate 182, p. 184, portrait by Hudson of Esther Hamner aged 13, 1752, in the private collection of Lady May-Gaye Bonus; see also the same design on paper by Garthwaite, 1747 (no. 5958.27; Department of Dress and Textiles of the Victoria and Albert Museum, p. 241).

18 N. Rothstein, *A Lady of Fashion: Barbara Johnson's album of styles and fabrics* (Thames & Hudson, London, 1987), p. 4 and p. 17 of the original album.

19 Ribeiro, *The Art of Dress*, p. 35.

20 M. Lovell, Copley and the Case of the Blue Dress (*The Yale Journal of Criticism*, 11, 1 Spring 1998), p. 56, p. 63 and p. 65. The portrait of Mrs Benjamin Pickman is in the collection of Yale University Art Gallery, that of Mary Turner Sargent is in

the Fine Arts Museum of San Francisco and that of Mrs James Warren in the Museum of Fine Arts, Boston.

21 M. Simon, *Fashion in Art: the Second Empire and Impressionism* (Zwemmer, London, 1995), p. 33 and p. 39.

22 Ibid. p. 40 and p. 39, quoting E. About, *Voyage à travers l'exposition des Beaux-Arts de 1855* (Hachette, Paris, 1855), p. 134; the painting of the Princesse de Broglie is in the collection of the Metropolitan Museum of Art, New York; that of Baronne James de Rothschild is in a private collection in Paris.

23 L. V. Fildes, *Luke Fildes, RA: a Victorian painter* (Michael Joseph, London, 1968), p. 24.

24 M. Snodin and E. Stavenow-Hidemark (eds), *Carl and Karrin Larsson, Creators of the Swedish Style* (Victoria and Albert Museum, London, 1997), p. 25.

25 See I. Spaander and P. van der Velde, *Reünie op't duin, Mondriaan en tijdgenoten in Zeeland* (Zeeuws Museum, Middleburg, 1994).

26 These Swedish village wall paintings were known in Britain by the early twentieth century. Three examples from the Halland region, including one dated to 1801, were brought to Surrey as part of the Haslemere Peasant Arts Collection, formed in the 1885–1926 period and survive in the collection at Haslemere Museum.

27 M. Evans, *Marianne and Adrian Stokes, Hungarian Journeys, Landscapes and Portraits: 1905–1910* (Magdalen Evans, London, 1996).

28 A. Stokes, *Hungary: painted by Adrian Stokes and Marianne Stokes, described by Adrian Stokes* (Adam and Charles Black, London, 1901), p. 30, pp. 165–167, p. 42, p. 176, p. 52, p. 179, p. 85, p. 38, p. 213, p. 313. With thanks to Jessica Harris.

29 W. B. Forster Bovill, *Hungary and the Hungarians* (Methuen, London, 1908), p. 238.

30 K. McConkey, *Impressionism in Britain* (Yale University Press and the Barbican Gallery, New Haven and London, 1995), p. 21.

31 This painting is in the collection of the Musée Crozatier, Le Puy-en-Velay, no. 894.10; with thanks to F.-X. Amprimoz, Director of the Musée Crozatier, Le Puy-en-Velay, France; see also Réunion des Musées Nationaux, *Costume-Coutume* (Réunion des Musées Nationaux, Paris, 1987), p. 236.

32 F. Gray, *Russian Stories – Ivan Bilibin* (University of Brighton, Brighton, 1993).

33 P. Weiss, *Kandinsky and Old Russia: the artists as ethnographer and shaman* (Yale University Press, New Haven, 1995), p. 4 and p. 21.

34 R. Billcliffe, *The Glasgow Boys: The Glasgow School of Painting, 1875–1895* (John Murray, London, 1989), p. 32.

35 Dewy Bates, *George Clausen, A. R. A.* (*The Studio*, 5, 25, 1895), pp. 6–8.

36 McConkey, *Impressionism in Britain*, p. 21.

37 Ibid. p. 27, quoting Sir George Clausen, Autobiographical Notes (*Artwork*, 55, Spring 1931), p. 19.

38 Ibid. p. 27, quoting Mrs Lionel Birch, *Stanhope, A. Forbes and Elizabeth Stanhope Forbes, ARWS* (no publisher given, 1906), p. 29.

39 C. Fox and F. Greenacre, *Painting in Newlyn* (Orion Galleries, Newlyn, 1985), pp. 58–59, quoting Stanhope Forbes's correspondence, 1 February 1884 and Cornwall from a Painters' Point of View, *Annual Report of the Royal Cornwall Polytechnic Society for 1900*, Falmouth, 1901, p. 8.

40 J. Faris, Anthropological Transparency: film, representation and politics, in P. I. Crawford and D. Turton, *Film as Ethnography* (Manchester University Press, Manchester, 1992), p. 172.

41 McConkey, *Impressionism in Britain*, p. 26.

42 Ibid. p. 139.

43 A. M. de Jong and M. Skougaard, The Hindeloopen and the Amager Rooms: two examples of an historical museum phenomenon (*Journal of the History of Collections*, 5, 2, 1993), p. 167.

44 Ibid. p. 175.

45 Fox and Greenacre, *Painting in Newlyn*, p. 58, quoting A Newlyn Retrospect (*The Cornish Magazine*, 1, 1898), p. 83 and Stanhope Forbes's correspondence, 25 December 1884.

46 Simon, *Fashion In Art*, p. 221 and p. 231.

47 K. Matyjaszkiewicz, *James Tissot* (Phaidon and Barbican Art Gallery, London, 1984), p. 69 and p. 72.

48 M. Easton, Dorelia's Wardrobe: 'There goes an Augustus John' (*Costume*, 8, 1975), pp. 30–34.

49 R. Shore, *Augustus John* (Phaidon, London, 1979), p. 7.

50 A. Ribeiro, *Dress in Eighteenth Century Europe, 1715–1789* (Batsford, London, 1984), p. 19.

51 G. Doré and B. Jerrold, *London – a pilgrimage* (Grant, London, 1872, reprint by David and Charles, Newton Abbot, 1971), p. 124.

52 A. Ribeiro, Antiquarian Attitudes – some early studies in the history of dress (*Costume*, 20, 1994), pp. 59–70.

53 D. Clayton Calthrop, *English Costume* (A. and C. Black, London, 1923), pp. ix–x, with thanks to Penelope Madden.

54 Gouache and ink illustration of *Victorian Dress* about 1850–60, in D. Clayton Calthrop, *English Dress from Victoria to George V* (Chapman and Hall, London, 1935).

55 D. de Marly, The Dictionary of Costume, R. Turner Wilcox, Batsford Reprint, 1979 (*Costume*, 20, 1986), p. 103.

56 B. Jones, *Design for Death* (Andre Deutsch, London, 1967).

57 See P. Binder, *Muffs and Morals* (Harrap, London, 1953).

58 K. Mann, *Peasant Costume in Europe* (A. and C. Black, London, 1931); and idem, *Design from Peasant Art* (A. and C. Black, London, 1939).

59 See N. Waugh, *The Cut of Men's Clothes* (Faber and Faber, London, 1964), *The Cut of Women's Clothes* (Faber and Faber, London, 1968) and *Corsets and Crinolines* (Batsford, London, 1970); J. Arnold, *Patterns of Fashion: English women's dresses and their construction, 1860–1940* (Macmillan, London, 1967, reprinted 1972), *Patterns of Fashion: Englishwomen's dresses and their construction, 1660–1800* (Macmillan, London, 1972), *Patterns of Fashion: the cut and construction of clothes for men and women, 1560–1620* (Macmillan, London, 1985).

60 National Museums of Scotland, Edinburgh, costume collection no. 1964.553. Avril Hart, recently retired from the Dress and Textiles Department of the Victoria and Albert Museum, published her research into trains which are similar to but not

precisely like this one in: The Evolution of the Mantua, in A. de la Haye and E. Wilson, *Defining Dress: dress as object, meaning and identity* (Manchester University Press, Manchester, 1999), pp. 100–110.

61 Victoria and Albert Museum, Dept. of Education, *Patterns of Fashion: Janet Arnold and the art of costume design*, a memorial study day leaflet, Saturday, 24 April 1999.

62 D. Langley Moore, *Gallery of Fashion, 1790–1822, from plates by Heideloff and Ackerman* (Batsford, London, 1949), footnote 3.

63 D. Langley Moore, *The Child In Fashion* (Batsford, London, 1953), p. 9 and p. 17.

64 T. Zeldin, *Taste and Corruption, France, 1848–1945* (Oxford University Press, Oxford, 1980), p. 209.

65 Ibid. pp. 209–211.

66 C. Breward, Femininity and Consumption: the problem of the late nineteenth-century fashion journal (*Journal of Design History*, 7, 20, 1994), p. 85.

67 B. Lynch, *A History of Caricature* (Faber and Gwyer, London, 1924), p. 10.

68 Ibid. pp. 59–60.

69 L. Ormond, *George du Maurier* (Routledge and Kegan Paul, London, 1969), p. 312, p. 311, p. 350 and p. 353.

70 *Phil May's Guttersnipes: 50 original sketches in pen and ink* (The Leadenhall Press, London, 1896).

71 Ormond, *George du Maurier*, p. 329.

72 The Royal Academy of Arts, *Honoré Daumier – The Arnold Hammer Daumier collection* (London, 31 January–15 March 1981), pp. 133–136.

73 Ormond, *George du Maurier*, p. 31.

74 As in *Phil May's ABC: fifty two original designs forming two humorous alphabets from A to Z* (The Leadenhall Press, London, 1897).

75 See http://libservb/ukc.ac.uk/cartoons/.

76 See A. Adburgham, *A Punch History of Manners and Modes* (Hutchinson, London, 1961); C. Walkeley, *The Way to Wear 'Em: 150 years of Punch on fashion* (Peter Owen, London, 1985).

77 A. Ribiero, Re-Fashioning Art: some visual approaches to the study of the history of dress (*Fashion Theory*, 2, 4, 1998), p. 323.

6 ✧ Approaches using visual analysis of photography and film[1]

The meaning of the photograph is understood to be inseparably tied to social consciousness, culture and custom. (Sue Braden)[2]

Introduction

EVERY kind of clothing has been captured on photographic film since the 1830s. Ethnographers and travellers photographed and filmed communities from the most remote corners of the world. From the great urban centres, images of elite high fashion and the most domestic family scenes leave us with records of every possible style and class of dress. Photographs and film footage seem obvious sources for dress history research and indeed photos have been used in dress history publications since Racinet used them as a basis for the chromolithographic illustrations in his *Costume Historique* of 1888. Since then their use within ethnographical and high fashion dress history publications has become standard. Film and video remain, however, new research tools still barely used in object-centred dress history, with the exception of specific studies on film fashions. Deciphering the coded signals behind the creation of all these images, as in paintings, is highly complex. Do they exaggerate, mock, deceive or manipulate and can they ever reflect the 'truth'?

This chapter examines this broad range of visual evidence in three sections. First, it will assess the history of ethnographic photographs featuring clothing and how such images have been used in dress research and then look at developments in Western, urban photography. The final section will discuss aspects of dress and the moving image.

Ethnographical photography

The same fascination with the strange and bizarre that gripped writers and illustrators of the earliest dress history books in the late sixteenth and seventeenth centuries were still at play when the first documentary photographs of indigenous communities were taken from the 1860s and 1870s. The same beliefs that 'Others' lived in an unchanging 'primitive' and 'exotic' world still persisted, but were by then suffused with new 'scientific' interest in the evolution of mankind and the development of notions of racial hierarchy. The problem has been over the inability of photographers to detach themselves from their own cultural roots and sensibilities, thus, for example, imposing Western stereotypic notions on gender roles upon photographs. Virginia Lee-Webb noticed that 'the status of both genders is indexed by their poses, clothing and possessions ... men as warriors, women in sexually suggestive poses'.[3]

The function of anthropological/ethnographical photography, according to Chelsea Miller Goin, is 'to attempt to describe visually a way of life – distinct people existing in a specific cultural landscape with specific material culture'.[4] The role of clothing and body adornment, as central within such cultural landscapes inevitably features in photography work by anthropologists and ethnographers. Anne Maxwell dates the earliest photographing of aboriginal peoples back to the 1860s when the Royal Institute of Anthropology of England and Ireland set about adapting ideas drawn from Darwin's *Origin of the Species* of 1859 to anthropological research. This involved classification of people according to their skin, hair and eye colour and the development of a system of anthropometric photography by Henry Huxley and J. H. Lampry. This was practised in 'India, Sri Lanka, Malaya, Africa and Australia in penal colonies and in the slave-owning states of North America before the Civil War'. Maxwell adds that it 'failed to take into account colonised people's feelings or to respect their privacy ... The more beleaguered a population, the more likely it was to be subjected to intrusive modes of interpretation.'[5] Firmly based on a European conviction of their own racial superiority, photographs often emphasised rituals or 'bizarre' appearance, such as tattooed, scarified, naked bodies, heavy jewellery, or dress that seemed extreme to the European eye. Such images were used to enhance scientific theories of biological and social evolution which identified the 'underdeveloped' people of the non-Western world as lying at the bottom of a racial hierarchy.

Missionary/colonial photography

Photographs taken by missionaries, colonial civil servants and the military in the late nineteenth and early twentieth centuries have left us with rare early images of indigenous people. Not a few missionaries recorded their newly converted flocks on camera for fund-raising public lectures (in the form of lantern slides). The Reverend George Brown used his photographs from the Pacific Islands in just this way. A tailor's son from Aldermaston near Reading, he spent forty-eight years in the Pacific, from 1860, as a member of the Wesleyan Methodist Mission. He was, according to Virginia Lee-Webb, 'a truly competent and prolific photographic artist'. He worked mainly in portraiture and 904 of his glass-plate positives survive in the Australian Museum, Sydney, showing the 'authentic' clothing and body decoration of communities from Samoa and Toga to New Guinea in the finest detail, as well as the introduction of missionary dress. Lee-Webb notes, however, that, despite his conventional colonial belief that he was taking his flock on a journey from 'primitive to civilised', the Revd Brown, unlike many others, respected his subjects and rejected the usual 'common tropes of the exotic "Other" in the poses of his sitters'. As Lee-Webb notes, these photographs 'are often our earliest and often our only remaining images to describe, through the missionary perspective, the communities and people they met'.[6]

Susan Conway's research *Hidden From History – court costumes and textiles of 19th century Lan Na* confirms this view. Searching for scarce nineteenth-century images of peoples in this remote area of what is now North Thailand, she found photographs taken by Dr Samuel Craig Peoples, who, with his wife, worked for the American Presbyterians in Lampang and Lan Na. Taken in the 1885–95 period, these very rare photographs show the Royal Family and Court circles of the region as well as Lan Na teachers at the Mission school in about 1900. These reveal that whilst male Royalty wore strongly Western European influenced Court dress with white jacket, trousers and plumed hats, Court women still wore their hand-woven *phasin* striped skirts.[7]

Military and civil service colonials stationed in remote regions of the British Empire were also keen to use a camera to record local populations. Elizabeth Dell, Curator of the Green Centre for Non-Western Art at Brighton Museum, has been researching a remarkable series of photographic albums taken by Colonel James Henry Green in the 1920s and 1930s. He was posted to the Union of Myanmar, as a recruitment officer for the British Army. He put together a large collection of local textiles and his own photographic albums to record the sartorial differences between the many indigenous communities of these remote Burmese. Green became so expert that in 1934 he submitted a dissertation to the Anthropology Department of the University of Cambridge.[8]

Anthropology/ethnography and photography

The use of photography within anthropology research was pioneered by Bronislaw Malinowski in his work in the Trobriand Islands, New Guinea, in the 1914–18 period. Here, according to Chelsea Miller Goin, he 'established fundamental methodologies and presentations in anthropological fieldwork', since seen as of lasting importance. These were based on 'the methodology of using participant observation to establish the scientific validity of its data'. Goin confirms Malinowski's angst at 'attempting to penetrate a form of life quite different from and incompatible with his own'. Malinowski used photographs of Tobriand women in traditional clothing to explain 'complex systems of sociological, economic and ceremonial principle', although Goin suggests that he may 'only have had superficial access' to information on women's seminal economic and cultural role in community life.[9]

In the 1930s Margaret Mead and Gregory Bates, working in colonial Bali 'to establish anthropology as a true scientific discipline' also used photography as one of their research tools. As part of their work recording Balinese trance dances and ceremonial calendrical processions, they conducted 'one of the earliest systematic studies of the use of photography in the social sciences'. Michael Hitchcock and Lucy Norris have examined the use of film and photography by Mead and Bates, who took 25,000 diapositive frames, for their study *Balinese Character: a photographic analysis* in 1942. Hitchcock and Norris believe that 'in adhering too closely to academic orthodoxy, they lost sight of certain visual criteria' and prefer the photography of Beryl de Zoete, a dance critic, who worked with Walter Spies, an artist and film maker, in Bali in 1934–35. De Zoete and Spies undertook a detailed and careful ethnographical dance research project which culminated in de Zoete's book *Dance and Drama in Bali* of 1938 based on over a hundred photographs taken by Spies. Hitchcock and Norris, investigating the Spies–de Zoete archive of photos and film in the Horniman Museum, London, believe that *Dance and Drama in Bali* 'represents one of the first major attempts to explain the performing arts of an Asian society with the aid of photography, and is as much an exercise in visual anthropology as in dance ethnography'.[10] These photographs leave us with detailed close-ups of Balinese dancers wearing elaborate masks, and woven and batiked garments. To any museum ethnographer seeking to display Balinese masks and dress, the de Zoete/Spies record is irreplaceable. To achieve these photographs, Spies, who was an experienced film maker, had to use strong night lamps. Intrusive as these may have been, Hitchcock and Norris firmly believe that their work was free of imperial clichés and without colonial misrepresentation of the Balinese.

De Zoete's interest in dance and music took her to Romania in the mid-1930s. Travelling from Bukovina in the north, through Transylvania and down to Oltenia in the south, she took research photographs of

29 Group of villagers attending a rain-making ritual, Romania, Beryl de Zoete, late
1930s

peasant dance festivals and rituals, including a funeral in Bukovina. These
show details of clothing, worn, to quote Sue Braden, as 'inseparably tied
to social consciousness, culture and custom'. The negatives of these photographs were given to the Horniman Museum and Library after her death
in 1962 and first printed up and shown to the public at the University
of Brighton in March 2000. Ioana Popescu of the Museum of the Romanian
Peasant in Bucharest has identified one series of images within these
photographs, showing a group of women making a large, flat human figure
from clay, as a rain-making ritual. The clay doll represents *Caloian*, the
deceased son of the Rain. The clay figure is buried in a small coffin and
as with a human burial, a funeral meal is then held in the home of the
'hostess' who organises the ceremony. *Caloian* is then exhumed and cast
into the river to join his mother, the Rain, who searches for him in the
forests. When the mother and son are reunited, rain will fall once again
on the dry plain regions. De Zoete's photographs show the women
organising this ritual (Figure 29) wearing unfashionable, cheap, urbanised
1930s dresses, whereas her photographs from Oltenia and Bukovina, for
example, show peasant women wearing embroidered blouses, long skirts
and aprons in far more 'traditional' Romanian peasant styles.[11]

Popular dissemination of photographs of the exotic 'Other'

A racist notion of the 'primitive' was commonplace in popular 'educational' books of the late nineteenth and early twentieth centuries. This popularist approach is revealed in the pages of *Peoples of All Nations – their life today and the story of their past*. This dates from the mid-1920s but used photographs dating back at least twenty years. This deeply racist, seven-volumed publication, was designed as a general, 'educational' encyclopaedia and featured 50,000 photographs, some in high colour. Covering 'all' nations, it included a *Dictionary of Races*, with ethnographical maps, purporting to amass 'an immense amount of information about the racial origins, geographical distribution, physical types and social customs of the people enumerated'. These are listed from Ababua, 'Bantu speaking people … of the Belgian Congo … they are a merry people and very hospitable' to 'Zyrians: Finnic people of moderate stature, with round heads, straight noses and blond or chestnut hair … They have a reputation of being skilful and unscrupulous traders'. All this is written by Northcote W. Thomas, 'anthropologist'.

The clichéd gender stereotyping highlighted by Lee-Webb is obvious in every page. Races covered include Britain's own 'Others', the Welsh, the Scots and the Irish. They are treated in patronising, sentimentalised tones. Indigenous non-Western peoples are treated with contempt. Comment on clothing is used all the way through this book to enhance the white middle-class readers' preconceptions of the 'primitive' and becomes another tool of racist, colonial prejudice. The quilted jackets worn in Turkistan by the Sarikolis are thus described as having 'ludicrously long sleeves' whilst 'the bravest of the Indian braves' is said to delight in 'bibs, beads and baubles'. Palaung women, photographed by Captain H. T. Parry, wear silver jewellery and black varnished bamboo hoops around their hips and over their dresses. The caption reads: 'Frocks and Frills in the Northern Shan States' (Figure 30; see p. 157). Other photographs throughout these volumes confusingly show studio photographs of pretty city girls posed in sanitised peasant dress. Their hair-styles and city boots always give them away.

With this weight of exploitative nationalist and colonial history behind them the use of such photographs to the dress historian is problematic. However, if the period terms on which they are offered are rejected, there are, even in *Peoples of All Nations*, rare images which should not be dismissed out of hand. In the Czechoslovak section, for example, Florence Farmborough's unsentimentalised photograph shows Ruthenian women selling strings of onions in a market, around 1910–20. The women wear long appliquéd sheepskin waistcoats, which would now be rare museum pieces, with their cotton print head ties, and clearly are discomforted by her camera (Figure 31). [12]

Photographs of 'Other' peoples by professional fine art photographers

The American photographer, Edward S. Curtis, has been celebrated for over sixty years for his definitive twenty-volume record of *The North American Indian*, begun in 1896 and finished in 1930. This has, however, been subject to highly critical post-colonial reconsideration in the 1990s by Anne Maxwell. She notes that whilst 'this work was an attempt to arouse popular interest in Native American cultures as a means of rescuing them from oblivion', Curtis's methods were profoundly incursionist. Where men had cut their hair short he provided wigs and costumes in pursuit of his ideal images. 'He was one of the few photographers of the late colonial period', she adds, 'who joined anthropological interests to artistic endeavours and so gave genocide an acceptable face'.[13] The manipulation of 'traditional' clothing played a central role in these processes.

The work of Laura Gilpin, famous for documentary photographic studies of the Navajo, has also been reassessed in this same light. In the 1930s, her photographic work made her so influential that she was invited to work with New Deal politicians on Navajo social issues. Her later book *The Enduring Navaho*, of 1968, which documents mid-twentieth-century Navajo history, has been reprinted ten times. The accusation voiced by James C. Faris is that her photography deliberately shows the Navajo as 'adapted, stoic, and non-resistant'. Yet, as Faris points out, when Gilpin was taking her first photographs in the early 1930s, the Bureau of Indian Affairs was systematically trying to break up the remaining remnants of Navaho culture. Thus Faris accuses Gilpin of denying political reality and seeking only 'to image a people in their landscape, in harmony with the setting, successfully adapted: a view of harmony which implied a very traditional and very clean Navajo or Navajo settlement; structured by the gaze of Western humanism'. Gilpin was a successful, well-connected, caring, fine art photographer. Nonetheless, Faris believes her images display only 'patronising humanism and ... pastoral romance', and worse.

> Her photographic corpus of Navajo and the lawsuit against her estate [bought by two of the photographed] says much more about the power relations between photographer and subject, and between Euro-Americans and Navajo than about any presentation of Navajo traditional cultural reality.[14]

An eye-view that manipulates clothing and appearance in this way

30 Women from the North Shan States, about 1920

31 Ruthenian onion sellers photographed in a Czechoslovakian market, about 1920

within these highly charged contexts is one that the dress historian needs to consider when using such images. Other artists/photographers in the 1930s were even less sensitive to these issues. In the African photos taken by the famous *Vogue* fashion photographer, Hoyningen-Huené, sitters are posed as art objects rather than real people. He published his *African Mirage: the record of a journey in 1938*, as a series of photographs documenting the landscape and people encountered during a journey from Alexandria to Lake Victoria and back across the Sahara to Algiers. He states clearly in his Foreword that 'I have purposely omitted all sordidness of realism in my photographs and have concentrated on the plastic and heroic side of an Africa which is slowly disappearing with the ever-increasing supply of European and Japanese manufactured goods'. In a Dinka/Zande village he photographed a young, tall, slim, very black-skinned girl called *Yo m*, describing her only in terms of her body colours and sexuality.

> She is naked but for a low belt of electric blue glass beads and a short black loin cloth. In one hand which is painted white to the wrist, like a glove, she holds an ebony and brass pipe, which she smokes languorously. Every movement of her is pure harmony and elegance in all its feminine refinement, each attitude exquisite, slow sensuality.[15]

Not all photographers worked in this manipulative way. Maxwell notes that the work of the ethnographer, Joseph Kossuth Dixon, who photographed Native Americans in the 1909–13 period and who believed that they and 'their cultures had a place in America's past and present, showed Native Americans as individual personalities rather than the usual stereotypes'.[16] The Transylvanian Museum of Ethnography in Cluj Napoca, Romania (Kolozsvár in Hungary up to 1919) has over 2000 glass negatives taken around 1910 by an English photographer, James Galloway. His sensitive portraits detail clothing and, for example, the complex plaited hair-styles of young unmarried peasants but sadly they remain virtually unknown.

The use of photographs in dress histories of non-Western clothing

The use of photographs in studies of the dress of indigenous non-Western communities is now commonplace, especially in studies which use colour photography to record exotic, rainbow-coloured garments and textiles. Few writers, however, explain how their photographs were produced or discuss their own working methodologies. Krystna Deuss's beautiful colour images in her *Indian Costumes from Guatemala* of 1981 are, for example, published without comment. Elaine and Paul Lewis in their book *Peoples of the Golden Triangle* of 1984, however, explain carefully their use of photography. As specialists in linguistics and anthropology, they use colour photography extensively. The Lewises lived and worked for sixteen years amongst the Karen, Hmong, Mien, Lahu, Akha and Lisu communities in North Thailand as missionaries of the Board and International Ministries of the American Baptist Churches. Their book features details of clothing and accessories through 'museum' artefact shots of silver neck rings, pendants and tattoo patterns. Studio shots by Heini Schneebeli and field photographs drawn from the Mayer-Lipton Hill Tribe Photography Collection show clothing being worn. Offering up a helpful example of good practice, the Lewises cite their methodology as a fusion of photography with 'written description of the people and their culture based on our own observations, consultation with specialists on each tribal group and anthropological studies'.[17]

The textile ethnographer Sandra A. Niessen, a specialist in Batak cloth and clothing from Indonesia, is angered by more than a failure to explain working methodologies. She asserts that once a vogue for the 'great art of a mysterious and sublime past' of Indonesian textiles took hold in museum displays and publishing, 'the miserable present was precluded and excluded. Even the people disappeared as their body wraps were displayed as two dimensional design works.' Niessen, using photographs dating back to 1907, therefore deliberately set out to show 'respect for how the Batak people have ingeniously manipulated their craft and their appearance to claim a place in a rapidly changing world'.[18] Thus she shows cloths being worn, and carefully included contemporary images of Toba Batak men in Western suits wearing glasses and women selling cloth in a market in Porsea, Toba, wearing watches. The Lewises too are careful to conclude their book with a section *Signs of Change* which includes photographs of women carrying 'ghetto-blaster' radios, putting on dance performances for tourists and climbing into trucks. Deuss too adds text, but no photographs, which raises the political and military persecution of Indian communities by the Guatemala authorities.

Dress in photography in Europe and North America

Photographs clearly showing clothing date back to work by Louis Daguerre in the late 1830s and to Octavius Hill, Robert Adamson and W. H. Henry Fox Talbot in the 1840s. Hill and Adamson shot the photographs for their six-volumed calotype photographic albums, *The Fishermen and Women of the Firth and Forth*, in 1844, at St Andrews and at Newhaven harbour, just outside Edinburgh. Sara Stevenson believes that the crowded harbour scenes, 'represent the most successful attempt to calotype an active crowd scene … the effort and calculation behind them is astonishing'.[19] Their close-up shots of the fisherwomen have left us, over one hundred and fifty years later, with vivid images of the fisherwomen in their striped petticoats, skirts and bonnets. In direct social contrast, Clementina, Viscountess Hawarden, took 850 photographs, between late 1857 and her death in 1864 showing details of the elite hoop-supported fashions of her day, worn by her three daughters posed on the terrace of their London house in South Kensington.[20] From then on photography provides the dress historian with images of women, children and men from every social class, age and country.

The 're-created' image

The starting point in using nineteenth-century photographs in dress history research might usefully be to weed out the 'art' images, created by photographers such as O. J. Reijlander and Henry Peach Robinson. Robinson was an adherent of the Picturesque movement in art and was deeply influenced by Pre-Raphaelite ideas. He saw nothing amiss in artificially re-creating images of rural peasantry in his photographs. Based in Tunbridge Wells in Kent from 1868, he worked on a series of art photographs of rural figures in romanticised landscape settings. Margaret F. Harker, Professor of Photography at the Polytechnic of Central London, writes that he 'interpreted popular pastimes and rural activities through pose, gesture and facial expression'. Finding that country girls either refused to be photographed or seemed incapable of carrying out his instructions, he used middle-class sitters instead, usually his family and friends. Harker explains that Robinson had a large collection of rural clothing that he had purchased from its original owners. He wrote in 1884

> it is not always easy to explain what you really mean when you meet a girl in a lonely country lane and you offer to buy her clothes … A country girl's dress is not often worth more than eighteen pence and if you turn the pence into shillings … you may make pretty certain of walking off with the property, or at all events, getting it sent to you the next day.[21]

The 'real' vanishes out of the dress historian's fingers rapidly here. What we are left with are 'artistic', bogus images, interesting because of their period Picturesque inventiveness but not as a source of the study of English rural dress of the 1860s to 1890s.

The dispute some twenty years earlier about the re-photographing of children taken in by Dr Barnado's homes in London in the 1860s centred around this same inventive practice. The charity had relied on sentimentalised publicity photographs which used raggedy 'before' photographs compared to cleansed 'after' images, for its successful fund-raising. Audrey Linkman, historian of documentary photography, comments that Barnado's 'commissioned the photographer, Thomas Barnes, to do this work' and that the resulting *carte-de-visite* photographs 'were sold in packs of twenty *cartes* for five shillings or singly for sixpence, from 1869'. Linkman explains that a public dispute developed when 'one mother, Mrs Holder, forced by poverty to send her daughters, Eliza and Florence, into the care of the charity, gave witness that her daughters had been sent to the home poorly, but decently dressed'. She complained further that 'although a *carte* showed her daughter selling newspapers in the street, she had in fact never done so'. Barnado's justification was that when the children were found their clothes were verminous and had to be destroyed immediately, thus necessitating the need to re-create the 'before' photographs. Linkman concludes that Barnado's was in fact simply 'imitating the conventional practice of art photographers of the day'.[22]

The re-creation of publicity images did not die away with Dr Barnado's. Angela Partington, for example, bases much of her informative article 'Popular Fashion and Working Class Affluence' on a comparison of a family snapshot of her mother in a day dress in 1951 with another photograph, of a famous Dior, New Look, black, cocktail dress, *Maxime*, supposedly of 1947. Partington uses the comparison to argue (convincingly enough) that working-class women, such as her mother, put together their own versions of the New Look on their own terms, rather than slavishly copying dominant class style.[23] It is unfortunate, however, that the Dior photograph she selected is not an original at all but a re-shot publicity photograph taken in 1970 for the *Sunday Times* by Cecil Beaton when he was consultant for the Victoria and Albert Museum's exhibition *Fashion, An Anthology*.[24] The sleek blonde chignon of the model, her style of make-up and the very large pearl beads of her necklace are not at all redolent of 1947.

This same process of re-photographing a Dior New Look dress was repeated again in 1997 to advertise the Imperial War Museum's much visited show, *Forties Fashion and the New Look*. Lord Snowdon was the photographer this time. His posters featured the ballerina, Darcy Bussell, dressed in the famous 1947 Dior *Bar* suit, a white, basqued jacket with a wide, pleated black skirt. Miss Bussell wears the hat at the wrong angle and her skirt hangs too limply, watering down the dynamism of Dior's original design. This show was so successful that its run was extended for several months. The late twentieth-century marketing value of the re-created fashion photograph was thus proven many times over. Its value to dress historians rests only in its history as re-created image. As Susan Sontag expresses it, 'a fake photograph (one which has been retouched, or tampered with, or one whose caption is false) falsifies reality'.[25]

Doctored images

Since every photograph can now be doctored and altered using digitised technology, how can they ever be trusted as reliable 'evidence' in the study of dress history? Such doctoring was already well established in the early 1900s when fashion dictated tiny waists and large hips. It was common-place, especially amongst society photographers, for waistlines to be artificially narrowed by skilful photographers. Once fashion photography became popularly used in women's magazines from the first decade of the twentieth century, a wide range of 'before and after' tricks were used to obtain the constructed body perfection demanded by seasonal fashion. Now the artificial 'adjustments' are all performed on the computer.

Of more profound political consequence was the common practice in Communist Russia from the 1930s, and in Central Europe from the late 1940s, for party leaders and functionaries who fell out of favour to be airbrushed out of group photographs. David King's study *The Commissar Vanishes – the falsification of photographs and art in Stalin's Russia*,[26] of 1997 identified specific personalities, such as Trotsky, whose images were air-brushed out of (and occasionally back into) official Soviet photographs once they had fallen out of political favour with Stalin. Milos Kundera's *Book of Laughter and Forgetting* details the fate of an official photograph taken at the moment when the Stalinist regime took over Czechoslovakia in February of 1948. The new Communist leader, Klement Gottwald, was photographed in his fur cap on the balcony of a Baroque palace in Prague addressing a vast crowd below. Kundera wrote that

> the Party propaganda section put out hundreds of thousands of copies of [the photograph] of that balcony, with Gottwald, a fur cap on his head and the comrades at his side, speaking to the nation. On that balcony the history of Communist Czechoslovakia was born.

Four years later Gottwald was hanged for treason and officialdom made sure that his image was rapidly airbrushed 'out of history'. Kundera concluded bitterly that 'they wanted to erase hundreds of thousands of lives from human memory and leave nothing but a single unblemished image of an unblemished idyll'. Kundera noticed that in the second version of the official photograph doctored after Gottwald's execution, someone else was wearing his fur cap.[27]

Fashion photography contains the most 'doctored' of all images of clothing. From the 1910s it has presented viewers with an entirely idealised, fictional construction of commercialised beauty and style. Fashion photo-graphs are the most commonly used form of illustration in dress history books, though nearly always without explanation of their utopian or avant-garde intent. Angela McRobbie raises the issue of the commercial power of the photographic fashion image in the 1990s. She suggests that photographic images created by 'star' stylists and photographers can now exert more style influence even than the work of fashion designers themselves. She shows that far from just disseminating the style of existing fashion garments, the photographer has become directly involved in creating the clothes too. In the reality of costly, risky, experimental fashion manufacture in the 1990s, 'the fashion item itself need hardly exist as an object for sale in the shops because its existence is more concrete, more assured and much more widely seen on the page' of avant-garde fashion magazines. Sheryl Garrett, editor of *The Face* in the late 1990s, explained to McRobbie that 'it's not a question of simply presenting clothes. Often we commission clothes to be designed to go with the overall art idea. It's more of an art direction approach to fashion.' If the fashion photographer becomes the closet designer rather than the recorder of existing 'fashion', the dress historian, in trying to interpret a fashion photograph, has to try to unravel the specific creative processes enmeshed in each image. Where is the line drawn between the input of the fashion designer, the stylist and the photographer? Paul Jobling's 1999 study of text and image in fashion shoots from 1980 onwards raises further challenging issues.[28]

Portraiture, and commercial and snapshot photography

Since every photographic image is percolated through the lens of the photographer and through her/his personal and cultural standpoint, can the photographer ever record 'authentic facts' or only her/his notion of 'facts'? Just like the work of artists, 'the meaning of the photograph is understood to be inseparably tied to social consciousness, culture and custom', as Sue Braden confirms.[29] Thus in trying to 'read' clothes from photographs some fundamental questions have to be considered. Why was the image taken, by whom, under what conditions, for what audience and for what use?

Images taken by professional portraitists were restricted to high society and respectable middle-class clientele until the Second World War. These clothes are often more fashionably styled and therefore easier to date. Most dress history books rely on this class of photograph, though usually without explanation of this narrow class focus. Commercial photography from famous studios such as *Seeberger* in Paris also produced high quality press images of *élégantes*. From 1907, three generations of this family sought out well-dressed high society women whenever they appeared in public. Attendance at the races at Auteuil or Longchamps afforded particularly useful photo opportunities, as they still do today. Couturiers sent their fashion models along to be admired by the crowds too, in the hope that their photographs would also appear in the press.

Seeberger images of the 1907–39 period mirror every nuance of style change as well as the seasonal calendar of French high society. The studio continued this work all through the German occupation of Paris from June 1940 to August 1944, working under Nazi censorship regulations. Today, rather than being used just for straight style analysis, these photographs chart the extent of collaboration that existed between *Tout Paris* circles and the elite of the occupying Nazi forces.[30] Despite Celestin Dars's insistence that this studio 'stopped attending the elegant gatherings and concentrated on outdoor and studio fashion photography with professional models',[31] *Seeberger* archives of the *Bibliothèque de la Ville de Paris* contain images that many, later, would rather have seen burned. The couturiers' milliner, Albouy, was photographed at the Auteuil races in the spring of 1941 with six of his models parading his extravagant hat collection for that season. The Marquis and Marquise de Polignac are shown on their annual June visit to Longchamps but, in 1941, their fellow racegoers were Nazi officers.[32] This library also owns press photographs taken during the Occupation by the photographer Zucca. These too go a long way to reveal the actuality of wartime social collaboration, as indeed the photographer may have intended. One series features the couturier Agnès at work in her salon at 83 Faubourg St Honoré in October of 1941. One image shows *La magicienne Agnès* presenting a collection made from German synthetic fashion fabrics, whilst another features the wife of Otto Abetz, the German 'ambassador' to Paris attending a fashion show. Agnès Rittener, although a member of the *Chambre Syndicale de la Couture Parisienne*, was certainly selected for this Nazi attention because she was of Austrian rather than French birth.[33]

Usefully for the dress historian, commercial images taken by high street photographers capture images of the clothes of 'ordinary' people, either portraits or images taken to mark important family events such as weddings, holidays, christenings and soldiers leaving for war. As stray photographs turn up in markets and antique shops, sitters are usually unknown, such as the young woman photographed in a summer dress of around 1880, by 'Mr Jabez Hughes, Photographer to the Queen and to H. R. H. the Prince of Wales, Regina House, Ryde, Isle of Wight'. We will never know if she was a resident of the island or a summer visitor choosing to have her likeness taken by the Queen's very own holiday photographer (Figure 32). Many surviving archives, however, such as records of photographers' studios and complete family albums, do fortunately contain customers' names, which can help in tracking down the personal histories of sitters. The work of local photographers, such as

left **32** Unknown sitter, about 1880   *right* **33** Commercial studio photographic portrait
of three fisherwomen from Llangwm, Pembrokeshire, Wales, about 1880

Charles Van Schaick in Black River Falls, Wisconsin, or Frank Sutcliffe of
Whitby in Yorkshire,[34] shows a clear empathy with people from their own
communities that neither patronises nor fakes.

From the 1860s, however, as middle-class tourism developed, high
street photographers searched for quaint rural images for commercial sale,
leaving the dress historian today with interesting if problematic groups of
photographs. Welsh women in steeple hats, such as fisherwomen from
Llangwm, Pembrokeshire (Figure 33), and farm labourers in smocks were
favourites, seen as the last vestiges of the British 'peasantry'. Another group
of women were selected because their clothing broke all the gendered
etiquette codes of Victorian society. The fisherwomen (flitherlasses) from
Filey in North Yorkshire became objects of curiosity because, in order to
climb the local cliffs safely, they tied up their short skirts to form knee-
length breeches. By 1900, postcards of oyster gatherers on Isle D'Oléron,
on the French Atlantic coast, were also just such a tourist gimmick
because beneath their fashionable, tight-waisted blouses, the young women

wore baggy knee-length breeches as they worked in the oyster beds. Whether or not the curvacious models featured in the photographs were 'genuine' is another matter.

Some of these images were indeed entirely faked. Avril Lansdell researched commercial photography in Tenby, on the South Wales coast, where women sold fish to visitors on the quayside dressed up in 'traditional' Welsh dress, complete with bright red shawls and steeple hats. One image of the 1870s taken by a local photographer, Sidney Webb, shows a pretty young woman posed as a cockle seller wearing a tall hat. Landsell believes that 'the hat and cap are fancy dress and the girl herself is too elegant to be a fisherman's wife'. She explains that the Pembrokeshire coast was becoming fashionable as a holiday area and that a *carte* such as this would have been a collectable souvenir in the days before picture postcards became common. Landsell defines all this as the 'cult of the picturesque'.[35]

Photography of urban poverty in Europe and the USA

Documentary photography of the poor would seem the perfect vehicle for dress history research because it shows clothing which has not survived and because much of this is supposedly based on images taken objectively and deliberately as a social record. In fact decoding these seems the hardest of all. Sue Braden discusses two documentary photographic approaches. She describes both as 'incursionist' because the documentary photographer (unlike the local photographer) is not part of the community which s/he is recording and probably not from the same social class, or even country that s/he is documenting. Braden notes the dangers of appropriating the image of the photographed without their consent or participation, which is precisely what offended Mrs Holder over the photographing of her daughters. Braden believes that such 'incursionists take with them the ideologies, conventions and often the context from their own world as they launch themselves upon the world of others'. She sees this as a form of 'cultural invasion'.

Braden has more sympathy for the work of photographers who 'become collaborators, integrated with the people and acting with them in collective authorship'. Often this interest in photographing 'other' communities, 'stemmed from philanthropic concern on the part of those who are economically better off, for those less well off than themselves'[36] and often as part of social reform campaigns. Some set out to arouse pity in the heart of the viewer. The work of John Thomson, who worked with his colleague, the journalist Adolphe Smith on the series *Street Life in London* from February 1877 to January 1878, fits this category. Having already published *Illustrations of China, and its People* (1873–74) Thomson and

Adolphe recorded the names and personal circumstances of their London sitters. Adolphe wrote that 'the Crawler' of St Giles was the elderly widow of a tailor, with no means of earning her living other than baby-sitting neighbours' children on street corners for a few crusts of bread. Her clothing is clear. She wears a piece of cloth around her hair, a worn-out striped shawl in which she cradled her young charges, and a thin, crumpled skirt.[37]

The historian of photography Audrey Linkman is convinced by Thomson's 'belief in the unquestionable accuracy of photographic testimony',[38] but Anne Maxwell suggests that, despite his progressive social concerns, Thomson's photographs also reflect typical masculine, Western European attitudes. Thus, when photographing in China,

> although Thomson remarked on the parallel between foot-binding and the prevailing European fashions in corsetry, he made light of the comparison; yet in these and many other ways European women were also victims of patriarchal excesses, some of them no less misogynist than those experienced by Chinese women.[39]

The fact that photographs survive today of young women who took on heavy work, men's work, in breweries and pits in the 1860s and 1870s is a consequence of this same social curiosity which focused on their idiosyncratic dress. *Carte de visites* of the pit girls from Wigan were famous for their depictions of women in heavy hob-nailed boots, full-length patched and raggy trousers and short thigh-length over-skirts. Linkman shows that such images were taken by Arthur Munby and by W. Clayton of Iron Street, Tredegar, in Wales, who photographed the girls who worked on slag tips. Munby's diary for 10/11th October 1860 gives a precious description of the clothing of a pit worker, Ellen Gounds, from Wigan Pier. She wore a wadded hood bonnet, 'a loose blue, patched cotton "bedgown" ... men's breeches she had worn for nine years, patched all over and warmly lined and wadded', and clean inside, with a short striped cotton skirt and heavy 'clogshoon'. Linkman writes that the women of Tredegar wore heavy-duty three-quarter-length dresses rather than trousers, with battered bonnets, decorated with brooches and feathers, held on with scarves tied under their chins. As with the fisherwomen photographs, there is more than a hint of sexual salaciousness as well as curiosity attached to these pictures. They represented the opposite to the conventional image of the middle-class young woman of the 1860s through to the early 1900s. Arthur Munby was the only photographer who also chose to photograph Wigan pit girls in their smart, hooped, Sunday-best dresses.[40]

Braden discusses the work of two famous American documentary photographers. Both took images of the poverty-stricken immigrant communities in New York at the turn of the twentieth century but from quite different political standpoints, which Braden believes coloured the images themselves. Jacob A. Reiss's images of immigrant slum dwellers were part of his campaign to improve housing conditions on the city's Lower East Side in the 1890s. Braden sees his work as full of humanity but also, 'based on pity' and with no intent 'to tamper with [the] established hierarchy'. Lewis W. Hine, however, was an active campaigner for social change from about 1908, especially on behalf of the National Child Labour Committee. Braden believes his photographs of the same communities, in direct contrast, were intended to 'engender indignation among the working classes on its own behalf rather than to imbue the middle classes with indignation on behalf of the conditions of working people'.[41]

During the Depression years of the 1930s, documentary photographers again used their cameras to make a permanent social record of the poorest in society. In the early 1930s Humphrey Spender documented living conditions in Stepney for Clemence Paine, a probation officer working for the liberal magistrate Basil Henriques. In 1937–38 he joined in Tom Harrison's *Mass Observation* social research project in Bolton. Deborah Frizell believes that Spender 'would invariably opt on the side of an instinctive understatement, never belittling or imposing "gloom" or falsely ennobling a situation or subject by pictorialist and technical interventions'. His photographs of life in these poverty-ridden working-class communities inevitably reveal details and conditions of clothing. His preference was for using a secret camera, despite his anxieties that 'you eliminate all relationship'[42] with the people at the other end of the lens.

Edith Tudor Hart took a series of photographs in mining villages in the Rhondda Valley, South Wales, and the West and East End of London in the same period. Some of these may have been intended for *Left: right – two worlds* , a book she was planning with the artist, James Fitton, and the graphic artist, Polly Binder, for Bodley Head but which was never achieved.[43] All were active members of the left-wing Artists' International Association founded in London in 1933. Some today might criticise Tudor Hart's work as 'incursionist' because she was Austrian, middle class and had trained at the Bauhaus, but no one can deny the sensitivity of the photographs she took in the late 1920s to 1950s nor her deep personal and active interest in issues of 'childcare, welfare and women's health'.[44] Tudor Hart's genuine commitment to exposing the consequences of poverty is evident. Clothing inevitably features in her work, too, and not Sunday best dress. One photo (Figure 34) shows a proudly smiling mother holding her little daughter in her arms, whilst their raggy clothes speak wordlessly of the poverty of the family. This image is signed TH and captioned on the back in pencil 'Mrs B (known to us) Clarendon St North Paddington. Family of 6 (5 children) in one room, rent 5/6, controlled, Typical case

Photographs by Edith Tudor Hart, mid-1930s *left* **34** 'Mrs B ..., Clarendon Street, North Paddington'
right **35** 'Is she having a better piece?', Caledonian Market

of that street with exception of rent which is lower than the average'. In
a second photo, captioned on the back 'Caledonian Market, London; nr. 14,
"... is she having a better piece ..."',[45] a woman in a dark coat and felt
hat distractedly holds up what looks like a second-hand, flannel nightdress
from a pile of cloth and garments (Figure 35). There are no 'types' in
Tudor Hart's photography.

Dorothea Lange's documentary photographs taken in Depression
America in the 1934–37 period for the State Emergency Relief Adminis-
tration and the Farm Security Adminstration's Historical Section,[46] despite
recent debate about social intrusion, also leave us with an emotive closeness
to the poverty of Depression rural America, created in large part by the
poverty of clothing.

Family and snapshot photography

From the 1920s 'home-made' photography became common practice. The
price of cameras dropped with the widespread consumption of the cheap
Box Brownie camera and thereafter the private snapshot becomes another
source of clothing detail. Although as yet little used by dress historians,

36 Family album wedding photograph, Wimbledon, 1934

when contained in original albums which reveal date, place, family names and even images of homes, snapshots can be immensely useful, as the work of Avril Lansdell has shown. Shots do still, however, inevitably lean towards the special album photograph taken in Sunday best dress, at weddings or on holiday, such as the wedding recorded in the middle-class family album of Mr and Mrs Robert in 1934 (Figure 36). Found in a discarded family album, this shows the wedding of Miss Gwendoline Calloway to Ernest E. Sawtell on 1 September, at Wimbledon Parish church. Usefully, the album contained a press cutting with full details of the wedding. This included comment that the two bridesmaids in picture hats were dressed in turquoise blue whilst the smallest one wore a mauve dress.

Decoding the class of sitters

Fundamental to any dress historical analysis to be drawn out of photographs has to be identification of the sitter's place in society. Photos are only of use to the dress historian if this can at least be attempted, otherwise there is no basis upon which to try to construct social or cultural meaning. By far the greater weight of portraits of the 1860–1925 period depict the middle and wealthy levels of society, producing a serious social disbalance of image. Further, the dress historian needs to remind her/himself that most commissioned portraits and family snapshots show sitters posed in best clothes. Severa emphasises that the function of nineteenth-century portrait photography was to propose 'a "proper" facade'. She suggests too that in middle-class America (as indeed also in Europe) 'it was of tremendous, almost moral, significance during the nineteenth century that one appeared cultured'.[47] For working-class sitters the driving impetus was respectability. For all, each within the etiquette codes of their own social milieu, clothes that indicated dignity and propriety were essential. Working-class and poor rural families in Europe and the USA, except those living in the direst poverty, managed to find some way to put on a semblance of a 'Sunday best' appearance for a photograph. It is rare to find crumpled raggedy clothes in studio portraiture, because no one would want their appearance recorded in such poverty-revealing clothing, hence the row about Dr Barnado's.

Trying to guess at class differences through photographs alone gets harder and harder from the late nineteenth century as working-class families joined the fringes of the new world of mass consumption. Lansdell is rightly cautious. 'Only if a photograph is very definitely annotated can one judge how new the clothes are and, so perhaps, place it in the social scale.'[48] To make judgements based on the 'fashionability' or otherwise of clothing seen in photographs alone can be a fearful trap. The notion, promoted by Veblen, that styles trickled down through society as each

37 Mrs Esmé Turner of Ilminster and Taunton, Somerset, 1909, in a widow's bonnet

68-065. **FORME**
en mérinos, noir,
nègre, mordoré.

Prix. . **13.90**

68-066. **FORME** mérinos,
bordée galon, Noir, nègre,
mordoré, castor. **15.75**
Prix. . . . . .

22-935.

22-936.
TAILLEUR en velouté de laine,
paletot longueur o^m,93 garni
imitation laquette mi-

38 Tailored costumes from the mail order catalogue of *La Samaritaine*, Paris, 1925

social rank emulated the one above it, would lead to the assumption that only the poorest would wear out-of-date clothes. This theory collapses when confronted with the clothes of the elderly of both sexes, or country dwellers, because some, whatever their wealth, remain in the fashions of their youth long after these have gone out of style. Mrs Turner of Ilminster and Taunton in Somerset was photographed in her old-fashioned widow's weeds in 1909. Even a highly skilled dress historian would probably mistakenly date the style of her bonnet to the 1890s (Figure 37). Queen Mary dressed in modified versions of the 1901 hobble-skirted style right through to the 1950s. Many other older women, too, from the aristocracy

39 Family snapshot photograph of three French women, about 1925, two in costumes, one in a coat

to the very poorest, refused to wear the short skirt of the 1920s. Photographs showing their ankle-length skirts can thus be completely misleading as a date indicator. Even reasonably fashionable middle-class women modified their styles to suit the circles in which they lived. Thus coat lengths featured in the 1925 mail order catalogue of the elegant Paris department store *La Samaritaine* are clearly shorter than the hemlines worn by three respectable French women photographed in the same year (Figures 38 and 39).

Photography within European and North American dress history

The first dress historian to make full use of photography was Alison Gernsheim, who had the advantage of access to the vast historical collection of her husband, Helmut, also a historian of photography. Her descriptive book *Fashion and Reality: 1840–1914* of 1963 reproduced studio portraits and was for many years the only source of such information.[49] Avril Lansdell, a museum-based dress historian with a specific interest in local history, published two invaluable books in 1983 and 1985.[50] These aimed to show the value of photographs to the dress and social historian and use *carte-de-visite* images, introduced into Britain in 1857, and the larger format of the Cabinet card, popular from the 1870s. Lansdell comments that there was such a passion for portrait photography in England 'that there were 168 portrait studios in London, twenty-seven of them in Regent Street alone, by 1861'.[51] She puts forward a carefully constructed methodology which uses dated, named photos whenever possible and which relates styles to the general fashion of the day. Lansdell targets 'popular' photography as her goal. As her work mostly deals with the 1860–1900 period, this inevitably means middle-class, conventional, family photography.

By the 1990s the value of using photographs within dress history was fully accepted and celebrated in Batsford's five-volumed series *Fashion In Photographs*, published in the early 1990s and covering Society photography from 1860–1920.[52] All authors were dress, rather than photography, historians. The series was produced in association with the National Portrait Gallery using examples from the 100,000 prints in its photography collection. Accompanying texts emphasised style development and tended towards the descriptive rather than the analytical. Authors acknowledged that the series was inevitably weighted to images of well-off, upper-class British society because those images form the bulk of the National Portrait Gallery's collection. Sarah Levitt was so struck by the narrowness of the social circles represented in the images that she commented that 'it became apparent that most of the sitters were on nodding terms with each other, if not close acquaintances'.[53] These detailed photographs are undoubtedly useful for curators and historians just as long as their narrow social confines are not forgotten.

Joan Severa's *Dressed for the Photographer* of 1995 covers a far wider social range of sitters. Subtitled *Ordinary Americans and fashion*, Severa adds her specialist dress history skills to her interpretations. She also explains her use of 'ordinary' as inevitably mostly covering the middle class, but adds that she also set out, wherever possible, 'to find as many images of known poor people as possible' with the aim of identifying different 'levels of affluence'.[54] Severa combed the archives of American museums and historical societies, concentrating on non-metropolitan communities. The State Historical Society of Wisconsin revealed the work of local photographers whose images show clothing in newly expanding communities in great detail. One example is the work of Andreas Larson Dahl, a Norwegian, who moved to Dane County, Wisconsin, in 1869, when he was twenty-one. Severa uses his photographs to document the clothing of the Norwegian immigrant farming community where Dahl lived and worked. 'At some point not long after his arrival he began travelling the countryside around Madison and small towns in the area photographing families, their homes and farms.' Photographs, such as the examples Severa shows dating from the 1870s, were used to send back to families in Norway to show how well their emigré relatives were doing. Names of sitters were carefully recorded. Most are photographed in plain and serviceable American-styled, utilitarian dress.[55]

Severa's focus is always on the hidden social coding to be drawn from the clothes. In her analysis of photographs of African-American women, for example, she makes valuable use of their dress codes to expose period race prejudice. Severa shows a stereotypical, commercial, racist studio image dated to 1899–1900, from the Library of Congress. The photographer is unknown. The original caption read: *An Old-Time Charleston 'Mommer' and Her Charge.* An elderly black woman, inevitably pictured with her white charge, a little girl, wears a 'cotton bandana' headwrap in a large check pattern, a white fichu with very large coin spots and a dark-coloured calico print with a tiny floral pattern. Helen Bradley Griebel (see Chapter 7) defines the headwrap as a 'symbol of servitude to the whites and an emblem of social and economic privation'.[56] Severa is clear too that this is 'familiar slave/servant wear'.[57] Severa then goes on to make a deliberate contrast with a Sunday-best photograph of Josephine Beasley, a slim, young black woman, photographed in Savannah around 1890–92 by a local photographer, J. W. Wilson. Free to choose how she was photographed, Mrs Beasley wears what was probably her 'best' outfit, an elegant, dark silk bodice and skirt, trimmed with glass beading and passementerie, fashionable for the 1890 period. She carries a large umbrella with a curved bone handle and wears a small fob watch. Severa checked census records and found that Beasley 'was a domestic who worked in Savannah, and her husband, Abram, was, like his father before him, a butler'. Severa stresses that 'the evidence of this photograph supports the claim that servants, working people, and lower middle class families did know how to dress well and made efforts in spite of modest circumstances'.[58]

Severa understands well the problems of trying to date clothing in photographs to precise years. How can one tell how long the sitter had worn a garment or whether the garment was new when s/he obtained it? Her knowledge of the history of dress occasionally tempts her to extrapolate one stage too far over identifying colours of garments. All the images are black and white, yet she proposes that the smart Chinese woman, photographed in a hooped dress of about 1863–66, is probably in black; that the sashes on two little sisters of 1870 are red, and that a bride from Black River Falls in 1891 is in 'black or navy blue'. Nonetheless, Severa, like Lansdell, provides a sound, basic methodological approach for using such photography in dress history.

When date and precise social identification of the sitter are known, there is no doubt at all of the value of the photograph to the dress historian. Every nuance of pose, accessory and garment is a cultural give-away. It was not by chance that the Duchess of Windsor achieved her famously elegant and sleek-headed hair-style evident in all her photographs. Her hairdresser, a Pole named Antoine, explained that

> she had her hair dressed three times a day; in the morning to go with a little hat, something quite simple; in the afternoon perhaps to go to the races; in the evening, for formal use a shape with a little ornament. This does not mean the ordinary woman's several-times-a-day hair-comb. It means a complete hairdressing by a coiffure or a maid. Each hair-do might take half an hour. The French fashion leader, the Princess Faucigny-Lucinge, had a similar schedule. This three-times-a-day business was not unusual amongst ultra-smart women.[59]

Contrasting photos of 1930s middle- and working-class women show less sophisticated and far more randomly cut, fluffier hair-styles.

Despite these drawbacks, when additional sources can be used to support analysis of photographs, they can become significant tools in the dress historian's search for the coded cultural meanings that lie within clothing. Mai Alman, for example, had her photograph taken with two girl friends feeding the pigeons in Trafalgar Square in 1960 (Figure 40). At first glance this looks nothing more than an ordinary tourist photograph. When information from personal interview is added, however, it becomes clear that this image reveals what would now be termed radical, counter-cultural dress.

40 Mai Alman (right) and friends in Trafalgar Square, London, in 1960

Mai Alman wears a man's beige, wool cloth, duffle coat, whilst her two Scandinavian girl friends wear typically feminine, fashionable coats of the period. Mai Alman was then 19 and had been an active member of the National Youth Campaign for Nuclear Disarmament since 1957, which is when she bought her duffle coat from an army surplus store in North London. She wore the coat on many protest marches and campaigns in direct opposition to the expected sartorial codes of young women of her period.[60] Similarly, the clothes worn by two young Hungarian girls (Figure 41) in a snapshot taken in Budapest in May 1991 would have gone unremarked in any Western European city. Their stylish short hair, narrow black trousers and plain black sweatshirts (one conspicuously pinned with three large safety pins), however, marked them out at that specific moment in the history of their city, as radically counter-cultural dressers enjoying the second spring of political freedom in post-Communist Budapest.

Film as a source for the study of dress and appearance, past and present

Of all the approaches to the study of dress and its history, the use of film is the most deeply divided between object-centred research and theory, though both emerged in the mid-1970s. Interest in dress in fictional film led to glossy books filled with film stills of Hollywood glamour costumes.

left 41 Two 'punk' girls in Budapest, 1991   *right* 42 Greta Garbo in 1933

Theory debate, developing out of feminist discussion, centred around the creation and manipulation of gendered 'star' images and the public consumption through 'the female gaze' by women audiences of star 'looks', such as those of Greta Garbo (Figure 42).

Object-centred research on Hollywood film designers, costumiers and the issue of style

1974–76 were key years for the development of artefact research into Hollywood film fashion. In 1974, Diana Vreeland, the retired editor of international *Vogue*, curated an exhibition at the Costume Institute of the Metropolitan Museum, New York, titled *Romantic and Glamorous Hollywood Design*. Its original catalogue was a modest, unillustrated listing. The intent was to show for the first time that the role of costume designers was central to the creation of Hollywood glamour. 'The diamonds were bigger, the furs were thicker and more ... everything was an exaggeration of history, fiction, and the whole wide, extraordinary world', wrote Vreeland.[61] This exhibition centred on surviving garments in the collections of the Design Laboratory of the Fashion Institute of Technology in New York and Burbank Studio's Historical Costume Collection. Where clothes from famous outfits were missing, the organisers had no qualms about commissioning the remaking of 'accurate' copies. A gold tissue, pearl and vulture feather dancing costume worn by Nazimova as *Salome*, designed for the 1923 Fox Film, thus made a reappearance.[62]

Object-based historians of film costume thereafter have sought public recognition for the specialist skills of design and making required to create these fantasy clothes. As Dale McConathy explained, 'Hollywood clothes were not really meant to be worn. Often dresses were so tight, so carefully moulded, that they could be worn only when standing up. The chief value of the Hollywood costume then was pictorial. It was made to be photographed.'[63] David Chierichetti, Vreeland's research consultant on the 1974 exhibition, published his own study *Hollywood Costume Design* in 1976. His text offers the costumiers' views, based on their work for the studios of MGM, Paramount, Warner Bros, Fox and RKO.

In 1976, Elizabeth Leese became the first British film historian to publish on film costume. Working as archivist at the British Film Institute in London, her *Costume Design in the Movies* covered a sharply chosen range of themes, from the work of specific designers to the relationship between Hollywood and Paris couture. She wondered why nobody has 'previously produced a factual book on costume design in the movies?' and set out to 'give some long-delayed credit to the designers for their contribution to the cinema'.[64] Books by Dale McConathy (1976), W. Robert LaVine (1980) and Margaret Bailey (1981)[65] would seem to have glutted the market, but 1997 still saw another 'new' book, *Fashion and Film* by Regine and Peter W. Engelmeier, which regurgitated the same information on the same Hollywood designers with use of the same standard film chronology.[66]

Dress in the early years of the development of the moving image

Actors in the earliest fictional film often wore their own clothes. Since many of these short films were built around scenes of the 'every day', frequently in domestic settings, such dress suited the scenes well. The pioneering English film maker George A. Smith captured the personal wardrobes of his wife Laura Eugenia Bayley and her sister Eva in many of the films they shot in Hove, Sussex, at the turn of the twentieth century. Here can be found some of the earliest examples of the use of clothing to develop narrative plots of flirtation and adventure. In Smith's *As Seen Through a Telescope*, of 1900, for example, a woman (Laura Smith) is seen with her two-wheeler bicycle wearing a long skirt, blouse and straw hat, typical cycling wear of the period. She is then shown lifting her foot up on to the cycle frame, whilst her male 'friend' ties her bootlace, spied on by an elderly snooper looking at them through a telescope. A little of the heroine's lower calf is revealed to the evident delight of the two male

observers in the film, and doubtless to the men in the audience as well
– a male-centred story for male consumption. One hundred years later,
however, this scene passes unnoticed, whilst through the eye-view of 1900
this scene is redolent with sexual innuendo. This is indicated both by the
fact that the woman is daringly riding a bicycle in the first place and
second, by the fleeting glimpse of her leg. Dress historians have made very
little use of such material as yet.[67] The use of amateur film, increasingly
taken from the early 1930s, such as that currently being collected by
specialists such as Frank Gray, Director of the South East Film and Video
Archives, based at the University of Brighton, remains another untapped
gold mine for the dress historian looking for images of the clothes of
'ordinary' families.

Hybridised Hollywood costume style

By the 1910s film directors had become acutely aware of the popular
commercial pull of more 'historical' and exotic film costumes, which
provided a perfect opportunity for erotic, fantasy, sexual display. A new
genre of hybridised film costume was born, a fusion of ballet and theatre
design, fashion and fantasy. Analysis of how these hybrid styles were
created and their impact both on the public and on the world of commercial
fashion has become of increasing interest to researchers from both sides
of the object-versus-theory divide. Edward Maeder's *Hollywood and History:
costume design in film* held at Los Angeles County Museum of Art in 1987
was one of the first to probe the issue of style hybridity. He showed, for
example, that for MGM's *Marie Antoinette* of 1938 starring Gladys George,
scouts were sent to Europe amidst a blaze of publicity 'to locate authentic
period and furniture'. 2,500 costumes were designed by Adrian in 1780s
style and George's much publicised *Marie Antoinette* gowns were said to
be based on portraits of the French Queen. Demands on costumiers were
so great that 'fifty women had to be brought to Los Angeles from
Guadalajara to sew on thousands of sequins'. No matter how much
'authenticity' was stressed in publicity material, the hybridised off the
shoulder décolletés ruined any semblance of 'realism'.

Maeder emphasises that movie fantasy and historical styles always had
to include such elements of high fashion of the day. Without these,
costumes lost their romantic appeal to feminine audiences: 'Costume
wardrobe creates the illusion of a past era by including elements from
period fashion but rarely abandons the distinctive traits of twentieth century
dress.' Thus 'the silhouette of the figure almost always remains contemporary ... the emphasis on breasts and their placement is always consistent
with what is fashionable when the film is made' and hence the 1930s'

shoulder line on 1780s' dresses. Above all, Maeder cites make-up and hair-styles as the absolute period give-away. His examples include Claudette Colbert as Cleopatra in 1934, with heavy glamour lashes and thin, plucked 1930s-styled eyebrows or Elizabeth Taylor in the same role in 1963, with heavy black eye make-up but with pale lips 'painted in the fashionably subdued hues of the 1960s, which subordinated lips to eyes'.[68] Most films, even ones set within their own periods, contain astonishing style anomalies, such as secretaries looking like millionairesses and expensive embroidery detail on collars, bodices and jackets to catch the close-up lens. All of this created a unique hybrid style, taken up ever since, to various extents, in television period dramas.

The final Hollywood ingredient in the construction of Hollywood glamour was the studios' creation of personalised star looks, with the help of dress designers, costumiers, dentists, dietitians, make-up specialists and photographers. The appearance of each star (male and female) was man-ipulated into a formulaic, gendered construct to enhance their commercial appeal to the general public. It is these themes, rather than clothing 'objects', which have interested feminist film historians, such Laura Mulvey, Jane Gaines, Charlotte Herzog, Christine Gledhill (1987), Sue Harpey (1994),[69] Pam Cook and Stella Bruzzi. When Cook looks at historical dress in British cinema, she highlights its duplicitous role, agreeing with Maeder that 'costume has to reflect contemporary fashion as well as suggest period'. She is clear that 'costume romances mobilise history as a site of sexual fantasy' and that this 'foregrounds history as masquerade'.[70]

Theoretical debate

In 1975 Mulvey, as part of the Second Wave of feminist film criticism, argued that the female gaze of the audience was manipulated by the way 'film reflects, reveals, and even plays on the straight, socially established interpretations of sexual difference which control images, erotic ways of looking and spectacle'.[71] Mulvey's views were based on psychoanalytical examination of the lure of the cinema to the general public. Thus she proposed that 'the cinema poses questions of the ways the unconscious (formed by the dominant order) structures ways of seeing and pleasure in looking'. Further, 'in a world ordered by sexual imbalance, pleasure in looking has been split between active/male and passive/female. The deter-mining male gaze projects its phantasy on to the female figure which is styled accordingly.'[72] In 1997 Stella Bruzzi stressed the importance of 'the debates surrounding the construction of gender and sexuality [derived] primarily in or from psychoanalysis'. Mulvey's dominant male/passive female boundaries are, however, questioned by Bruzzi in her assessment of Jane Campion's *The Piano* of 1993. In this film written and directed by women 'the agent of the gaze is female, and its object is the male body'.[73] Bruzzi also assesses in the same way the Queer gaze, the development of 'blackness' in the cinema and explorations of androgyny through film costume.

All these writers share a belief in the key role played by clothing within the movies. Audiences, like the readers of drawn cartoons, learn to interpret formulaic class, gender and race stereotyping through the director's/costume designers' use of specific coded garments and 'looks'. Gaines confirms that 'costumes are fitted to characters like a second skin'.[74] Bruzzi is convinced that the role of costume in the movies is so central that the whole essence of characters can be constructed through costume and that clothing in the movies has a role far more fundamental than merely a secondary 'brides-maid status'. She thus argues that 'clothing exists as a discourse not wholly dependent on the structures of narrative and character signification'. She cites the 1850s plain black bonnet, mourning dress and the hooped petticoat worn by Ada, the heroine, throughout *The Piano*, which is set in New Zealand, as her example. Bruzzi believes Campion 'adopts clothes and their relationship to sexuality and the body as primary signifiers'. Smith and Williamson had done this too a hundred years earlier but, as Bruzzi notes, throughout *The Piano* clothing is used by the heroine in defiance of gender expectations of how she should dress and behave.[75]

The relationship between the worlds of Paris couture and Hollywood cinema

Paris couture, as the natural home of sartorial opulence, was involved with the invention of Hollywood glamour from the early days. Both dress and feminist film historians have explored this relationship but from entirely different angles. Both industries were (and are) vast enterprises which base their commercial success on the creation of idealised images of women and men for consumption by a vast global audience. It is not therefore surprising that their relationship has been competitive and deeply nation-alistic. By the late 1990s, the two worlds had united in one powerful commercial embrace. Top fashion houses encourage Hollywood stars to sit in the front row of their shows whilst couturiers provide them with free clothes for high profile public appearances, such as the Oscar Night award ceremony, which is globally televised. Many are eager to 'place' their garments and other products (branded logos to the fore) in popular movies.

In the 1930s, however, the relationship was far less cosy. Paris couturiers had worked for Hollywood from as far back as 1915 when Lucile and Poiret designed for Roberta Hickman. In 1931 Chanel was asked by Samuel

Goldwyn to organise a department of over one hundred workers 'supervised by Chanel's representative Jane Courtois',[76] dressing Barbara Weeks, Ina Claire, Joan Blondell and Madge Evans. Gloria Swanson seems to have broken this relationship which was never successful. What Leese and others who have looked at this relationship do not detail is that Chanel's foray into Hollywood coincided with the moment when her couture salon was severely hit by financial problems due to the Wall Street Crash of 1929 and the imposition a year later of a 90 per cent import tax on Paris haute couture garments going into the USA under the Hawley–Smooth bill. By 1935, as her couture business picked up again, Chanel was employing 4000 workers and making 28,000 model garments a year and she no longer had any need for Hollywood approval.[77]

Others, however, continued to relish the international publicity gained from designing for the movies. Bruzzi comments aptly that 'designing for a film is, for a couturier, an ambiguous process of maintaining a balance between self-promotion and immersing the designs in the film'.[78] Christian Dior at the height of his success designed clothes for Marlene Dietrich in *Stagefright* (1949) and Myrna Loy in *The Ambassador's Daughter* in 1956, which included a fashion show of outfits from his latest collection.[79] Givenchy designed most famously of all for Audrey Hepburn in films such as *Funny Face* (1957) and *Breakfast at Tiffany's* of 1961.

America began to insist from the mid-1930s that it was Hollywood designers who innovated new fashion lines which the French couturiers then followed. The origins of the popular romantic Victorian revival look of the 1934–40 period became a centre of controversy which is still debated today. Was it created first in Hollywood or Paris? Was it or was it not Travis Banton's befrilled frock for Joan Crawford in *Letty Lynton* in 1932 that propelled *la mode romantique* on to the international fashion scene? In 1978, Charles Eckert, the first to rediscover this period controversy, quoted an American fashion buyer from the *Saturday Evening Post* of 1935. The *Letty Lynton* dress 'swept Paris not only after it had appeared in the film but after it had been sold in New York shops'.[80] Edward Maeder cites Laura Blayney, a movie journalist, who also attended the Paris collections in 1935, at the moment when evening and formal afternoon gowns were succumbing to the Victorian 'billowy-skirted silhouette'.[81] Marcel Rochas confessed to her that he had been inspired by the Walter Plunkett designs for the film of *Little Women* of 1933, set in 1869, whilst Molyneux stated that he owed his new full skirts to Adrian's designs for *The Barretts of Wimpole Street* of 1934, set in 1845–46.

Bruzzi, referring to the same *Letty Lynton* dress, also believes that Hollywood cinema took over style leadership in the 1930s and 1940s, when 'the distance between costume and couture fashion was minimised'.[82] In terms of international cultural status it was clearly then (and indeed now) in the interests of Hollywood and the American nation as a whole to believe this, just as the New Deal was encouraging Americans to recognise the worth of the country's own artists and designers. By 1939, Mainbocher, the Paris couturier of American origin, had been forced by the war to return to New York. By then Howard Greer and Adrian, both vastly successful Hollywood costume designers, had also become couturier/ready-to-wear designers completing the fusion of the Hollywood/Paris fashion axis.[83]

Dress historians in France, however, see the debate differently. Françoise Mort writes that the Paris couturier Marcel Rochas insisted that it was his work that 'influenced Adrian to design the Letty Lynton dress for Joan Crawford in 1932'.[84] Guillaume Garnier's assessment of the origin of *la mode romantique* indicates that in 1934 Molyneux had designed full-skirted costumes for *Les Barretts de Wimpole Street*, a play at the *Theatre des Ambassadeurs*. The couturier Robert Piguet 'sent his staff to see the performance'.[85] Thereafter he too became taken by this revival style which, as Garnier points out, was already current in a series of romantic, waltz-centred French films produced by the early 1930s. By 1934 early forms of the Victorian revival style were so firmly established across the international fashion industry in Europe that even a mainstream middle-class store such as the *White House* of Regent Street was selling a debutante summer dress in 'green and white checked organdie' with Victorian revival ruffles on neckline, hip and hem (Figure 43).[86] England claimed it was Norman Hartnell's famous Winterhalter-inspired collection for the new Queen's visit to France in 1938 that launched the mode. This feud was about commercial rivalry and issues of national identity and pride, and above all about international cultural rivalry over ownership of the creation of international feminine style, a rivalry that has escalated through vast commodified international rivalries ever since.

Movies, styles and mass consumption

What is clear is that clothing codes filtered off the screen into daily life, inserted there by individual consumption choices and by the retailing of commercial products. Christopher Breward is right when he suggests that films which were 'marketed directly at women ... with a self-conscious appeal to areas of so-called "feminine" interest such as romance, glamour, and material wealth ... interact with women's perception of themselves in terms of fashion, consumption, sexuality, maternal and marital duty and work'.[87] The stars tapped into the spin-off profits to be made from advertising beauty and fashion products. Thus in 1955, Jane Powell, MGM's guest star in *Deep in My Heart* featured in a *Lustre-Creme* shampoo

left 43 Debutante dress in Victorian revival style, catalogue of *White House*, Regent Street, London, 1935   *right* 44 Jane Powell, MGM star, advertising *Lustre-Creme* shampoo, 1955

advertisement in *Picturegoer*, which read 'When America's most glamorous women – beauties like Jane Powell – use Lustre-Creme Shampoo, shouldn't it be your choice above all others, too?' (Figure 44).

Another direct spin-off was the production of copy-cat ready-to-wear clothing and accessories. The film historian, Charles Eckhert, has charted the influence of Bernard Waldman and his Modern Merchandising Bureau. By the mid-1930s this company was designing and commissioning the manufacture of thousands of 'movie' fashions, working in conjunction with all the major studios except Warners. Their garments were sold all over the USA as were many other middle and mass market copied styles. In Britain too *Women's Film Fair* and *Screenland*, for example, offered paper patterns and even ready-made versions of film styles. 'Don't *FilmFair* fashions looks attractive in this effective display arranged by Messrs Lewis's at their Birmingham store? The mannequin in the foreground is wearing the Margaret Sullivan picture frock' declared *Film Fair* in 1936.[88] Eckert confirms that in the USA alone, 'tens of millions of Americans provided the captive audience for the unique experiments in consumer manipulation, that the showcasing of products in films and through star endorsements constituted'.[89] Charlotte Herzog argues that movie scenes showing fashion shows even 'taught women how to look and act like mannequins' and that they exploit 'the way women as the primary audience see themselves in order to subtly suggest sales of clothes to them'.[90] Even if women could not afford the copy-cat clothes and hats, they could style their hair and make-up to those of their favourite stars, they could copy the way cigarettes were smoked on the screen and the ways the stars wore coats, scarves and tipped the brims of their hats over the forehead – and all at no cost. There still remains a dearth of empirical dress history studies on these themes of style leadership, copy-cat production and the processes of personal 'consumption' of movie fashions and style, all themes which carry important international cultural significances.

Documentary film of fashion

In 1976, Elizabeth Leese researched the history of newsreels of fashion to understand their significance as style diffusers to a mass audience. From as early as 1910, footage of fashion parades was included as a regular feature of newsreels in European and North American cinemas, verifying that the nascent cinema industry understood well the public appeal of elite fashion images. The earliest fashion film that Leese found was *Fifty Years of Paris Fashion, 1859–1909*, a parade of period and contemporary dress shown in London in 1909. She notes that in 1910 Pathé and Gaumont newsreels contained only two or three minutes of fashion, but by October 1911 *Bioscope* magazine had announced that 'Messrs Pathé are commencing a series showing the coming models from Paris. The present one gives coloured pictures of hats, dinner gowns, tailor-made costumes, walking dresses, negligees and teagowns.' These films used the Pathé stencil colour process, invented in 1908.[91] 1916–17 saw the production of *Florence Rose Fashion* films in New York, also for Pathé News. Florence Rose was the fashion page editor of the *New York Evening Mail*. These fortnightly films were also seen in Chicago and Boston. As this was in the midst of the First World War, when contact with London and Paris couture houses was curtailed, the newsreels stressed that all clothes were American made and designed.

Paul Poiret and Lucile, rival couturiers in pre-war Paris, were the first to realise the marketing potential of documentary film. Poiret took a filmed version of his collection with him to New York on his famous sales visit in 1913. It was confiscated as obscene in New York by the Customs authorities. In 1914, Lucile, the English couturier Lady Duff Gordon, who had salons in London, Paris and New York, used film extensively for publicity purposes. She advertised her own fashions in 1914 in film trade papers and her designs were still regularly featured in *Gaumont News* through the 1920s.[92] Ine van Dooren, when working at the Netherlands Film Museum in Amsterdam, put together a useful compilation of early colour film of fashion and fashion shows of the 1900–25 period. The models walk in front of the static camera, sit and take off shawls and coats. The models walk easily enough in their hobbled skirts when period comment (and much current dress history) insists that they were shackled by their narrow, ankle-length hems.[93]

Leese shows that fashion newsreels retained their popularity and that by 1938–40 the *Florence Rose* series had evolved into eleven-minute techni-colour films called *Fashion Forecast*. These were narrated by the international editor of *Vogue*, Edna Woolman Chase, and shown all over the US. All these newsreels stressed elite fashions, particularly those of Paris, allowing audiences vicarious access into elite fashion salons and diffusing images of couture style to a mass female audience, until newsreels were killed off by rivalry from television broadcasting and fashion magazines in the 1960s. So far none of this material has been investigated in any depth by dress historians.

Documentary and ethnographical film

The 1930s witnessed the blossoming of documentary film to highlight and record the plight of the working urban class in the years of the Depression, such film work was undertaken for the *Mass-Observation* organisation by Humphrey Spender, just before the Second World War. This period also marked developments in amateur 'home' film making. Archives such as those of the South East Film and Video Archive at the University of Brighton contain thousands of invaluable documentary films charting local celebra-tions of Royal Jubilees, street parties to mark the ending of the Second World War in 1945, family birthday parties and holidays. Many of these show clothing of both men and women in detail and remain, as Frank Gray, the Director of the Brighton-based archives, believes, a vastly under-used study source.[94] Ethnographic documentary film inevitably also records images of clothing and personal appearance. Thus, in Hungary in the 1920s, István Molnár, using film to record the intricacies of peasant dances in preparation for his book *Hungarian Dance Traditions*, also captured clothing on film. Even though the music could not at that point be recorded, details of peasant dress certainly were.[95] But again this field is mired with problems.

Crawford and Turton are concerned again over the crisis of representation in documentary ethnographic film as with photography.[96] Concerns centre on the same themes of visual imperialism, which is seen as stemming from carefully selected colonialist images which have in the past been presented as the 'truth'. Anthropologists making films today are desperately conscious of the dangers of imposing their own cultural eye-view on their work, including their own attitudes to issues of gender, class or race. This problem has been finally overcome by avoiding it altogether. As one consequence of the development of the video camera, with the camera in their own hands, indigenous communities can now make their own films of themselves, on their own terms.

As with photographs, the safest route through interpretation of dress in film, whether fictional or documentary, is again to use a comparative methodology. It would be of positive benefit to the field, too, if dress historians came to terms with the wealth of untapped interpretative possibilities that lie within what might seem the most banal home or holiday snapshots and movies. Now that film stills can be downloaded via digitised systems there is less and less excuse for the continued failure of dress historians to use them in their work. New museum practices offer them examples of good practice. Here documentary film is increasingly being used to give 'life' to static objects – to a dress mounted on a tailor's dummy or to a carved mask pinned down in a case. The African gallery at the Horniman Museum in London, which opened in 1999, effectively uses video film of Dogon ritual dancers wearing the masks shown in a case nearby. Similarly, in its *Forties Fashion and the New Look* exhibition of 1997–98, the Imperial War Museum successfully selected newsreel footage of a fashion model being fitted with hip pads, *waspie* corset and massive petticoats to show just what went beneath a New Look couture ball dress. New Look dresses were shown close by. Such examples point to future innovative directions for the use of film and video footage by dress historians.

Notes

1 With thanks to Frank Gray for his advice on this chapter.

2 S. Braden, *Committing Photography* (Pluto Press, London, 1983), p. 1.

3 V. Lee-Webb, Missionary Photographers in the Pacific Islands – divine light (*History of Photography*, 21, 1, Spring 1997), p. 16.

4 C. Miller Goin, Malinowski's Ethnographic Photography and Exhibitions, Image, Text and Authority (*History of Photography*, 21, 1, Spring 1997), p. 67.

5 A. Maxwell, *Colonial Photography and Exhibitions: representations of the 'native' people and the making of European identities* (Leicester University Press, London, 1999), pp. 41–42 and p. 59.

6 V. Lee-Webb, Missionary Photographers in the Pacific Islands, p. 16 and p. 20.

7 S. Conway, *Dress and Cultural Identity: court costumes and textiles of 19th century Lan Na* (Ph.D., University of Brighton, 2000), Appendix C/C/9 papers of Dr Samuel Craig Peoples, Payap University Archive, no. RG. 008/90.

8 E. Dell, The Green Centre for Non-Western Art (*The Royal Pavilion, Libraries and Museums Review*, Brighton, April 1997), p. 13.

9 Goin, Malinowski's Ethnographic Photography, p. 71.

10 M. Hitchcock and L. Norris, *Bali, the Imaginary Museum: the photographs of Walter Spies and Beryl de Zoete* (Oxford University Press, Oxford, 1995), p. 60, p. 65 and p. 79.

11 These photographs were first shown in the exhibition *Field-Work, Beryl de Zoete's Roumanian Photographs, 1900–1940* at the Gallery, University of Brighton, March–April 2000.

12 J. A. Hammerton (ed.), *Peoples of All Nations: their life today and the story of their past*, 7 vols (Educational Books, London, n.d. (*c.* 1925)), vol. 7, p. 5327, p. 5337, p. 5372, p. 5026 and p. 5058; vol. 1, p. 1087 and p. 1528.

13 Maxwell, *Colonial Photography and Exhibitions*, p. 110.

14 J. C. Faris, Laura Gilpin and the 'Endearing' Navajo (*History of Photography*, 21, 1, Spring 1997), p. 60 and p. 65.

15 G. Goyningen-Huené, *African Mirage: the record of a journey in 1938* (Batsford, London, 1938), preface and p. 20.

16 Maxwell, *Colonial Photography and Exhibitions*, p. 119.

17 E. and P. Lewis, *Peoples of the Golden Triangle* (Thames & Hudson, London, 1984), p. 7.

18 S. A. Niessen, *Batak Cloth and Clothing: a dynamic Indonesian tradition* (Oxford University Press, Oxford, 1993), p. viii.

19 S. Stevenson, David Octavius Hill and Robert Adamson, in M. Weaver (ed.), *British Photography in the Nineteenth Century: the fine art tradition* (Cambridge University Press, Cambridge, 1989), p. 51.

20 V. Dodier, *Clementina, Lady Hawarden: studies from life, 1857–1864* (Victoria and Albert Museum, London, 1999).

21 M. F. Harker, *H. P. Robinson – Master of Photographic Art, 1830–1901* (Basil Blackwell, Oxford, 1988), p. 73 and p. 66, quoting H. Peach Robinson, *Picturemaking by Photography* (Piper and Carter, London, 1884), p. 54.

22 A. Linkman, The Workshy Camera: photography and the labouring classes (*Costume*, 25, 1991), pp. 48–49.

23 A. Partington, Popular Fashion and Working Class Affluence, in E. Wilson and J. Ash (eds), *Chic Thrills: a fashion reader* (Pandora, London, 1992), pp. 159–160.

24 Victoria and Albert Museum, *Fashion: an anthology* (HMSO reprint, London, 1972), plate 7.

25 S. Sontag, *On Photography* (Penguin, London, 1979), p. 8.

26 D. King, *The Commissar Vanishes* (Metropolitan, New York, 1997).

27 M. Kundera, *Book of Laughter and Forgetting* (Penguin, London, 1983), p. 3 and p. 24.

28 A. McRobbie, *British Fashion Design: rag trade or image industry* (Routledge, London, 1998), pp. 164–165. See P. Jobling, *Fashion Spreads* (Berg, Oxford, 1999).

29 Braden, *Committing Photography*, p. 1.

30 L. Taylor, Paris Couture, 1940–1944, in Wilson and Ash, *Chic Thrills*, pp. 127–144.

31 C. Dars, *A Fashion Parade – the Seeberger collection* (Blond and Briggs, London, 1979), p. 6.

32 *Bibliothéque de la Ville de Paris*, Seeberger Archives, NA Album 4 (o)43.7, April to June 1942.

33 Ibid. Zucca Archives NA Album 4(o)258.41, no. 4, October–November 1941.

34 See M. Hiley, *Frank Sutcliffe: photographer of Whitby* (Gordon Fraser Gallery, London, 1974).

35 A. Lansdell, *Fashion à la carte, 1860–1900* (Shire, Princes Risborough, 1985), p. 73.

36 Braden, *Committing Photography*, p. 1.

37 J. Thomson and A. Smith, *Street Life in London, 1877–78* (Sampson Low, London, republished EP Publishing, London, 1973).

38 Linkman, *The Workshy Camera*, p. 50.

39 Maxwell, *Colonial Photography*, p. 64.

40 Linkman, *The Workshy Camera*, p. 44; the Munby Collection is in the library at Trinity College, Cambridge; see also Liz Stanley (ed.), *The Diaries of Hannah Cullwick, Victorian Maidservant* (Virago, London, 1984).

41 Braden, *Committing Photography*, p. 2 and p. 4.

42 D. Frizell, *Humphrey Spender's Humanist Landscapes: photo documents, 1932–42* (Yale Centre for British Art, New Haven, 1997), p. 17 and p. 26, quoting Humphrey Spender, *Worktown People: photography from northern England, 1937–38* (Falling Wall Press, Bristol, 1982), p. 21.

43 Polly Binder archive, *Book of Work: 1930–1954*, p. 32, entry reads: 'Left, Right (Two Worlds) montage social-political book with James Fitton; idea started November 1934, possibly for Bodley Head (started collecting cuttings)'. Polly Binder archives, author's collection.

44 Open-Eye Gallery, *Edith Tudor-Hart: a retrospective* (Open-Eye Gallery, Liverpool, 1987), p. 8.

45 Polly Binder archives, author's collection.

46 See K. Beckerman, *Dorothea Lange: the documentary tradition* (Louisiana State University, Baton Rouge, 1980).

47 J. Severa, *Dressed for the Photographer: ordinary Americans and fashions, 1840–1900* (Kent State University Press, Kent, Ohio, 1995), p. xv.

48 A. Landsell, *Fashion à la Carte: a study of fashion through carte de visite* (Shire, Princes Risborough, 1985), p. 176.

49 This was republished as *Victorian and Edwardian Fashion: a photographic survey* (Constable, London, 1981).

50 See A. Lansdell, *Wedding Fashions 1860–1980* (Shire, Aylesbury, 1983) and idem, *Fashion à la carte.*

51 Ibid. p. 11.

52 M. Lambert, 1860–80; S. Levitt, 1880–1900; K. Rolley and C. Aish, 1880–1900; E. Owen, 1900–20.

53 S. Levitt, *Fashion in Photographs, 1880–1900* (Batsford, London, 1991), p. 11.

54 Severa, *Dressed for the Photographer*, p. xviii.

55 Ibid. p. 339.

56 H. B. Griebel, The West African Origin of the African-American Headwrap, in J. B. Eicher (ed.), *Dress and Ethnicity* (Berg, Oxford, 1995), p. 125.

57 Severa, *Dressed for the Photographer*, p. 536.

58 Ibid. p. 479.

59 Antoine, *Antoine* (W. H. Allen, London, 1946), p. 121, with thanks to Alexandra Palmer.

60 Correspondence, October 1994.

61 W. R. LaVine, *In a Glamorous Fashion: the fabulous years of costume design* (Allen and Unwin, London, 1981), p. vii.

62 The Costume Institute, *Romantic and Glamorous Hollywood Design* (Metropolitan Museum, New York, 1974), catalogue no. 145.

63 D. McConathy, *Hollywood Costume: glamour, glitter, romance* (H. N. Abrams, New York, 1976), p. 31.

64 E. Leese, *Costume Design in the Movies* (BCW Publishing, London, 1976), p. 6.

65 McConathy, *Hollywood Costume*; LaVine, *In a Glamorous Fashion*; Margaret Bailey, *Those Glorious Glamour Years* (Seacacus, New York, 1981).

66 R. and P. Engelmeier, *Fashion and Film* (Prestel, Munich, 1997).

67 F. Gray (ed.), *Hove Pioneers and the Arrival of the Cinema* (Faculty of Art, Design and Humanities, University of Brighton, 1996), p. 28. These films are in the South of England Film and Video Archive, University of Brighton; with thanks to Frank Gray.

68 E. Maeder, The Celluloid Image: historical dress in film, in E. Maeder, *Hollywood and History: costume design in film* (Thames & Hudson and Los Angeles County Museum, Los Angeles, 1987), pp. 34–35, p. 9 and p. 50.

69 L. Mulvey (ed.), *Visual and Other Pleasures* (Macmillan, London, 1989); C. Gledhill (ed.), *Home is Where the Heart Is: studies in melodrama and the women's film* (British Film Institute, London, 1987); S. Harpey, *Picturing the Past: the rise and fall of the British costume film* (British Film Institute, London, 1994).

70 P. Cook, *Fashioning the Nation: costume and identity in the British cinema* (British Film Institute, London, 1996), pp. 75–77.

71 L. Mulvey, Visual Pleasure and Narrative Cinema, in Constance Penley (ed.), *Feminism and Film Theory* (Routledge, New York, 1988), p. 57. This article was reprinted from *Screen* (16, 3, Autumn 1975).

72 Ibid. p. 7 and p. 9.

73 S. Bruzzi, *Undressing Cinema: clothing and identity in the movies* (Routledge, London, 1997), p. xvi and p. 62.

74 J. Gaines, Costume and Narrative: how dress tells the woman's story, in J. Gaines and C. Herzog (eds), *Fabrications, Costume and the Female Body* (Routledge, London, 1990), p. 181.

75 Bruzzi, *Undressing Cinema*, p. xiv, p. 57 and p. 60.

76 Leese, *Costume in the Movies*, p. 14.

77 D. Grumbach, *Histoires de la Mode* (Seuil, Paris, 1993), pp. 35–36.

78 Bruzzi, *Undressing Cinema*, p. 26.

79 For further details see M. Delpierre, M. de Fleury and D. Lebrun, *French Elegance in the Movies* (Musée de la Mode et du Costume, Paris, 1988).

80 C. Eckert, The Carole Lombard in Macy's Window, in Gaines and Herzog, *Fabrications*, p. 105.

81 Maeder, *Hollywood and History*, quoting L. Blayney, Do Movies Influence the Paris Designers? (*Movie Classic*, 8, June 1935), p. 34.

82 Bruzzi, *Undressing Cinema*, p. 4.

83 See S. Tomerlin Lee, *American Fashion: the life and lines of Adrian, Mainbocher, McCardell and Norell* (Deutsch, London, 1976).

84 F. Mohrt, *30 ans d'Elégance et de Creation* (Jacques Damase, Paris, 1983), p. 90.

85 Musée de la Mode et du Costume, *Années Trentes* (Musée de la Mode et du Costume, Paris, 1987), p. 40.

86 The White House, *Moderna* (Regent's Street, London, May 1934), p. 11.

87 C. Breward, *The Culture of Fashion* (Manchester University Press, Manchester, 1995), pp. 197–198.

88 E. Wilson and L. Taylor, *Through the Looking Glass: a history of dress from 1860 to the present day* (BBC Books, London, 1989), p. 100.

89 Eckert, The Carole Lombard in Macy's Window, p. 120.

90 C. Herzog, 'Powder Puff' Promotion: the fashion show-in-the-film, in Gaines and Herzog, *Fabrications*, p. 150 and p. 136.

91 With thanks to Frank Gray for this information.

92 Leese, *Costume Design in the Movies*, pp. 10–14.

93 I. van Dooren, *Compilation of Fashion Film up to 1925* (The Netherlands Film Institute, Amsterdam, 1993).

94 With thanks to Frank Gray.

95 Néprajzi Filstúdió, *Ethnographic Film Catalogue* (no publisher given, Budapest, 1995), p. 21.

96 P. I. Crawford and D. Turton, *Film as Ethnography* (Manchester University Press, Manchester, 1992), p. xi.

7 ✧ Ethnographical approaches[1]

Amongst the Big Men, clothing is a taboo subject. They don't want it known they even care about it. (Tom Wolfe)[2]

Introduction

E THNOGRAPHY offers approaches for analysing clothing and body ornament which stem from the study of the technological and cultural roots of specific peasant and small-scale communities. Such approaches construct theories on the function and development of culture based on analysis of social organisation and the intellectual and behavioural processes of human society. Thus the broad field of anthropology, out of which ethnography has grown, is 'sustained by its ambition to describe the full range of human cultural and biological variation'.[3] All aspects of the human life cycle have been meticulously examined from belief, kinship and economic systems to complex ritual associated with cosmology and annual agricultural cycles. Music, language, dance and every kind of material cultural object from domestic equipment to hunting and farming tools and religious artefacts have long been scrutinised. Central within this discourse today is assessment of the cultural meanings of textiles, clothing and body decoration, though this has not long been the case.

The 1850–75 period saw the founding of the study of ethnography in Europe and was the point at which

> a systematic, well-documented comparative social anthropology was born, and an interest in the manner, customs, institutions and beliefs of small-scale cultures and of the great cultures of South America and the East ceased to be confined to travellers, antiquarians and satirists. To take the study of them seriously became no longer merely a proof of eccentricity.[4]

Today ethnographers have dramatically broadened their field of interest and now see their remit as covering all communities within world cultures, including those of urban Western Europe, as the work of the French ethnographer, Beatrix de Wita, discussed in Chapter 3, has already shown.

The growth of interest in clothing and textiles

In its early stages of development the study of anthropology soon came into conflict with prejudice fuelled by an eye-view that recognised only the superiority of European art and culture set within imperial interests. Ignorant judgements which labelled 'primitive' artefacts as pagan and savage were freely asserted and accepted. Peasant-made artefacts were dismissed as child-like, 'Other', naive, popular or emulative. All these objects were seen by the public at large to take a lesser, lower and secondary place in the hierarchy of cultural forms, whether music, dance, sculpture, masks, clothing or textiles.

In 1975 even Van Nespen, the Curator of the *Oudheidkundige Museum*, Antwerp, who was Commissioner of one of the first major pan-European ethnographical exhibitions sponsored by UNESCO and the Council of Europe, felt obliged to write an explanatory defence of the cultural value of the peasant art and artefacts included in the show *Love and Marriage.*'The aesthetic standards of popular art are not the same as for art in general, where every work of art is or should be an individual creation; on the contrary, popular art lives for and through the society that makes it and as such it is appreciated and experienced.'[5] Barbara Kirshenblatt-Gimblett in 1987 confirmed 'the importance of examining the values and internal logic of folk art production in proper relation to its larger cultural setting'.[6]

The hunt for this larger cultural setting has sought, as she suggests, an understanding of the function of such artefacts set within their own belief systems. Anthony Shelton, for example, urges that in order to understand the cultural forces of indigenous communities such as the Huichol of north-west Mexico, Western observers have to accept that the Huichol world 'is not the world we perceive' and that it 'appears very different to that which confronts the Western observer'. In the complex Huichol world of 'primary unconscious processes', Shelton explains, for example, that there is a direct involvement in maintaining or adjusting 'a system of ethics inherited from their ancestral deities, which organises the world and defines appropriate activities and relations within it'.[7]

Ethnographers have long recognised that material cultural artefacts are essential ritual tools within such belief systems. In 1958 two major Hungarian ethnographers, Edit Fél and Tamás Hofer, reiterated the cultural centrality of peasant artefacts within village life. Objects in peasant culture, they explain, 'solemnize human relations and sanctify them, through application laid down by custom'.[8]

The emergence of textiles and dress studies within the fields of anthropology and ethnography

Within these developing approaches within the fields of anthropology and ethnography, Ronald Schwarz commented on the dearth of in-depth analysis of cloth and clothing. In 1979 he noted that accounts of clothing were usually only descriptive and that 'in our rush towards specialization and new forms of integrating anthropology with other sciences, clothing was left in the closet'.[9] Ruth Barnes, an ethnographer based in the Ashmolean Museum, Oxford, with a specialism in South-East Asian dress and textiles, confirms this historical problem. She highlights the damaging impact on textile research of the Royal Anthropological Institute's handbook to fieldwork, *Notes and Queries*, first published in 1874.[10] This established a methodological approach which was followed thereafter for many years. Intended to provide a rational, scientific research method, it proposed a formulaic structure with sections titled 'General', 'Domestic life', 'Laws and customs', 'Religion', 'Folklore' and 'Language'. Barnes believes that this method 'succeeds in creating an abstract structure that does not take its lead'[11] from the actuality of the lives being studied. Clothing fell under the general category of material culture and although items were carefully collected and identified, little real interest was shown in trying to understand their coded meanings and cultural functions.

By the mid-1960s there was a recognition that clothing research had been marginalised for far too long and that its value as a basic cultural signifier was still neither adequately recognised nor researched. In 1979, Schwarz, in an entertaining but angry article, 'Uncovering the Secret Vice: towards an anthropology of clothing and adornment', declared that 'clothing is a subject about which anthropologists should have much to say yet remain mysteriously silent ... Descriptions of clothing are so rare in some texts of social anthropology ... that the casual reader might easily conclude the natives go naked.'[12]

Unusually he directly raised the issue of male anthropologists' bias against dress study despite the fact that many decorated their homes with strange sartorial artefacts. In seeking an answer as to 'why clothing is so rarely the object of systematic enquiry', when anthropologists write so much about 'clitorectomy and ambiguity, sorcery and profanity, patrilineality and locality', he quoted Tom Wolfe. 'Amongst the Big Men, clothing is a taboo subject. They don't want it known they even care about it ... Sex, well all right, talk your head off. But this, these men's clothes.'[13]

Annette Weiner and Jane Schneider raised the self-same problem ten years later in their introduction to their book *Cloth and the Human Experience*. Recognising that cloth produced by women makes a contribution of central importance to ritual, social and political life in so many societies, they ask why ethnographers (by implication here meaning male ethnographers) 'often overlook this possibility, whether from a disinterest in women's activities, or in fibers and fabrics (as distinct from food) or both'. They believed that the negative consequences of this attitude had led to the use of 'simplistic and inadequate'[14] analytical categories which mistakenly push women and their cloth and clothing manufacture into a 'domestic' social corner whilst men's arenas, which have been far more fully researched became unduly emphasised as more importantly public, spiritual and political.

Ruth Barnes too discovered that some male ethnographers paid little attention to the textiles and clothing they themselves had collected. Two British Colonial administrators, Hutton and Mills, amassed large ethnographical collections for the Pitt Rivers Museum from the Naga Hills on the Indian/Burmese border during the interwar period. Of the 4000 specimens, which included horned head-dresses made and worn by young men when headhunting, overall two-thirds of the objects were cloth, dress accessories or body ornaments. All were most carefully documented, yet Barnes found that in the numerous books and articles published by the two collectors, dress was dealt with only 'in a few pages in their introduction'.

Since Hutton and Mills collected so much, it seems surprising that they wrote so little about these artefacts, especially about the large, impressive cloths with geometric patterns worn as wrap-around cloaks or skirts, which were woven by Ao Naga women. Barnes wrote in 1992 that Mills and Hutton 'did not look at Naga life from the female perspective and they were not especially alert to the symbolic position of gender'. This led Mills to overlook the centrally important gender role of these ritual cloths. When Barnes undertook her own investigation she found that 'the cloth is the essential marker of achievement in the household, a sign of spiritual blessing ... by weaving the cloth [women] produce one of the essential emblems of the acquired merit',[15] a merit which Barnes argues is as significant within Ao Naga culture as the status headhunting gives to men. Thus, she argues, Mills's view of the gender relationships and division of social power in this community developed a major inaccuracy.

Barnes repeated her observation again after researching a collection of textiles from the Lamaholot Islands of Eastern Indonesia put together in 1928/29 by Ernst Vatter and now in the *Städtisches Museum für Völkerkunde*, Frankfurt. Despite also amassing a large group of fabrics, including ritual ikat cloths whose patterns he researched with care, Barnes found that, like Mills and Hutton, 'he did not attempt to interpret the designs in detail but restricted himself to a description of what he saw and collected'.[16] Building on Vatter's work, Barnes undertook her own fieldwork investigating a complex type of bridewealth ikat cloth from the village of Lamarela woven exclusively by women, samples of which were among the Vatter collection. She is able as a consequence again to assess the social and cultural place of women through these woven artefacts. She identifies their ritual place as essential displays of power and clan affiliation. By re-examining their encoded patterns and ritual usage she revealed these overlooked ikat cloths to be an enfolding cultural force in Lamarela. They are, she explains, highly significant indicators of the juxtaposition of tradition and change which is 'a characteristic quality and strength of the community'[17] as a whole.

One book which significantly does not fit into this historical and gender-biased pattern of research was Petr Bogatyrev's *The Functions of Folk Costume in Moravian Slovakia*. Originally published in 1937 in Czechoslovakia, it was not translated into English until 1971, but thereafter made a major and lasting impact on research methodologies. Bogatyrev, a linguistics specialist, was a distinguished teacher of ethnography at the University of Moscow, working closely with Prague structural anthropologists. He undertook research into peasant dress in Slovakia and Moravia whilst teaching in Bratislava.

In 1971, in an introduction to the translated version, the semiotician, Ogibenin, evidently still felt the need to rationalise Bogatyrev's unusual interest in peasant clothing. He does so by explaining clothing's semiotic direct links to the author's well-established ethnographical field of linguistics. 'What Bogatyrev has judiciously surmised, though not explicitly stated, is that wearing clothing is as universal, constant, and consequently as natural a feature as, for example using language for communication, or within language, as common and universal as using vowels, and consonants to discriminate between words.' Ogibenin notes that Bogatyrev's far-seeing approach was close to Lévi-Strauss's later views on structural anthropology which aimed at 'interpreting society as a whole in terms of theory of communication'.[18] Using the interwar research of A. Václavík and Josef Klvana and others, Bogatyrev's fascinating study touches on every aspect of Moravian village life as reflected through dress. He shows how integral the form and function of village clothing were to gender and age roles identity, magico-religious ritual and the processes of cultural change. Bogatyrev's dress research was a rare and early exception.

From the mid-1960s a campaign has been fought within ethnographical circles to win professional recognition for clothing's powerful and central cultural meanings, a campaign conducted by ethnographers such as Annette Weiner, Mary Ellen Roach-Higgins, Jane Schneider, Justine Cordwell, Ruth Barnes and Joanne Eicher, amongst the women, many of them American. Thus over the last thirty years, the same struggle for subject recognition that took place in the fields of social and economic history, took place too in the world of ethnography. This has pushed the study of textiles and dress into the mainstream of ethnographic research and has succeeded in establishing an accepted place for dress and textiles within the hierarchies of ethnography.

Developments since 1965

Roach and Eicher's study *Dress, Adornment and the Social Order*[19] of 1965 was an effort to pull together a broad selection of readings on dress, some old, some new, largely for teaching and research purposes. A massive annotated research bibliography was appended to encourage research development. The authors' prime interest was boldly stated. Their intent was to use dress 'to cast light on the total picture of human behaviour … [because] … the portable character of clothing and associated decorative items makes these highly visible and flexible in building the setting for behaviour'.[20] Selected texts were grouped into issues of 'the origins and function of dress', 'diversity in cultural patterns', 'social organisation and dress', 'dress and the individual', and 'stability and change in patterns of dress'. The mix of authors was the broadest, from extracts from Cecil Beaton's 1954 *Glass of Fashion*, to Ferdinand Zweig's 1952 study of the role of clothing in the lives of British workers and Charles Hughes's *Changes in Eskimo Clothing*.[21] Despite the book's carefully themed structure, Ronald Schwarz complained that it was 'an eclectic collection of excerpts and articles. There is no critical analysis of the field nor do the editors attempt to develop a general theory.'[22]

Three landmark international conferences soon laid the groundwork for just such theoretical development. The first, in 1973, was the IXth International Congress of Anthropological and Ethnological Sciences, in the USA. Its proceedings were published in 1979 and Schwarz's role was prominent. The second, *Towards an Anthropology of Dress*, held in 1983 was organised by the French *Centre National de La Recherche Scientifique*. The third also took place in 1983, at Troutbeck, New York, organised by the American women anthropologists, Annette B. Weiner and Jane Schneider. Like the CNRS gathering, this was attended by art historians, textile experts and historians as well as anthropologists. The publications from these three conferences have been profoundly influential. Twenty-two dress-related papers from the 1973 Congress were edited into a book in 1979 by Justine M. Cordwell and Ronald A. Schwarz under the title *The Fabrics of Culture – the anthropology of clothing and adornment*. The editors acknowledged again that 'compared to other dimensions of human behaviour, we anthropologists are relatively silent about the meanings and function of dress and adornment'.[23]

Their book, which interestingly starts with a quote from Bogatyrev, sets about amending this state of affairs by providing examples of good practice. Five approaches were taken, many set within African cultures. 'Clothing, culture and communication' was the first. Section two, 'Signs, symbols and the social order' tackled themes related to the symbolic meanings of clothing within specific cultural boundaries. Section three, 'Man, masks and morals', was concerned with the part ceremonial dress and masking play in the maintenance of social and moral order. Section four examined cultural change and the impact of imperialism, colonialism and modernisation on dress whilst the final theme assessed 'Technology and textiles' in terms of production, distribution and consumption.

Ten years later, many of the same themes were explored again at the French Congress in 1983. Papers were drawn from a wide community of historians, archaeologists, ethnographers, art historians and fashion de- signers with the clear intention of moving beyond descriptive and historical approaches. The papers here, more Eurocentric and museological, were clustered into strands titled 'Innovation, diffusion, evolution: the phe- nomena of fashion'; 'Dress codes'; 'Methods of inquiry and analysis of sources'; and 'Problems of description and classification'.

Six years after the Troutbeck conference Weiner and Schneider pub- lished their study *Cloth and the Human Experience*, confirming their view that 'on a world-wide scale, complex moral and ethical issues related to dominance and autonomy, opulence and poverty, political legitimacy and succession, and gender and sexuality, find ready expression through cloth'.[24] All the contributions came from American researchers, more than half of whom were anthropologists. The book emphasised the symbolic poten- tialities of cloth in its material form, the rituals attached to the manufacture of cloth and the ritual links between textiles, their manufacture and the human life cycle and symbols of political power.

Current research themes in dress and ethnography

Ethnographic research has therefore sought to show that textiles and clothing are powerful indicators of the most subtle, complex and important facets of the life of small-scale and peasant communities, acting as stabilisers reflecting the unity and strength of cultural practices and the social cohesion of a community. Research approaches are both historical and contemporary. The processes of the cultural absorption of outside and urban influences now attract much research interest which indicates that these vary enor- mously over vast time-spans and that each case is a reflection of the community's own very specific circumstances. These may focus on very specific local circumstances but may also set a small community properly within the broad framework of sources of outsider influences.

A 1997 exhibition at the Ashmolean Museum, Oxford, *Textiles and the Indian Ocean Trade*, for example, celebrated the results of Barnes's historical research into sources of some imported Indonesian textiles. India's supreme strength in the manufacture and international export of printed cotton cloth along trade routes out of India to Arabia, East Africa and the Red Sea was already well known. So too was the textile history associated with the Indian trade route to Indonesia, [25] but what had not been appreciated was the ancient history of this activity. The Ashmolean Museum holds a collection of 100 samples of block printed Indian cotton donated by the Egyptologist Percy E. Newberry in 1946, who had found his small samples in Egypt. They had been 'imported as utilitarian cloth, to be worked into items of dress or furnishings'. Through carbon dating it is now agreed that many of these Indian cottons found in Egypt are far, far earlier in date than could have been imagined. One, astonishingly, is now dated to around AD 895 whilst twenty-two are now dated to the fourteenth century AD.[26] Following this revelation, the museum then carbon dated a collection of large Gujarati block printed cloths collected in Sulawesi, Eastern Indonesia, where they had been used as ceremonial cloths and were objects of much ethnographical interest. Up to now, Barnes explains, 'it had been assumed that [Indian] cloth surviving in South East Asia could not be earlier than the 17th or 18th century'. Her research proved this assumption to be a gross error. Carbon dating proved that some of these cloths imported into Indonesia also dated from the fourteenth and fifteenth centuries. With these new early dates in place, the political, economic and cultural history of the Indian textile trade and the development of its cloth patterns and their historical ethnic settings in South-East Asian cultures will now have to be reconsidered.

Contemporary ethnographical research is of no less significance than these historical explorations and is largely but not exclusively weighted towards assessment of the consequences of the complexities of globalisation on world cultures. Alfred Gell, for example, reclaims the use of the term 'primitive' to describe the contemporary wood carved canoe prows of the Trobriand islanders from Papua New Guinea. He does so in recognition of the fact that 'they continue to fabricate primitive art because it is a feature of an ethnically exclusive prestige economy which they have rational motives for wishing to preserve'. Yet he is clear that the carvers are in fact 'not at all themselves "primitive"; they are educated, literate in various languages, and familiar with much contemporary technology'.[27]

Historical and contemporary settings therefore both provide the basis of today's ethnography which is increasingly using research into textiles and clothing as a means of exploring the fundamental issues outlined at these three major conferences. These themes include reassessments of terms such as 'traditional' and 'authentic', issues of gender, ethnic and national identity, the aesthetics of ethnographical artefacts and finally issues of modernity and globalisation as they impact on tribal and peasant communities.

Analysis of 'tradition' through cloth and clothing

The term 'tradition' in ethnographic research 'has come to mean an item or action inherited intact from the past'.[28] This seemingly straightforward comment is, however, suffused with complexities. By implication the terms 'inherited' and 'intact' carry with them notions of a cultural longevity and stability that we know now bear little relation to the reality of 'tribal' or peasant life, both of which have always been subject to change. From the idyllic illustrations to European fairy tales, such as those of the Russian illustrator Ivan Bilibin in the early twentieth century, we have in the West imbibed childhood images and fictitious visions of an unchanging, rural peasantry living in isolated utopian simplicity. The falsity of such myths has been exposed by ethnographers often through analysis of dress.

The Hurons of Quebec, for example, are famous for their moose hair embroidery on leather. Whilst ethnographers believe that geometrical moose hair embroidery was at one point an indigenous skill, its development was not. A French Ursuline order founded as early as 1639 opened a seminary for Indian girls. It was here that the Huron 'tradition' for fine needlework was established with many designs based on delicate seventeenth-century French embroidered floral patterns. Once the imported silks and metallic threads of the nuns fell into short supply local raw materials such as moose hair and quills replaced them, but with patterns still made up within the European aesthetics of the Ursuline sisters. This embroidery survived in convents in Quebec for nearly two centuries. By the 1870s, once Quebec was opened up by railways and commerce, wholesale orders for American and Canadian cities, workers in the Yukon gold fields and the increasing number of tourists provided a wider consumer market for hair embroidered moccasins and fancy goods. By 1898 workshops were producing 140,000 'traditional' pairs a year,[29] by then embroidered by both Indian and French Canadian outworkers. This Huron 'tradition' continues today.

Though roots may sometimes have been ancient, peasant culture across Europe was always wide open to Western European, urban, 'high art', and now global, influences, absorbing and appropriating them on its own terms. Hungarian ethnographic research reveals that a 'local' style develops over a period of three to four generations. Tamás Hofer and Edit Fél explain that 'it can develop fully or reach a peak, after which stagnation and decline may set in'.[30] As peasant communities all over the world come under increasing outside pressures from tourism and economic change, the meanings of culturally descriptive terms such as 'traditional', 'pure' or 'authentic' are consequently being questioned.

A refusal to deal with this issue of the 'uncontaminated' peasant dress versus 'incorporated' style change has long been a contentious issue. When a collection of over six hundred 'peasant' artefacts from all over Europe was put together in Haslemere, Surrey, in the 1885–1926 period to provide inspiration for local arts and workshops, every effort was made to seek out the 'authentic'. Thus the Haslemere Peasant Arts Collection contains a seventeenth-century carved wooden wassail bowl from Norway and, for example, a nineteenth-century shift worn by Erzinian Mordivian women from Simbirsk Province in Russia (Figure 45). This is embroidered in thread coloured with natural madder red and indigo blue dye.[31] No hint of the bright chemical dyes, urban sequins or fancy braids, which found an eager market amongst much of the European peasantry from the 1890s, is to be found in the Haslemere collection. These represented the very stuff of urban contamination. The founder of the collection, the Reverend Gerald Davies,

45 Erzinian Mordivian embroidery, Simbirsk Province, Russia, probably mid-nineteenth century

was convinced that authenticity within peasant artefacts centred on 'the endeavour by Peasants to make beautiful the objects which surround and serve them in their daily life' and that such objects had to be made 'to keep, or at most to give'. Thus ceramics made by a potter for sale within his village community failed to meet Davies's notions of 'authentic' and were 'excluded, since even in the hands of the Peasant potter, it is an Art so special as to have been practiced only by the expert and with the aim of selling'.[32] The very same debate was apparent amongst ethnographers in Romania in the early 1980s and early 1990s. The Institute of Ethnography's official research policy excluded the collecting and analysis of 'non-authentic' peasant clothing, such as modernised village blouses, which were by then to be found in many areas of Romania. Cut and embroidered 'traditionally' but made of light-weight, creped cotton, or even nylon, rather than heavy linen and hempen cloth, these were not considered 'worthy of collection whilst pure examples of authentic garments still remained to be studied in the field'.[33] Thus although village women from the 1970s and 1980s were making blouses up in nylon they were not collected. Some showed much ingenuity in this modernising 'transformation' phase, which still continues. One example, cut to the traditional T shape which has been dated by Romanian ethnographers back to pre-Roman Dacian origins, was made up in a cheap and basic white nylon factory fabric already printed with a black floral border pattern. The maker, adapting this to village forms, has placed the border print on centre front and cuffs and hand embroidered the design in coloured threads (Figure 46). Such items seem unlikely to be lovingly catalogued in Romanian ethnographical museums for a good few years yet.

John Picton, of the School of African and Oriental Studies at the University of London, focused debate on change and the 'traditional' in his boundary-breaking 1995 exhibition *The Art of African Textiles: technology, tradition and lurex* which explored the design, making, meaning and consumption of textiles. His deliberate use of the word 'lurex' in the show's title was indicative of his innovative approach. This exhibition was one of the first on African textiles to examine in depth export print cottons made in Holland and Britain for the African market[34] such as the *ABC Oval* design, wax Duplex printed on to cotton by the African Printing Division of Brunn-schweiler, Manchester. This design sold well in the early 1980s (Figure 47). Picton's innovative approach led him to re-examine his own earlier attitudes. Twenty years earlier, his 1979 book *African Textiles* had 'dwelt upon the traditions inherited from the past and on achievements within a given and largely restraining technology, with the developments of the present century considered only in regard to the use of new yarns and other materials within the technology'.[35] Ten years later for the 1989 second edition of the same book, he decided to remove the term 'traditional' altogether.

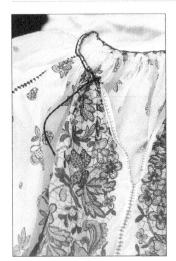 

left **46** Romanian peasant blouse, village made, probably 1980s, printed, over-embroidered nylon fabric   *right* **47** *ABC Oval*, wax Duplex printed cotton print fabric, made in Manchester for export to West Africa

At best it was redundant: it served no useful purpose and signified nothing that was not already obvious. At worst it was misleading, supposing an essentially 'authentic' African practice ... Traditionality was, indeed, exposed as a fiction denoting an invented and perhaps largely spurious authenticity. It was no longer acceptable as a representation of social practice to contrast the 'traditional' with the 'contemporary'.[36]

So Picton's 1995 exhibition dealt boldly with cotton export prints as well as the full range of indigenous fabrics because imported cottons have been worn across the whole continent from West to East since the late nineteenth century. Picton produced new research on their earliest manufacture and design, explaining the Dutch origin of the imitation Javanese wax batik export cloths, and finding hand blocked, Dutch printed samples made for West Africa which dated as far back as 1846–49. Picton proved through surviving sample books that by 1884 the firm of Vlisco in the Netherlands was designing and making for a specific East African market. By 1905 Brown Flemming Ltd, Dyers and Printers of African and Colonial Specialities, were designing export prints in Glasgow to the localised tastes of African consumers. Picton gives an example dated to 19 April 1905 of a design 'based upon postage stamps and the various ports of the Colonial Gold Coast'.[37] Picton stresses strongly that these designs 'were and are fused into the specific African market they were designed for' and are designs which 'effectively mediate local concerns that can be described, variously, as decorative, commemorative, proverbial, didactic and funerary'.

This exhibition thus directly challenged a clichéd stereotypic eye-view of 'traditional' ethnic African textiles as consisting only of mud-block prints, indigo-dyed or strip-woven cottons. Picton commented that

> one might argue, of course, that as these fabrics are the products of European industry, they have no real place here ... Moreover, this opinion might seem to be reinforced by the colonial encouragement of any attempt to subvert hand-production by the import of cheap alternatives, thereby transferring wealth from Africa to Europe.

Picton, however, strongly believes that these views are a misrepresentation because the businesses of wax prints 'were contingent upon a local agency with a far greater determining role than has hitherto been realised, and secondly that the employees of these firms are in employment by African patronage'.[38] Local agencies included, for example, commissioning dealers who ordered specific designs to cater for the tastes and demands of their own very specific customers.

A 1997 study shows that the established and 'traditional' design aesthetic of these African export prints, now well over a hundred years old, is itself beginning to be abandoned as new changes sweep in. Since 1989 the British firm of Brunnschweiler has been using computer aided systems to produce imi wax designs for Africa in which largely abstracted floral or geometrical motifs are manipulated very quickly on the screen into more and more complex contemporary designs. Shona Heath's research shows these new designs to be 'a response to active (African consumer) demands for "modern" but meaningless bright, original and unusual designs'.[39] This development reinforces Picton's view of the redundancy of notions of 'the traditional'.

Dress and gender

Interpreting cloth and clothing as 'an indicator and a producer of gender'[40] has now become an established factor within ethnographic research methodology. We know now that even seemingly insignificant items may carry with them important ritualised gender functions. Barnes and Eicher are clear that 'gender distinctions are a crucial part of the construction of dress, whether they are made on biological or social grounds'.[41] Investigations show that these emblematic gendered uses of cloth are central to the well-being of spiritual as well as practical life. Weiner and Schneider propose a dual-stranded approach whereby cloth and clothing is identified first as a cultural signifier/indicator of gender difference and second, as a carrier/producer of socialised gender meanings.

In looking at the first signifying strand of their approach, it is clear that a central function of gendered clothing is to differentiate between the sexes visually. Bogatyrev in 1937 termed this 'sex-distinction' through dress. Here codes also identify the wearer's sexual status through indicating their precise marital status. The clothes worn by a Central European peasant woman were rigidly coded in this way from girlhood through to old age. Colour, pattern and form sharply defined her role as daughter, wife, mother and widow. The codes were so refined that dress was used to transmit the most subtle gender messages. Clothes acted as well-understood, actively invoked, symbols of gender. In Hungarian villages during courtship rituals, a young man would 'accidentally' leave his precious embroidered frieze coat in his intended's house: 'If early next morning he found the coat out on the porch, it meant he had been rejected'. Handkerchiefs were made by women and given as ritual gifts to men. A village girl would give her fiancé a new embroidered ritual handkerchief each week before their wedding. Their perfect stitching, which her future mother-in-law would certainly examine, signified her virtuous character and refined feminine skills. Hofer and Fél recount the story of a woman who

> looking out of her window at dawn saw, tied to her single beloved rose-bush, the handkerchief of her husband, who worked in the city but found the unaccustomed labour hard to bear. The signal told her at once what words could not tell, that her husband had returned but for some grievous reason could not talk to her. Running outside, she found his body hanging in the stable where he had committed suicide.[42]

Bogatyrev searched but could not find any overt erotic function in Central European peasant dress. Unlike Western society where notions of dress and eroticism seem to be increasingly fused, he found that 'ordinarily the wearers do not talk about the erotic function, nor are they sufficiently aware of it themselves'. Rather he found the erotic function to be fused with the aesthetics of dress. 'Both functions have the same goal, i.e., to attract attention'.[43] However, links between clothing, fertility, sexuality and the magic function of dress were easy to find. Bogatyrev shows of the linen shift, for example, that it

> was such an intimate part of women's clothing that even some husbands never saw one in their whole lives … Perhaps precisely because of the secretiveness associated with it, the shift was thought to have curative power, especially for men or cattle hexed by the evil eye.

The origin of this belief Bogatyrev surmises is 'the shift being directly in contact with the body, serves by Frazer's law of contact and contagion, as a conductor of the magic power which is stored in the naked body'.[44]

Weiner and Schneider's second strand of approach deals with dress and cloth as a carrier/producer of socialised gender meanings and has been widely appreciated. Bogatyrev had already shown that gendered clothing was used in peasant communities to resolve events that broke socially accepted sexual rules, upsetting basic values and beliefs. How does a village whose values are built on communally celebrated life cycle rituals of marriage and then childbirth deal with the problem of illegitimacy, for example? Bogatyrev found that well-understood clothing codes were put into play as a vehicle of public condemnation. Within most East and Central European peasant communities one of the signs of a single girl's virgin status was that she went bareheaded, with her long hair braided into one or two plaits. It was only upon marriage that her hair was put up and covered with the coveted married woman's cap. There is much ritual play and celebration at weddings when the bride's crown is removed and she is 'capped' for the first time. Bogatyrev discovered that in East Slovakia married women refused to allow a pregnant single girl to go bareheaded. Humiliatingly 'they cut her hair and wrap her head in a kerchief'. In 1933 in Western Moravia, 'if a fallen girl marries, she may not go to the altar wearing a wedding crown. She must wear a cap instead since she has excluded herself from the circle of her other girl friends.' Such unmarried mothers even had to sit in a special place in church. Men did not escape approbation either. Bogatyrev recounts a story dating back to around 1870 when a married miller (a position of wealth and dignity within a village community) fell in love with a village girl who became pregnant. His furious wife

> hid behind the church belfry and as the pregnant girl passed, snipped off the girl's two braids and nailed them up for all to see. They hung there for a long time till somebody took them down. The miller couldn't take all the looks and the gossip so he sold his mill and moved somewhere far away.[45]

What Bogatyrev is stressing here is the enforcement of sexual stability and gendered behaviour patterns through the publicly visual language of gendered clothing.

Barnes and Eicher point out too that 'far from being a value-free activity, the construction of the dress article may hint at the essence of its meaning'.[46] Ethnographers have therefore studied gender divisions between makers of cloth which vary from one culture to another. C. A. Bayley, a Cambridge University historian, in his study of *swadeshi* weavers in India notes that 'the qualities with which cloth was seen to be imbued by Indians had implications not only for the status of those who used it, but also those who produced and serviced it'.[47]

In much of India the specialist weavers of ritual silk cloth are men but this is not always so. Researchers, such as Barnes, are particularly interested in women makers of sanctified cloth which is used in ceremonials of power-making because of the cultural weight carried by these textiles. Research, as we have seen, indicates that women's socio-cultural role within tribal and peasant communities has been underestimated and misread because not enough attention has been paid in the past by male ethnographers to their often equal role in manufacturing these sacred textiles and clothes. Schneider and Weiner note that 'women are by no means the universal producers of cloth but in many societies they monopolise all or most of the manufacturing sequence, giving them a larger role than the men ... Emblematic and communicative uses of cloth are, finally, as common among women as men.'[48] Barnes's study of the making and ritual function of Lamarela cloth supports this view.

In Central Europe both sexes made ritual cloth and clothing, but there were profound gender divisions between what they made. Thus women at home wove wool, silk and linen, and then cut and embroidered it into bed covers and dowry pillows for the ceremonial marriage bed, into shirts for the future groom and into blouses, shifts, aprons, petticoats, skirts for themselves, their daughters and god-daughters.

Hofer and Fél note that 'in regions where weaving and embroidery were highly developed, as in the villages of the Kalotaszeg region, Transylvania [in Hungary until 1919], mothers began to prepare the dowry when their daughters were about eight or ten years old ... the preparation took about ten years'.[49] A feature of the dowry was a huge pile of large white linen pillows, stuffed with goose down and made to be piled high ritually on the marriage bed. These were all embroidered across one end only with geometric and floral designs either in madder red or indigo blue linen threads. The decorative ends were carefully placed on public view for the inspection of future mothers-in-law (Plate VI).

Only male craft artisans were allowed to join the craft guilds, many of which dated back to the Middle Ages. They were the makers of heavy overgarments, the leather and frieze tailored coats, waistcoats, capes and jackets and boots for both men and women. All these items were embroidered or appliquéd, status giving and costly, some very costly. In the 1875–90 period in Hungary, the high point of manufacture of men's embroidered frieze coats, 'master tailors employed between twelve and sixteen assistants ... No less than 800–1000 ... were said to have been sold at one country fair.'[50] However, whether made by men or women, at home or in a professional workshop, many garments carried ceremonial, ritualised meanings.

At another level of cultural practice, ethnographers are now aware of the tripartite enfolding of meaning that wraps together, first, women's cloth production and clothing, second, their sexuality and, third, the annual cycle of seasonal–agricultural change. In Hungary women's aprons and ribbons corresponded to those of the priest for important Church festivals such as Christmas, Easter, Lent, Harvest and so on. These festivals also corresponded to the agricultural seasons and often celebrated them. Shelton found a similar tripartite process amongst the Huichols in north-west Mexico where 'cultivation is conceptualised as the cutting open of the womb of [a female water deity] in order to impregnate her with seeds'. He found reference to the water deities within designs on the shoulder bags which the bride makes and gives to her future groom. 'By offering ... this apparel, the girl expresses her affiliation to the water deities and thereby draws attention to her procreative qualities.'[51]

What is evident is the depth of significance attached to gender indicators and the way in which they are fused within a complex web of other codes, particularly ethnic codes.

Dress and ethnic identity

Coded forms of dress are also used to mark a sense of 'belonging', whether to a family, community and eventually a nation. Largely thanks to the authoritative and pioneering work by women anthropologists already cited here, using dress as a means of debating issues of ethnicity has now also become an accepted methodology. Joanne B. Eicher established an influential research centre at the University of Minnesota, working to establish this field of research since 1965. In her 1995 volume *Dress and Ethnicity* nonetheless she still felt that although 'ethnic dress has been noted as an aspect of ethnicity ... it has been neglected analytically'.[52]

Eicher and Sumberg's view is that 'dress is often a significant visible mark of ethnicity, used to communicate identity of a group or individual among interacting groups of people'.[53] Bogatyrev discussed the concept of ethnicity in his analysis of 'our costume' amongst the peasantry of Moravian Slovakia. 'There is a strong emotional element expressed ... costume and wearer are closely, intimately connected in it.' He observed a concept both personal and communal, one which changes through time and the circumstances of village life which can be an emotion so strong that 'when it comes to ridiculing or insulting [another] community, it is sufficient to ridicule that community's *signs*, such as its costume ... which in turn insenses the insulted group to defend these signs'.[54]

Emotional attachment thus plays a central role in the retention of ethnic dress. Thus very localised styles are still worn in parts of the Netherlands today, such as the little town of Veere, on the Friesian island of Walcheren, where one or two elderly residents still proudly wear their regional dress on a daily basis, with its white linen cap and complex gold head ornaments (Figure 48). Their dress still remains close to styles photographed in nearby Middelburg market around 1910 (Figure 49). The small communities of Koniakow and Istebna above the town of Cieszyn, in Polish Upper Silesia in the Beskid mountains have also clung tenaciously to their indigenous peasant costume, despite Austro-Hungarian rule, Polish rule, two World Wars and the imposition of forty years of Communism (Figure 50). In the 1960s women from this Highlander community still commonly wore simple loose white linen blouses over black pleated linen skirts and indigo blue, block printed aprons. A strip of fine lace from the cap covered their foreheads, with a large white scarf worn over the head. Local dress is still proudly worn to Church festivals and with not a tourist in sight. These mountain slopes straddle the border between Poland and Czechoslovakia which splits an ethnic community in two. Villagers still say today that they see themselves as Upper Silesians rather than Poles.[55] Hence on special days even young girls put away their jeans and trainers to wear modernised versions of the old styles. Married women still cover their hair with the lace-fronted caps that were once believed to keep thunder and lightning away from the home. Indigo blue print skirts have been replaced by ones of lurex and rayon, worn with elaborate beaded belts and laced up, velvet bodices, adopted from lowland town styles.

left 48 One of the last residents of Veere, on the island of Walcheren, the Netherlands, to wear local Zeeland dress as a daily habit, photographed in 1998   *right* 49 Postcard, Middelburg market, island of Walcheren, Zeeland, the Netherlands, about 1910

50 Villagers leaving church in Koniakow, near Cieszyn, Upper Silesia, Poland, in 1961

51 Villagers at an Easter Fair from Istebna, near Cieszyn, Upper Silesia, Poland, 1995, still in regional dress

Men's styles have changed far less, still retaining their heavy felted trousers and bright red woollen waistcoats. The same process of ethnic self-definition is still taking place here (Figure 51). Within this process the wearers' personal eye-view of themselves, their place in their community and their community's place within the state, is defined through such localised small-scale community dress and its ritualised etiquette codes.

Ted Polhemus, an American trained as an anthropologist, has, however, confused definitions of ethnicity with his loose use of the term 'tribal' in his popular publications on 'street style'. These parallel the appearance and body adornment of today's street and counter-cultural groups, whom he calls 'style tribes', with aboriginal communities. Although perfectly aware of the role of specific cultural practices and values used to identify ethnic differentiations, Polhemus nevertheless writes that 'a tribe can use the customised body as a means of expressing complex values, beliefs and ideals ... this is as true of our contemporary style tribes as it is of the ancient tribes of the Third World'.[56] He was not the first to draw these easily appealing but highly misleading parallels between tribal people and punks bedecked with Mohican hair cuts and nose rings.[57] His notion of 'style tribes' to describe multifarious punkish, New Age and fetish counter-cultural groups has, however, now unfortunately become lodged in the common parlance of the media and fashion press. Finally Polhemus's obsessive fascination with fetish dress, as revealed in his book *The Customised Body*, seems to have become not anthropology at all but a rationalisation of intellectualised soft pornography, which overstresses the cultural significance of fetish dress and further extends existing confusions over terms and meanings.

It is revealing that no reference to any of Polhemus's work is made in Daniel Wojcik's carefully researched 1995 study *Punk and Neo-tribal Body Art*. This was published by the University of Oregon, where Wojcik is Professor of English and Folklore. He defines the differences between the body decoration and dress of aboriginal communities and that of urban groups which he carefully identifies as 'neo-tribalists'. He writes that 'by adorning and altering their bodies in symbolically powerful ways, both punks and neo-tribalists may proclaim their discontent, challenge dominant ideologies, and ultimately express the yearning for a more meaningful existence'.[58] This, as he explains, is very far removed from the functions of body adornment and clothing within small-scale communities.

A far more meaningful approach to ethnicity than that of Polhemus is taken by Helen Bradley Griebel, trained in the field of folklore and folklife. She used clothing as a focus of study in her 1995 research into African-American ethnic identity which examined the origins and ethnic meanings of the African-American woman's headwrap. At issue is, first, the degree to which the material culture of enslaved West Africans brought to the United States survived at all and second, what, if any, ethnic significance does this hold amongst African-Americans today.

Griebel found that whilst some believed that 'the slaves lost many of their tribal habits and customs, along with their technics, through a process which anthropology terms acculturation',[59] more recently others have shown that the contrary 'overall, direct formal continuities from Africa are more the exception than the rule in any African-American culture'.[60] Griebel is highly critical of most African-American dress history which leaps to easy assumptions of the African roots of this head covering and remedies this by examining 'several hundred accounts' and images taken from the writings of early travellers to Africa. She found further evidence of the direct West African origin of the headwrap in *The Charleston, South-Carolina Gazette and Country Journal* of 25 April 1769 in an advertisement seeking the return of a runaway slave, from Guinea. 'RUN-AWAY from my plantation ... a NEW-NEGRO WENCH, she had on when she went away a new oznaburg coat and wrapper, and a black striped silk handkerchief.'

Griebel argues for a direct African (rather than Africa-via-the-West-Indies) origin for the headwrap but finds that it had a complex African–European birth. She believes European trade contacts in West Africa encouraged the development of the headwrap, finding that it 'comes into being some time after the start of the European trade expansion in Africa', thence travelling with slavery directly to the USA and that 'by the late eighteenth century, the headwrap was a nationally recognised characteristic feature of African-American women, marking their social and economic status as well as their ethnicity'. Griebel concludes with words that effectively validate the use of dress in this area of research. Moving beyond the descriptive and the historical,

> its use today serves to memorialise those American ancestors who wore the head cloth covering as a mark of servitude to whites and as an emblem of social and economic privation; but modern black women imbue it with an additional symbol of ethnic identity, as a reclamation of their West African heritage.[61]

National identity through clothing

'National' dress carries quite other significances than ethnic or gender-based clothing, for it bears the weight of representation of an entire nation. The term is slippery in meaning and often confused with peasant or ethnic dress but stems from an urban, knowing, intellectualised awareness of the concept of nationhood. Its sources are urban, politicised, elitist and educated. The process of inventing a 'national' dress usually involves the appropriation of peasant styles as romanticised and utopian icons of democratic struggle and national cultural revival. Styles are based on ethnically based elements which are always modified if not indeed artificially invented. These clothes fall into three categories, 'national struggle', 'national cultural revival', and finally 'commodifed national dress' which can be manifested at the same moment. All designs are inevitably romanticisations.

'National struggle' styles

The creation and use of 'national struggle' dress is politically driven and becomes a symbol of the struggle of a minority for national independence from occupying rule. Scottish Highland dress became a national identity symbol during the Jacobite campaigns in the late sixteenth- to eighteenth-century period. Its origins are ancient. A small fragment of third-century tartan found in Falkirk, central Scotland, shows a simple check 'of the type now known as the "Shepherd's Plaid"', woven into two shades of natural wool. This confirms opinion that such cloth carried regional not clan associations. The long belted tartan plaid cut with a length wrapped round the shoulder evolved as Highland peasant dress in the sixteenth–seventeenth centuries. Taken up by clan chiefs and their supporters, it was this, together with a white cockade, or a white rose, that became symbols of Jacobite identity as expressed by the Jacobite poet, Alexander MacDonald:

> Better for men is the Proud Plaid
> Around my shoulder and put under my arm,
> Better than though I would get a coat
> Of the best cloth that comes from England.

After the savage putting down of the Jacobite uprising in 1745, the 'Disclothing Act' was passed in 1747 which outlawed the wearing of Highland dress and imposed harsh punishment – transportation 'to any of His Majesty's plantations beyond the seas, there to remain for the space of seven years'. The Act forbade the wearing on whatever pretext of 'Highland clothes [that is to say] the Plaid, Philabeg, or little kilt, Trowse, Shoulder belts, or any part whatever of what peculiarly belongs to the Highland garb; and that no tartan or party-coloured plaid shall be used for Great Coats or Upper Coats'. Hugh Cheape writes that 'the strictness of the sanction reflected the serious fear and sense of political threat inspired by tartan'.[62] This Act, which outlawed 'national' Highland Scottish dress, was not repealed until 1782. By then neither the kilt nor tartan was seen any longer as symbolic of Jacobite threat.

Betty M. Wass, an African Studies specialist, researched the symbolic use of dress in the course of the colonial struggle for independence, that of Nigeria against the British. Her research showed that since 1940 as the independence movement grew stronger, and especially since Nigeria's independence from Britain in 1960, both men and women in urban, upper-class Yoruba circles increasingly rejected the Western European fashions their families had worn in colonial times. Since 1940, and specifically for special occasions, they chose to wear indigenous Yoruba dress. Wass identifies this practice which was widespread in Nigeria as a reflection of 'a renewed interest in pre-colonial customs and manners' and therefore a 'cultural assertion, the revived appreciation of traditional things'.[63]

Another example of the deliberate use of 'national dress' from the same colonial resistance period and also used as an anti-British propaganda tool, arose during the Greek Cypriot national liberation struggle from 1955–59. The Political Committee of the EOKA Movement (PEKA) organised an economic boycott of imported British and Commonwealth goods. PEKA's most publicised campaign involved the boycott of imported British fashion fabrics and their replacement with locally woven, finely striped, Cypriot peasant *alatziés* silks and cottons, which also supported local industry (Figure 52). PEKA termed this form of national identity dress,

52 Blouse and skirt in local *alatziés* silk, Cyprus, 1955–59

researched by the ethnographer, Eleni Papademetriou, 'passive resistance' clothing. PEKA urged that

> in this different form of our liberation struggle, of equal importance and greatness ... the Greek daughter of Cyprus will take the leading role and set the example ... she must throw her weight into this great battle for Cyprus. To keep her home, her office or her factory clear of all kinds of British made products ... Therefore we propose a decent and proper appearance ... let her prefer local fabrics.

The leading Cypriot fashion journalist Lana Mataff remembers 'Eoka boys' on their motor bikes, some in *alaja* striped cotton shirts, roaring around the Nicosia streets, pulling down the very fashionable imported paper nylon petticoats worn by the trendier teenage girls, to humiliate the wearers and discourage this 'British' fashion trend.[64] Politically correct, indigenous Cypriot fabrics and dresses included handwoven lengths of narrow striped *alaja* cottons and plain-coloured, fine, slubbed Cypriot silks. PEKA, like all such nationalist movements, had a total vision of their ideal woman. They issued a declaration on 18 August 1958 warning patriotic Cypriot women that 'it was a disgrace to see Greek women imitating foreign city women of suspect morality and social learning, as we see them in the cinema, in the way they smoke, gamble, in their shameless way of dress, their manners etc'.[65] Despite these stern strictures however, PEKA wisely made no effort to enforce the wearing of any kind of re-created Greek Cypriot ethnic dress with its fitted long-skirted waistcoat worn over white blouse and baggy trousers, because urban Cypriot women had been steadily abandoning these styles from the 1880s. In Cyprus such a drastic change, however patriotic, would have been one step too far. The compromise solution of wearing fashionable Paris-based styles but made up in *alaja* did, however, catch on. Garments were made either at home or by skilful Cypriot dressmakers. A stranger to Cypriot politics could be forgiven for not recognising that the elegant styles proposed in *The Times of Cyprus* in the 1950s were in fact 'passive resistance' designs.

In this case it was Cypriot women who engineered a pragmatic solution by inventing a compromise national identity style, half liberation struggle and half Paris, through which they felt able to express their EOKA-oriented patriotism, their femininity and their international chic all at the same time.

A reverse situation existed in East and Central Europe after the war. Under Stalin, peasant dress, as representative of the clothing of 'the people' was imposed as a form of 'national' dress across all the satellite states of the Soviet Union. In Poland, for example, where it was falling rapidly into disuse in all but the remoter regions, gaily dressed 'peasants' in 'national' dress were seen on all political demonstrations, on propaganda posters, stamps and on wrapping of exported goods. State Folk Dance companies travelled abroad when so many could not. Polish Communist party-speak of 1952 explained that it was the role of ethnographers 'living in modern democratic Poland, to take up the great work of revaluing, absorbing and directing into proper channels of truly national art, that great but latent store of popular creation'.[66]

'Cultural revival' style

'Cultural revival' styles are concerned with the 'collision of tradition and modernity', and a determination to preserve a national heritage seen as threatened by the processes of industrialisation, and now by globalisation. Wendy Salmond argues that this leads to a 'revival and reassessment of native traditions'.[67]

Once again Scottish dress comes back into focus. In 1782 the Dis-clothing Act was finally repealed. By the early nineteenth century the short kilt had been introduced into the newly formed Scottish regiments of the British army and in addition a new urban, intelligentsia-based national style had been created within the context of 'the Romantic gaze' and the Celtic Revival movement. This movement was not a campaign waged by or on behalf of the vanquished Highland communities. They were by then a powerless minority being forcibly removed from their villages by the Highland Clearances and by poverty which drove them on to emigrant ships or into the industrial cities looking for work. The trigger for the style's aristocratic and bourgeois adoption as a 'national' dress was George IV's coronation visit to Edinburgh in 1822. Advice on suitable dress had been sought from the novelist Walter Scott and, only seventy years after Culloden, clan chiefs and their large retinues lined up in newly invented 'clan' tartans, with full embellishments of sporran and bonnets. The King, as his Indian/Chinese styled Pavilion in Brighton attests, was a man fond of fantasy. Cheape believes his imagination was stirred 'by the Highlander as warrior-hero, a beau-ideal'[68] and so he appeared too, despite his large size, in full fantasy Highland dress. It is this style which has remained as 'national dress' ever since. Trevor-Roper calls it 'a bizarre travesty of Scottish history'.[69] Chapman is clear that

> 'Highland Dress' has always subsequently had a feel either of central inter-
> ference (alien upper middle class, special occasions, choir, Ceilidhs and
> tourists), or of the Scottish diaspora (where ready access to symbols of
> unEnglishness was far more important than any consideration of the genuine
> authenticity of such symbols).[70]

By the late nineteenth century the wearing of 'Highland' dress and tartan fashion fabrics had become a highly commodified 'national' style with expensive outfits and textiles available for middle-class consumers from large and elegant retailing outlets. *Regents House* of Sauchiehall Street, Glasgow, for example, advertised their 'Beautiful clan dress materials' made by Daly and Co. in the catalogue of Glasgow's International Exhibition of 1907 (Figure 53). It is significant that in the 1890s when the Glasgow Four sought inspiration for a new form of Scottish identity design, including dress and embroidery, the last source on their mind seems to have been this commodified, gentrified, sanitised 'national identity' fabric and clothing.

A far more sinister appropriation of rural dress as national cultural symbol was the adoption in Nazi Germany during the 1930s of the German/Austrian peasant dirndl skirt, favoured by Hitler (Figure 54). Worn at 'festivals' and family celebrations, with dark wool or velvet bodice and floral printed apron by girls and young women, it became a symbol of the feminine ideal – Aryan, healthy, 'natural' and preferably blonde. The style became so popular that it was featured in dressmaker pattern books, such as *Der Golden Schnitte*, the Golden Rule, published in Hamburg in

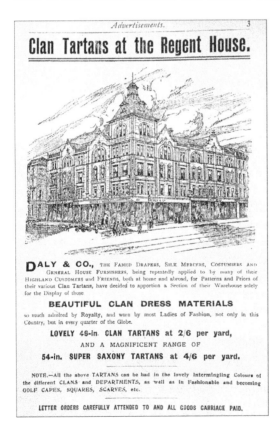

53 Advertisement for clan tartans from *The Regent House*, 199 Sauchiehall Street, Glasgow, 1907

left **54** Hitler with young girl in dirndl dress, late 1930s   *right* **55** Designs for dirndl-styled dresses, late 1930s, Germany

about 1938. Dirndls for all ages are shown, some adapted to a more urbanised style, with the use of country-styled gingham dress instead of skirt, bodice and blouse but still worn with the pinafore as usual (Figure 55).

The use of the Russian peasant head-dress, the *kokoshnik*, is another example of 'cultural revival' national dress, this time from the late nineteenth century, at Salmond's moment of 'collision of tradition and modernity'. Aristocratic and intelligentsia supporters of the Russian arts and crafts and national revival styles turned to their own peasant culture in their search for utopian national symbols. Peasant dress, as we have seen in Chapter 4, was collected, exhibited, used as inspiration for fine art, for the Ballet Russe, within Ivan Bilibin's famous illustrations of Russian folk tales, and taken up in the form of costly fancy dress and formalised national Court styles by the Russian aristocracy. Above all river pearl bedecked *kokoshnik* head-dresses, the head-dresses of married women from the Novgorod, Kourst and Kaluga regions, became significant icons of cultural national identity in late Tsarist Russia, enhanced by exhibitions of the findings of three major ethnographical expeditions to the region between 1902 and 1904.[71] The most famous of all the Tsar's pre-Revolutionary Balls at the Winter Palace in St Petersburg was the 1600–50 Fancy Dress Ball of spring 1903. Whilst men attended in their full dress regimental uniforms, women wore fancified *kokoshniks*. Nadine Wolnar-Larsky's was designed by Diaghilev, made up by Fabergé, and mounted with all the Larsky family jewels[72] (see Figure 15, Chapter 4). Boris Yeltsin was photographed on his election trail in the mid-1990s surrounded by elderly women supporters in reproduction *kokoshniks*. This head-dress has been appropriated for national identity propagandist purposes since the 1870s as much by avant-garde artists and designers as by Tsarist, Communist and now post-Communist political interests.

The Scottish kilt too is currently shifting its cultural and political significance. As political debate about issues of devolution and independence in Scotland have intensified over the last five years, and as Scotland has regained a far greater level of cultural confidence, a new generation of radical Scots have reclaimed the wearing of the kilt from the embrace of nearly two hundred years of establishment, commodified gentrification. The early to mid-nineteenth-century invented styles of day and evening etiquettes of tailored jacket, sporran, *skean-dhu*, knee-length woollen socks and fancy laced, lightweight shoes, have given way to contemporary usage. Now many younger men wear their kilts casually and informally for everyday use, with a heavy buckled belt, T shirt or casual jacket, woolly socks falling around the ankles and heavy soled boots or trainers (Figure 56). Interestingly this is not a style to be seen in the corridors of the new Scottish Parliament in Edinburgh, where sharp suits and bright silk ties are used to promote a sense of urgent modernity. However, significantly in terms of national identity image, the highly charged party political broadcast of the Scottish National Party for the 1997 general election used romanticised William Wallace-style figures with Celtic music. This reclaiming of the kilt must also be in part due to the immense popular success of films such as *Braveheart* and *Rob Roy* and to the popularity of the 'uniform' of the Scottish 'tartan army' of football supporters who cut such a dash in France during the World Cup in the summer of 1998 in their kilts and 'Jimmie bunnits'. The singer Travis and the actor Ewen McGregor represent the sartorial inclinations of this new generation. What we are seeing here is that after nearly two hundred years, a reclamation of the wearing of the kilt is taking place. This is pulling Scottish 'national' dress out of the hands of the old establishment elite. Now young Scotsmen wear their kilts according to their own cultural codes and on their own national identity terms, which includes wearing kilts with T shirts and trainers.

56 Scotsmen in national identity dress,
on a visit to Holland, 1999

For Scottish women, however, here is a problem. For formal occasions, less and less choose to wear the invented Victorian 'tradition' of a white ball dress, worn with silk tartan shoulder sash. For day wear they have to invent their own. Winnie Ewing, long-term Scottish National Party parliamentarian and now the 'mother' of the new Scottish Assembly, for example, wears her own invented 'national' dress. This is an effective combination of a full-length dark tartan skirt worn with navy blue jacket, long matching tartan scarf and bold Celtic or modern brooch.

The English, men and women alike, have no 'national' garment or even accessory to wear *en masse* that could present 'Englishness' or that could in any way carry the same emotional intensity as the kilt, Celtic brooch or *kokoshnik*. When an English image is required for 'national' or official purposes, the figure of *Britannia*, or the Beefeaters of the Tower of London or the Horse Guards in their red uniform and black busbies are produced and worn incongruously by women as well as men. These uniforms are used to create images of 'tradition', 'stability' and 'heritage' but also represent an outdated imperial militarism. A popularist solution to this problem of the lack of English 'national dress' has been the appropriation of the St George's or Union Jack flag. English football supporters have transformed it into a 'garment' by wrapping it around the body like a ceremonial cloak or painting it across their faces.

In Wales the stereotypical national identity garment is the feminine tall steeple hat derived from invented traditions of the early nineteenth century. These were commodified for tourist consumption from the 1840s. The hat, with accompanying red flannel cloak and dark skirt, is still worn for occasional national identity purposes. Welsh men have no Welsh identity garments to choose from.

In the mid-1930s, in a set of designs for children, a pattern book, *Leach-way Fancy Dress for Grown-Ups and Children*, encapsulated the three most popular images of national identity dress from Wales, Scotland and England. Under the byline 'we all know and like these people', Wales was represented by a little girl in a steeple hat and Scotland by a boy in a kilt and black velveteen jacket. England was sweepingly and typically represented by the 'national' figure of *Britannia*, in a white sateen robe with a gilt helmet, gilt sandals, carrying a trident and 'a shield of painted cardboard' featuring the Union Jack (Figure 57).

57 Fancy dress designs for English, Welsh and Scottish 'national dress' for children, about 1935

At the turn of the millennium, an interesting development is taking place in Eire, where the massively successful revival of traditional Irish dancing has led, in the last few years, to a reconsideration of 'traditional' dress for competitive dancing. Over the last one hundred years the design of these short-skirted dance garments has spiralled from plain dresses into an orgy of bright, very large, primary coloured 'Celtic' patterns. These are lovingly appliquéd by mothers on to the stiff, short, full dance skirts. The plain, dark coloured, softer styles of the internationally successful *Riverdance* company were deliberately designed in direct opposition to this tradition and this has led to a reappraisal of these national identity garments. In 1999, Gail Flood, a young fashion designer from Dublin, and a dancer herself, sought a creative contemporary compromise between the two styles and used subtle mixes of dark rich velvets delicately printed in silver or embroidered with bold but simpler patterns of a Celtic base (Plate VII).[73]

'Commodifed national dress'

Recent new themes of research have been examining the globalisation of culture and impact of the global economy on tribal and peasant communities. A much debated theme is the impact of tourism upon ethnic dress and textiles in 'host' communities. Clothes and textiles now flow increasingly from peasant and aboriginal communities into the maw of the global economy. David Howes deals with consuming the 'Other', the reception of 'exotic goods' (peasant, aboriginal) in the West and the consequences of their production upon maker communities. Daniel Miller has been energetically promoting just this kind of consumption-based research within anthropology, noting that approaches had shifted by the 1990s when:

> the study of commodities and consumption was no longer cast as the radical repudiation of primitivist refusal. It has become the mundane acceptance that most peoples who are being studied are either themselves engaged in such activities as a central aspect of their lives or are affected by other people's consumption as mediated through global capitalism.[74]

The commodification of images of 'national dress' for tourist and export consumption is enmeshed within constructions of the varied categories of 'tourist art'. At early stages of tourism, 'host' communities find a market for some of their own 'traditional' artefacts – such as jewellery and textiles. Although the 'destination' use may be unrelated to the original function of the goods, these 'traditional' goods can find an eager market. Eric Cohen defines this as 'complementary commercialisation'. At the next stage 'host' communities produce similar-looking but still locally styled products for direct commercial sale, with no local use in mind. Cohen describes this second process as one of 'encroaching commercialisation, where external forces sponsor the reorientation of a still viable craft for tourism'.[75] The Akha traders selling old and newly made silver jewellery to tourists in the night market at Chiang Mai, in North Thailand, fit this category. Dan Jones, travelling through the area in 1998, sketched the traders dressed in their regional dress to appeal to tourist customers (Plate VIII). The quality of craft skills already begins to diminish at this stage as artefacts are made for sale and not personal or ritual local use. These objects are also made locally, but to order usually for middlemen and designed to suit more clichéd tourist demands. Commercially made raw materials are often used, as is the case with the Mexican blouses described below. At the end of the line, in the third stage of change, entirely new artefacts are produced to suit tourist or export demands. Carol Hendrikson defines these nicely as goods 'whose meanings and uses have generally been reframed … in anticipation of the knowledge, desires and lifestyle of the new consumers'.[76] Sometimes these tourist goods are even made externally and shipped in for sale with no direct cultural relationship to the 'host' community at all. Extreme examples would include 1950s plaster-cast, Welsh lady figures with barometers in their stomachs and cheap plastic Welsh dolls, all labelled 'Foreign Made' yet sold to tourists in Wales (Figure 58).

58 Welsh tourist souvenirs from the 1890s to the 1960s; left to right: plaster barometer figure, 'foreign made', 1950s; a ceramic cruet set, probably 1930s; plastic doll, 1950s; porcelain teacup, 1890s

59 Tourist tea cloths, with national identity dress motifs:
from Alsace, France, 1999; and from Warsaw, Poland, mid-1980s

National dress features strongly in such objects, pandering to tourist notions of 'folk' art and their demands for products of 'use' within their own home cultures. Other examples are easily found such as figures of Spanish dancers on ash trays or made into lamps and costumed 'peasant' dolls found for sale all around the world. These images of 'national' dress are energetically applied to a vast range of tourist souvenir artefacts such as tea cloths (Figure 59), place mats, jewellery, T shirts, ceramics and postcards, etc. The process started from modest mid-nineteenth-century beginnings through the sale, for example, of porcelain teacups for a bourgeois tourist market featuring Welsh ladies (see Figure 58). By the second half of the nineteenth century potteries in Stoke and Glasgow were mass-producing figures of the romanticised Highlander which graced the parlour mantelpieces of many working homes (Figure 60). Today an avalanche of 'national identity dress' products greets the global tourist in remote villages, city tourist shops and the sales outlets of concerned charity organisations such as Oxfam. Celia Lury neatly ranks these objects into three categories, elite 'traveller-objects', then 'tourist-objects' and finally at stage three, 'tripper-objects'.[77]

60 'Burns and his Highland Mary', flat
back, hand painted, Stoke pottery,
about 1850

Two examples of the making up of embroidered 'ethnic' blouses for globalised consumption as 'national dress' will be considered here in support of the approaches of Miller, Howes, Cohen and Hendrikson. In the 1970s Ronald Waterbury studied the making of embroidered blouses for tourists in Oaxaca, Mexico. The ritual function of such garments, heavily embroidered with magico-religious patterns of double-headed birds, animals and stars[78] was related to significant wedding festivities. They were presented to the bride by her future parents-in-law. Waterbury found that local manufacture steeply declined in the 1930s. As urban styles filtered into the region, this indicated, even then, a loss of the ritualised ethnic meaning which had been attached to these garments. Far from dying out, however, a revival occurred in the 1950s, encouraged by Mexican state policies and set in place by local entrepreneurs. The trigger was tourism. By the late 1960s demand for exports became so great that 'the "tourist" demand for hand-embroidered "peasant" garments outstripped the capacity of a traditional, undifferentiated organisation of production to make them'. Manufacturing methods were soon changed to an exploitative, mechanistic, piecework putting out system, whereby each worker undertook one of a set of separated operations instead of making a complete garment. By 1978, 'the largest operator in San Antonio estimated that he put out to about 900 workers in 15 different communities'.[79]

By then the cultural meanings of the blouse had dramatically changed in the eyes of local consumers: 'Almost nobody wears it.' Young San Antonio girls who dance in the local folk dance group 'have to borrow the blouses they perform in, and would never wear one at any other time'.[80] The processes of change finally destroyed any ethnic significance these garments had held for the Oaxaca community. In the end they even lost their regional identification because retailers in the tourist markets piled them up as 'national dress', labelled vaguely as 'Mexican wedding dresses'. Whilst for tourist consumers they become an exotic, utopian souvenir of 'the Other', in reality they have become a homogenised global commodity, answering the desperate needs for work and income for the Oaxaca garment makers, and satisfying the profit demands of local entrepreneurs and their export associates.

In Ceauşescu's Romania in the 1970s and 1980s this same loss of sartorial ethnic identity overtook peasant dress also under pressure of global commerciality, which turned it into a commodified 'national dress' far removed from the actuality of garments worn by surviving peasantry (see Figure 46). The impetus for change here was not tourism but a dictatorial political policy driven originally by Stalin and current all over Eastern and Central Europe after the imposition of Communism. This policy established vast state folk craft organisations, such as UCECOM (the Central Union of Handicraft Cooperatives) in Romania which had a network of 320,000 workers and outworkers by 1979.[81] These functioned basically for political propagandist purposes, to provide the politically correct peasant images already discussed.

Without large-scale tourism there was no mass or eager market for these products. UCECOM recognised as early as 1969 that 'the market in Roumania for its products "was dying"'. Neither town dwellers nor the peasantry – the makers – wanted these products so new consumers had to be found elsewhere. Elsewhere was the global market, 'Australia, the USA, Japan, China and fifty-seven other countries'.[82] But global desires were different and thus hybridised clothes had to be created with a dose of peasant embroidery incorporated within a dash of glitzed-up Western European fashion. Standards of skill were kept high but many entirely new 'fashion' products, such as 'Western' styled dresses, were introduced. Factory-produced, crinkle-crepe cotton muslin, rather than hand-woven linen, became the base fabric, a major change of ethnic character.[83]

Many organisers and designers working in these schemes sincerely tried to keep 'authentic' skills alive and to find work for women in isolated communities. Ironically their efforts at conservation became one further element of the 'undressing'[84] process which has so dramatically transformed the appearance and ethnic identity of the Romanian peasantry, as they discard their indigenous dress and turn to 'world' fashions.

Both in 1970s Oaxaca and Ceaușescu's Romania, commercialism, whether driven by capitalism, or by Communist ideology, became the force that has 'globalised', and thereby displaced, the cultural function of these embroidered peasant blouses and the socio-economic position of their makers.

The reception of foreign clothing into ethnic communities

David Howes, a Canadian anthropologist, emphasises in his study *Cross-Cultural Consumption* that instead of absenting '"foreign" objects [his] focus ... is on their presence and instead of treating cultures as meaningful wholes existing in pristine isolation, the emphasis is on their interface'.[85] Howes is also convinced that notions of an overwhelming global homogenisation or Cocacolarisation of culture are far too simplistic because when goods are transported from one culture to another their function alters.

> Imported objects often become imbued with alternative meanings upon incorporation into a new cultural setting or local reality ... one often finds that the goods have been transformed, at least in part, in accordance with the values of the receiving culture.[86]

He defines this recontextualisation by the culture of reception as 'hybridisation', a term above all others which can be most effectively examined through cloth and clothing. In the global process of hybridisation, goods flow from 'the West' out to the rest of the world where they are absorbed, altered and even resisted, as we have seen. The cultural significance of imported 'Western' clothing within receiver communities has been addressed by Carola Lentz, a German anthropologist. In 1983–85, she studied the clothes of young Indian migrant workers from one village in Ecuador. Almost all of the men from the highland village of Shamanga work in the coastal cities as street traders, or as seasonal workers in the sugar plantations. She proves that the incorporation of modern 'world'[87] clothing styles is 'a central factor in the weighting of city and village life in the survival strategies of the Indians and their struggle for ethnic identity'.[88] One aspect of this fascinating study will serve here to indicate the strength of her findings.

Indian male village dress consists of wide trousers and loose shirts, hand-made from light, white cotton, covered with ponchos of coarse sheep's wool. Their coloured, woven stripes indicated the locality of origin and marital status of the wearer. Young male migrants found that wearing it caused them to be labelled as 'uncivilised animals' by *mestizos* (people of mixed Spanish and Mexican origin) in their villages as well as in the cities and plantations. In order to gain work and to avoid this ethnic discrimination as much as possible, they therefore adopted urban fashions. However, this has far from resolved their problems because the young Indian men, to use David Howes's terms, transformed the meanings of these clothes in accordance with the values of their own receiving culture. These young fashion rebels selected therefore 'only a few particularly obvious aspects from the wide variety of contrasts between foreign dress and their own'. Further, once adopted, items became fossilised and as Lentz explains 'often develop[ed] a remarkable resistance to subsequent shifts in urban fashion'. This ironically negates the purpose of this incorporation process because ethnic differences are still easily seen. Carola Lentz gives many examples of incorporated 'world' dress in the clothes of these young men. One is the cheap, nylon, baseball cap.

> Young migrants like to wear this cap not only on the coast, but, to impress their peers, in the highlands as well … Although unintentional, this cap has become a signal identifying Indian migrants on the coast, as have bell-bottom trousers, nylon shirts with large floral patterns or old-fashioned plastic bags from airlines.

These young Indian men, she concludes, are using 'clothing to protest against the ethnic status quo'.[89] Bogatyrev gives an earlier example. In Russia before the First World War rubber galoshes began to reach the villages. Far from being seen as practical objects in which to walk in the mud, young men wore them as symbols of urban modernity for holidays and in sunny weather. 'The dominant function of the galoshes in the villages was aesthetic', wrote Bogatyrev. 'In galoshes every lad is handsome.'[90] This altered view of such urban products stemmed from their role within the village community as markers of modernity.

Ethnographic approaches to the study of contemporary Western European urban dress

Ethnographic approaches have now in a far wider way also entered assessment of the consequences of change and modernity in contemporary urban society. Chapter 3 has already shown that Beatrix de Wita, a member of the *Centre d'Ethnologie Française*, caused a stir in the French media with her 1988 ethnographic research because her focus was not on a Third World ethnic community but rather on the wealthy bourgeoisie of the western suburbs of Paris. Using her professional ethnographical skills, she examined their ethnic roots, kinship, belief and value systems across three generations, language, coded patterns of gender behaviour, economic setting, education, the material culture of home, clothing and rituals such as the debutante ball. De Wita found that above all never do bourgeois clothes serve to express idiosyncratic behaviour ... The way they dress testifies to the fact that they belong to the milieu ... indeed it may be that the sought-after distinction does not so much operate in relation to the Other; above all it enables the *bourgeoisie* to recognise and to be recognised by her own people.[91]

De Wita tracked, as we have seen, the sartorial indicators of bourgeois belonging amongst a group of young married women, just as Bogatyrev had done in his Moravian–Slovakian project. At around the same date, Yves Delaporte was also using clothing codes and choices to examine the value systems of another social milieu of Paris, but a very different one, that of a group of disadvantaged thirteen- to seventeen-year-old adolescents with no pocket money and no means to buy the fashionable clothes they wanted. The aim behind his study *Fashion and Poverty* was to assess the methods and meanings behind the appropriation of an elite style by a poorer social grouping and their methods of doing this – using substitution, transformation and do-it-yourself making. Still living at home, with their parents only able to buy them the most basic cheap items, they were forced to resort to a range of means of acquiring their sartorial desires. Delaporte looked at how they transformed their clothes and appearance without money. Some boys took illegal under-age work to earn money, a minority thieved and 'some directly stole the goods they desired, especially small sized accessories such as badges, fantasy sunglasses, nail varnish and make-up'. Delaporte found a lot of sharing, borrowing and remaking. Girls cut up cheap grey sweatshirts into top and miniskirt, boys unable to afford fashionable white baseball boots for street wear, painted their regular blue school gym shoes white with their mothers' window cleaning fluids. When John Travolta heeled boots were the vogue, they added heels on to their ordinary shoes themselves. Major items such as coveted leather jackets were borrowed from older relatives or friends, and thus were often too large. Delaporte comments that 'it is possible that leather jackets were stolen in the metro or after concerts'.

He noticed, like de Wita, that accessories carried a heavy weight of coded signals but perhaps more so amongst these adolescents where make-up and accessories take a position of high importance 'precisely because they are the easiest to acquire and bricolage'. Far from wearing the 'imperceptible' make-up of young bourgeois women, he found that girls made mascara out of carbonised matches and red nail varnish from ink from red felt tip pens. If they could not afford tights they dyed their legs with tea. Boys used olive oil from the kitchen instead of hair cream to shape their street-wise hair-styles.

Driving forces were 'above all, rejection of any way of dressing that made them look old (adult)'. However, skills at bricolaging counted for nothing 'if in any way the adapted styles contradict the value systems of the group'. Delaporte believes that this is why punk styles, even though they could have been bricolaged from the cheapest products, were not taken up by these adolescents. 'The ideology behind punk style with which their clothes are associated presents too much of an opposition' to the generally accepted taste patterns which informed the dominant ideology amongst these adolescents.[92]

These two Parisian research projects from the 1980s show that ethnographic interest has extended itself well beyond its old boundaries and is tackling not only the consequences of change but also of modernity in the village, city and global contexts. Miller, as discussed in Chapter 3, has challenged anthropologists to rethink their basic approaches to objects. He argues that 'a new maturity in the anthropological study of consumption may represent a new maturity for the discipline as a whole'.[93]

Aesthetics and ethnographical dress and textiles

The aesthetic 'value' of ethnographic artefacts, including dress from 'Other' cultures and how that should be judged, valued and displayed by ethnographers, has long been a source of contention and remains so today. The distinguished anthropologist Raymond Firth commented that 'anthropologists dealing with iconography often face a problem of categorisation: 'Is this really *art*? ... The concept "art" as such is alien to the practice and presumably the thought of many of the peoples studied by anthropologists, who try to present the people's own iconic classification as a whole.'[94]

As a starting point anthropologists would warn against imposing Western aesthetic values and interpretations on to artefacts made in 'Other' cultures. 'Taking it as axiomatic that people from different cultures live in different visual worlds', Jeremy Coote argues that 'it is a basic task of the anthropology of aesthetics to investigate how people from different cultures "see" the world'.[95]

Verity Wilson in her meticulously researched 1986 study of Chinese dress comments on the lack of critical thought on 'aesthetic features' of Chinese garments. She never once uses the terms 'artists' or 'arts' in relation to these clothes or sartorial traditions. She also scrupulously avoids eulogistic description, even of the Emperor's gorgeous Dragon robes, in order not to impose a Western cultural eye-view on her artefacts. Instead she explains exactly how Court robes, silks and embroideries were designed and made. In the 1750–1800 period, for example, designs for Chinese Court dress for all ranks was officially regulated and controlled in colour, cut and pattern 'by the Board of Rites annually'.[96] She describes the weavers at the Imperial silk workshops straightforwardly as workers and not artists.

More popularly pitched ethnographic dress and textile books, particularly those by textile makers, are far more liberal with aesthetic judgements and with their use of the words 'art' and 'artist', though these are never defined. Titles such as *The Art of Arabian Costume, Art Traditionnel du Japon* and Brandon's *Country Textiles of Japan: the art of Tsutsugaki*, are typical.[97] Brandon is clear that both the makers of elite resist-dyed silks for the Court and the makers of the utilitarian country resist-dyed fabrics are 'skilled urban artisans' and 'anonymous craftsmen'. However, the eulogistic adjectives she uses would never appear in the work of Picton, Barnes or Wilson. She describes these Japanese textiles as 'stunning' works, possessing 'both a strength and beauty of their own', descriptions which by no means advance her argument.

A related debate is also currently still raging, as it has since the days of William Morris, W. R. Lethaby and Walter Crane. If ethnographic artefacts, such as a Huichol woven bag, are now called 'art', what is the distinction between art and craft? Few have ever argued of an Edo period Japanese silk *kosode*, made with its subtle complexity of techniques and with centuries of Buddhist/Shinto poetic meaning hanging from every woven plum blossom and waterfall motif, that it was anything other than an art form. But are Lamarela ikat cloths or Chilkat dancing blankets 'art' too? There has been a view that tools and the functional utensils of domesticity, including textiles and clothing, are straightforwardly material cultural craft forms with only minor decoration. This view maintains that their creators lacked the aesthetic sensibilities which would make them 'art' objects. Others argue that practical tools and textiles have an aesthetic of their own, just as they have cultural meanings of their own, that this is just as 'worthy' to be recognised as 'art' as the finest sculpture or mask.

Where exactly is this invisible line between 'art' and non-art objects to be drawn and who is to draw it? The possible role of anthropologists as arbiters has long been overtaken by the auction houses. Whipped along by the pragmatic reality of the huge prices some ethnographic artefacts now fetch at auctions in the international art world, certain ethnographic objects have long since attained the heights of 'art'. These are not usually textiles, dress or utensils (hence the application of the term 'crafts') but rather 'art' sculptures and masks. It is their enormous monetary value that has validated these artefacts as 'art pieces' alongside the Picassos and Brancusis. Who could thereafter deny them the status of 'art object'? They have become upwardly commodified by sellers, auctioneers and consumers moving from craft to art, from 'savage' to sophisticated.

Some museums and most commercial dealers now use the term 'art' as a norm even for textiles and dress. For many the term here has also become a 'given' usually without even any sense that it needs justifying.

The Museum of Cultural History of the University of California, Los Angeles, held its *Igbo Arts – community and cosmos* exhibition in 1985. Its advertising described every cultural form shown as 'African arts' from body decoration, hand-held objects, house posts, shrine sculptures, masquerade costumery, to dance and music. A Horniman Museum exhibition of 1991, *Yoruba: a celebration of African art*, however, made a clear distinction between art and craft objects. Its 'modern art' section included work from the famous Oshogbo School shown alongside 'Popular Art' – trade signs, posters and naive paintings. Indigo cloth was termed 'craft work'.[98] John Picton called his Barbican Gallery exhibition of 1995 *The Art of African Textiles* and exceptionally and carefully explains his use of the term 'artists' as he applies it to African textile makers.

> While it is taken for granted that art is a form of social practice ... it must be recognised that so much of the literature on African art has been constituted in terms that leave out the voices of the artists, patrons, critics and teachers ... One recognises, of course, that there are artists and Artists ... The convention in Europe is to call the first kind of person a 'craftsperson', but as the work in this exhibition demonstrates, the making of a piece of cloth is never just the making of a piece of cloth: all textile design is shot through with commentary, irony, concept and parody ... In that case it is impossible to sustain the art/craft distinction on the basis of the work itself.

So Picton abandoned the term 'craft' altogether. He adds that his deliberate aim of trying to identify usually anonymous makers (the artists) further confuses the issue because this process problematises 'the Romantic idea of the Artist, even while enabling individual identity to be made apparent'.[99]

Anthropologists have long debated the application of the term 'art' within the field of anthropology. Raymond Firth argued that it is the point at which pattern and shape move from the decorative to the sacred through abstraction of form that turns an object into 'art': 'The ritualization of the abstract constitutes a general principle in the emergence of art from craft.'[100] Edmund Leach's definition was not dissimilar: 'Primitive art is nearly always associated with ambiguous, dangerous, sacred, interesting, mysterious, exciting, or sinful episodes which are restricted to ritual occasions.'[101] Jeremy Coote and Anthony Shelton in their 1992 study *Anthropology, Art and Aesthetics* build on Firth's view, noting that since the 1970s 'there has been a resurgence in the anthropological study of art' though this 'has yet to significantly influence the mainstream, let alone other disciplines – except, perhaps, to a limited extent, art history'.[102]

Whether or not objects are termed 'art' or 'craft', a further divide has opened up related to display methodologies. *Museum International*, summing up the concerns, declared that 'almost nothing displayed in museums was made to be seen in them. Museums provide an experience of most of the world's art and artefacts that does not bear even the remotest resemblance to what their makers intended.'[103] Commercial galleries do not hesitate to display selected artefacts in exactly the same way as Western, classical or oriental art objects, on a pedestal by themselves. Yet this process, whether in the pedagogical and leisure context of a museum or in a commercial gallery, reshapes the artefact's whole *raison d'être*. Jane Young, an anthropologist, adds that artefacts when 'displayed in dramatic fashion on a pedestal [become] divorced from their cultural context, in a manner which suggests that they represent "high art" such as that crafted by artists in mainstream society'. Young decries this as 'denying the location of the object within its manufacturing and use context, and thus losing their fundamental function as indices of cultural practices and values'.[104]

Discussion of the aesthetics of objects is largely avoided in ethnographic studies. Even the otherwise meticulous Bogatyrev hedges around what he terms 'the aesthetic function' of the dress he studied in Moravian Slovakia. He never defines what he means by this term, but states that its importance grows in holiday and ceremonial dress. The most direct comment he makes is that 'attracting attention to a given item [of dress] is one of the basic aspects of the aesthetic function'.[105]

Even when Coote and Shelton encouraged contributions which took this approach, few of their researchers responded, dealing instead with a range of allied but different issues. Ruth Barnes set out to take a cautious art historical approach to her analysis of Melanesian ikat cloth. Stating that her analysis of cloth from Lamarela in Melanesia was an attempt to 'establish a connection between function and design', she commented that 'the patterns and their arrangements ... might be read as art-historical documents'. However, she soon moved on to approaches that were more directly applicable to her interests, for example, Lamarela myths, gender divisions in the community and the delicate balance to be seen in the production of village textiles which epitomises the balance between tradition and change. This is her central theme, one which she sees as 'a characteristic quality and strength of the community'.[106] It is revealing that whilst Coote and Shelton, with no explanation, call these makers of Lamalera ikat cloth a 'group of artists',[107] Barnes never once herself uses the term. The two editors of *Art, Anthropology and Aesthetics* do address the issue in their own contributions. Coote writes that the anthropology of aesthetics

> consists in the comparative study of valued perceptual experience in different
> societies. While our common human physiology no doubt results in our

having universal, generalised responses to certain stimuli, perception is an active and cognitive process in which cultural factors play a dominant role. Perceptions are cultural phenomena ... a society's visual aesthetic is, in its widest sense, the way in which people in that society see.[108]

Shelton uses the Huichols of north-west Mexico as his research base and explains that their 'aesthetics is not just concerned with passive reflection (as in the West) but with an active attitude to maintain or adjust a system of ethics inherited from their ancestral deities, which organises the world and defines appropriate activities and relations within it'.[109] Shelton shows textiles as being central to the aesthetics of 'seeing' other cultures and identifies a set of highly complex social, spiritual and creative forces involved in the creation and consumption of Huichol patterns on bags and bracelets. He writes that 'Huichol aesthetics unlike its Western contemporary counterpart, does not appear to make any distinction between signified and signifier'. Further it not only represents iconic images of deities 'but becomes a manifestation of them'. Thus Huichol woven bags exchanged during marriage ritual 'signify, or actualise, the intangible things that are being exchanged: fertility and regeneration in one cycle, or

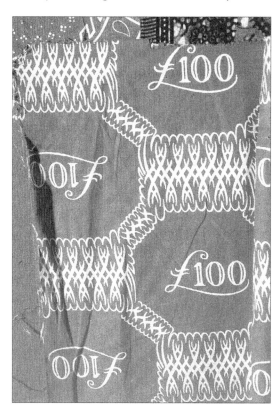

61 Sample of roller printed cotton, featuring pound signs in yellow on dark red ground, Lagos, for Nigerian market, about 1975

productive and reproductive qualities and abilities in the domestic sphere of exchange'.[110]

None of these issues is resolved and perhaps this is as it should be, since so much of the debate on the relationship between art, aesthetics and ethnography runs on parallel rather than converging lines. The development of an aesthetic understanding of the cultural eye-view of the 'Other' is, however, clearly called for. At an exhibition of Nigerian textiles in a polytechnic art gallery in 1978, a lecturer in fine art (a painter) found himself standing in front of one of the African export-print samples. This Yoruba, machine-made, imi wax print featured bright yellow, repeated motifs of £-signs on a plain maroon background, an excellent example of proverbial, auspicious and witty Nigerian 'good luck' imagery (Figure 61). On being asked what he thought of it he exploded with fury: 'I can't think why anyone would put such crap on public view in an art gallery!' Perhaps, here, an open-minded tolerance of the interest and specialisms of others was again required.

Conclusion

Textiles and clothing are proving to be one of the most useful vehicles through which to explore issues of ethnicity, gender and tradition versus modernity and acculturalisation. De Wita's conclusions about the lifestyle of the Paris bourgeoisie today are not so different from those reached by Barnes in the Indonesian village of Lamarela. 'The whole person of the bourgeois', she comments, 'from appearance to voice modulations, is ... imbued with the values and cultural schemata of the group'.[111] Barnes concluded that the ikat cloths she researched revealed 'a characteristic quality and strength of the community'.[112] Though these two communities could not be more socially and culturally different, their use of fabric and clothing as 'indicators of cultural practices and values' is shared.

Through such approaches, ethnographers and anthropologists show how textiles and clothing are invested with symbolic meanings which have to be considered as one whole. Only then can cloth and clothing be fully recognised for what it is – a powerful cultural enforcer, carrier, enhancer, transmitter and celebrator.

Notes

1 With thanks to Susan Michelman and Elizabeth Dell for advice on this chapter.

2 R. A. Schwarz, Uncovering the Secret Vice: towards an anthropology of clothing and adornment, in J. M. Cordwell and R. A. Schwarz, *The Fabrics of Culture* (Mouton, The Hague, 1979), p. 42, quoting Tom Wolfe, The Secret Vice, in idem, *The Kandy-Coloured*

Tangerine-Flake Streamline Baby (Farrar, Straus and Giroux, New York, 1965), pp. 254–261.

3 A. and J. Kuper, *The Social Science Encyclopaedia* (Routledge, London, 1996), p. 25.

4 E. Service, *A Century of Controversy: ethnological issues from 1860–1960* (London, Academic Press, 1985), p. viii, quoting W. Burrow, *Evolution and Society: a study in Victorian social theory* (Cambridge University Press, Cambridge, 1966), p. 80.

5 Ministerie van Nederlandse Cultuur en Nationale Opvoeding, *Love and Marriage: aspects of popular culture in Europe* (Ministerie van Nederlandse Cultuur en Nationale Opvoeding, Antwerp, 1975), p. 11 and p. 16.

6 B. Kirshenblatt-Gimblett, American Jewish Life: ethnograhic approaches to collection, presentation and interpretations in museums, in P. Hall and C. Seemann, *Folk Life and Museums: selected readings* (The American Association for State and Local History, Nashville, 1987), p. 151.

7 A. Shelton, Predicates of Aesthetic Judgement: ontology and value in Huichol material representation, in J. Coote and A. Shelton, *Anthropology, Art and Aesthetics* (Oxford, Clarendon, 1995), p. 241.

8 E. Fél, T. Hofer and C. Csillery, *Hungarian Folk Art* (Budapest, Corvina, 1969), p. 3.

9 Schwarz, Uncovering the Secret Vice, p. 28.

10 With thanks to the library of the Royal Anthropological Institution.

11 R. Barnes, Women as Headhunters: the making and meaning of textiles in a southeast Asian context, in R. Barnes and J. B. Eicher, *Dress and Gender: making and meaning* (Berg, Oxford, 1993), p. 30.

12 Schwarz, Uncovering the Secret Vice, p. 23.

13 Ibid. p. 41 and p. 42, quoting Tom Wolfe, The Secret Vice, pp. 254–261.

14 A. B. Weiner and J. Schneider, *Cloth and the Human Experience* (Smithsonian Institution Press, Washington, 1989), p. 25.

15 Barnes, Women as Headhunters, pp. 30–31, pp. 36–37, p. 41 and p. 42.

16 R. Barnes, Textile Design in Southern Lembata: tradition and change, in Coote and Shelton, *Anthropology, Art and Aesthetics*, p. 160.

17 Ibid. p. 176.

18 P. Bogatyrev, *The Functions of Folk Costume in Moravian Slovakia* (Mouton, The Hague, in the series *Approaches to Semiotics*, ed. A. Sebeok 1971), p. 52 (originally published as vol. 1, *Publications of the Ethnographical Section of Matica Slovenska*, Turçiansky sv. Martin, 1937), p. 13 and p. 21, quoting C. Lévi-Strauss, *Structural Anthropology* (Basic Books, New York, 1963), p. 83.

19 M. E. Roach and J. B. Eicher, *Dress, Adornment and the Social Order* (John Wiley, New York, 1965).

20 Ibid. p. 3.

21 Ibid. pp. 111–117, quoting F. Zweig, *The British Worker* (Penguin, London, 1952), pp. 157–165 and pp. 308–311, from C. C. Hughes, *An Eskimo Village in the Modern World* (Cornell University Press, New York, 1960).

22 Schwarz, Uncovering the Secret Vice, p. 28.

23 Cordwell and Schwarz, *The Fabrics of Culture*, p. 1.

24 Weiner and Schneider, *Cloth and the Human Experience*, p. ix.

25 See for example J. Irwin and K. Brett, *The Origins of Chintz* (HMSO, London, 1970) and J. Goody, *The East in the West* (Cambridge University Press, Cambridge, 1996).

26 The Ashmolean Museum, Dept. of Eastern Art, *Textiles and the Indian Trade*, 22 July–28 September 1997, exhibition leaflet, text by R. Barnes, University of Oxford; see also R. Barnes, *Textiles and the Indian Ocean Trade* (Ashmolean Museum, Oxford, 1997), 2 vols.

27 A. Gell, The Technology of Enchantment and the Enchantment of Technology, in Coote and Shelton, *Anthropology, Art and Aesthetics*, p. 63.

28 J. B. Eicher and B. Sumberg, World Fashion, Ethnic and National Dress, in J. B. Eicher (ed.), *Dress and Ethnicity* (Berg, Oxford, 1995), p. 229.

29 G. Turner, *Hair Embroidery in Siberia and North America* (Pitt Rivers Museum, Oxford, first published in 1954, reprint 1976), p. 48.

30 Ibid. p. 7.

31 D. Crowley and L. Taylor (eds), *The Lost Arts of Europe: the Haslemere Museum collection of European peasant art* (Haslemere Educational Museum, Haslemere, 2000), p. 68.

32 Ibid. p. 25; G. Davies, *The Peasant Arts Museum at Haslemere* (Haslemere Educational Museum, Haslemere, 1910).

33 L. Taylor, State Involvement with Peasant Crafts in East/Central Europe, 1947–97: the cases of Poland and Romania, in T. Harrod (ed.), *Obscure Objects of Desire: reviewing the crafts in the twentieth century* (Crafts Council, London, 1997), p. 59.

34 See P. Lees and L. Taylor, *Yoruba Printed Cottons and the European Connection* (Brighton University, Brighton, 1983). This also juxtaposed 'traditional' Nigerian adire cloth with export prints, drawn from the Brunnschweiler and the late Fred Wilde collections.

35 J. Picton and J. Mack, *African Textiles* (British Museum, London, 1979).

36 J. Picton, *The Art of African Textiles: technology, tradition and lurex* (Lund Humphries, London, 1995), p. 11.

37 Ibid. pp. 25–28.

38 Ibid. p. 29.

39 S. Heath, *A Study of the Contemporary Production, Consumption and Meaning of British Wax Prints Intended for West Africa* (unpublished B.A. Hons, Fashion Textiles Design dissertation, University of Brighton, 1997), p. 34.

40 Barnes and Eicher, *Dress and Gender*, p. 7.

41 Ibid. p. 2.

42 T. Hofer and E. Fél, *Hungarian Folk Art* (Oxford University Press, London, 1979), p. 18.

43 Bogatyrev, *The Functions of Folk Costume in Moravian Slovakia*, p. 75.

44 Ibid. p. 52, quoting A. Václavík, *The Backwoods of Luhaçovice … contributions to the ethnographic borders of Valachia, Slovakia and Hana* (Luhaçovice, 1930), p. 150.

45 Ibid. pp. 72–73.

46 Barnes and Eicher, *Dress and Gender*, p. 5.

47 C. A. Bayley, The Origins of Swadeshi, in A. Appadurai (ed.), *The Social Life of Things: commodities in cultural perspective* (Cambridge University Press, Cambridge, 1986), p. 293.

48 Schneider and Weiner, *Cloth and the Human Experience*, p. 4.

49 Hofer and Fél, *Hungarian Folk Art*, pp. 23–24.

50 Ibid. p. 37.

51 Shelton, Predicates of Aesthetic Judgement, p. 217 and p. 219.

52 J. Eicher, Dress as Expression of Ethnic Identity, in Eicher, *Dress and Ethnicity*, pp. 1–4.

53 Eicher and Sumberg, World Fashion, Ethnic and National Dress, p. 301.

54 Bogatyrev, *The Functions of Folk Costume in Moravian Slovakia*, pp. 96–97.

55 Author's interview with Margozata Kieres, Curator, Beskid Ethnographic Museum, Wisla, September 1994.

56 T. Polhemus and H. Randall, *The Customised Body* (Serpent's Tail, London, 1996), p. 8.

57 See V. Hennessy, *In the Gutter* (Quartet Books, London, 1978).

58 D. Wojcik, *Punk and Neo-tribal Body Art* (University of Mississippi Press, Jackson, 1995), p. 36.

59 H. B. Griebel, The West African Origin of the African-American Headwrap, in Eicher, *Dress and Ethnicity*, p. 120, quoting J. A. Porter, *Modern Negro Art* (Howard University Press, Washington, 1943), p. 4.

60 Ibid. p. 211, quoting S. W. Mintz and R. Price, *The Birth of African-American Culture: an anthropological perspective* (Beacon Press, Boston, 1992), p. 60.

61 Ibid. p. 220, p. 221 and p. 225, quoting L. A. Windley, *Runaway Slave Advertisements: a documentary history from the 1730s to 1790s* (Greenwood Press, Westport, c. 1983), vol. 3, p. 644.

62 H. Cheape, *Tartan and the Highland Habit* (National Museums of Scotland, Edinburgh, 1991), p. 3, p. 25 and p. 32.

63 B. M. Wass, Yoruba Dress in Five Generations of Lagos Family, in Cordwell and Schwarz, *The Fabrics of Culture*, p. 346.

64 Interview with Lana Mataff, June 1997, Nicosia, Cyprus.

65 E. Papademetriou, Liberation Struggle, 1955–59: 'passive resistance' in fashion, an alternative revolution, quoting The Greek Woman, PEKA, Cyprus, 6 June 1958, p. 83 and p. 89, in the Municipal Art Gallery of Nicosia, *Revolutions, 1950–1960–1970* (The Popular Bank Cultural Centre, Nicosia, 1997).

66 The Ethnographic Museum, *Polskie Tanic Ludowe*, Tadeusz Zygler's catalogue introduction (Krakow, 1952), p. 30.

67 W. Salmond, *Arts and Crafts in Late Imperial Russia* (Cambridge University Press, Cambridge, 1996), p. 1.

68 Cheape, *Tartan and the Highland Habit*, p. 50.

69 H. Trevor-Roper, The Invention of Tradition: the Highland tradition of Scotland, in E. Hobsbawm and T. Ranger, *The Invention of Tradition* (Cambridge University Press, Cambridge, 1983), p. 30.

70 M. Chapman, 'Freezing the Frame': dress and ethnicity in Brittany and Gaelic Scotland, in Eicher, *Dress and Ethnicity*, p. 24.

71 F. Gray, T. Verizhnikova and R. Watkinson, *Ivan Bilibin: Russian stories* (University of Brighton, Brighton, 1993), p. 14.

72 L. Taylor, Peasant Embroidery: rural to urban and East to West relationships, 1860–1914 (*Journal of the Decorative Arts Society*, 14, 1990), p. 48, from N. Wolnar-Larsky, *The Russia That I Loved* (Elsie MacSwinney, London, 1937).

73 G. Flood, *An Exploration of the History and Design of Irish Dancing Costumes from 1890–1990* (unpublished B.A. Textiles dissertation, National College of Art and Design, Dublin, 1999).

74 D. Miller, Consumption and Commodities (*Review of Anthropology*, 24, 1995), p. 143.

75 E. Cohen, The Commercialisation of Ethnic Crafts (*Design History*, 3 and 4, 1989), p. 162.

76 C. Hendrikson, Selling Guatelmala: Maya export products in US mail order catalogues, in D. Howes (ed.), *Cross-Cultural Consumption – global markets, local realities* (Routledge, London, 1996), pp. 106–107.

77 C. Lury, The Objects of Travel, in C. Rojek and J. Urry (eds), *Touring Cultures: transformations of travel and theory* (Routledge, London, 1997), pp. 77–80.

78 D. and D. Cordry, *Mexican Indian Costumes* (University of Texas Press, Austin, 1973), p. 141.

79 R. Waterbury, Embroidery for Tourists: a contemporary putting-out system in Oaxaca, Mexico, in Weiner and Schneider, *Cloth and the Human Experience*, p. 265 and p. 253.

80 Ibid. p. 269.

81 Taylor, State Involvement with Peasant Crafts In East/Central Europe, p. 55.

82 Ibid. p. 56, quoting ICECOOP-IMPORT-EXPORT, The Foreign Trade Enterprise of the Handicraft Cooperatives, Roumania (publicity booklet, Bucharest, n.d. [*c*. 1979]).

83 See for example *Portul Românesc*, supplement to *Moda* magazine, UCECOM, Budapest, 1981.

84 A. Gáborján, *Hungarian Peasant Costumes* (Corvina, Budapest, 1988), p. 56.

85 Howes, *Cross-Cultural Consumption*, p. 2.

86 Ibid p. 5.

87 Eicher and Sumberg use the term 'world fashion' in this context, noting that 'designating items as "Western" for people who wear them in other areas of the world, such as Asia and Africa, is inaccurate. Instead, the terms, "world fashion" or "cosmopolitan fashion" are more apt': Eicher and Sumberg, World Fashion, Ethnic and National Dress, p. 297.

88 C. Lentz, Ethnic Conflict and Changing Dress Codes: a case study of an Indian migrant village in Highland Ecuador, in Eicher, *Dress and Ethnicity*, p. 290.

89 Ibid. pp. 270–283.

90 Bogatyrev, *The Functions of Folk Costume in Moravian Slovakia*, p. 100.

91 B. De Wita, *French Bourgeois Culture* (Editions de la Maison des Sciences de l'Homme and Cambridge University Press, Paris and Cambridge, 1994), pp. 66–67.

92 Y. Delaporte, Fashion and Poverty: 'do it yourself' adaptions of style by adolescents in the outskirts of Paris, in *Vêtement et Sociétés*, 2, *Ethnographie* (special number 92–93–95, LXXX, 1983), p. 129, p. 127 and p. 132.

93 Miller, Consumption and Commodities, p. 143 and p. 157.

94 R. Firth, Art and Anthropology, in Coote and Shelton, *Anthropology, Art and Asethetics*, p. 26.

95 Coote and Shelton, *Anthropology, Art and Aesthetic*s, p. 9.

96 V. Wilson, *Chinese Dress* (Victoria and Albert Museum, London, 1986), p. 10 and p. 98.

97 H. Colyer Ross, *The Art of Arabian Costume* (Arabesque Commercial, Fribourg, 1981); S. and D. Buisson, *Art Traditionnel du Japon* (Edita Lausanne, Lausanne, 1983); R. M. Brandon, *Country Textiles of Japan: the art of Tsutsugaki* (Weatherhill, New York, 1986), pp. 3–4 and p. 105.

98 Horniman Museum and Public Park Trust, leaflet for the exhibition *Yoruba: a celebration of African art*, 1991.

99 Picton, *The Art of African Textiles*, p. 13.

100 Firth, *Art and Anthropology*, p. 45.

101 Shelton, Predicates of Aesthetic Judgement, p. 234, quoting E. Leach, Levels of Communication and Problems of Taboo in the Appreciation of Primitive Art, in A. Frost (ed.), *Primitive Art and Society* (Oxford University Press, Oxford, 1973), p. 227.

102 Coote and Shelton, *Anthropology, Art and Aesthetics*, p. 1.

103 *Museum International*, editorial (185, 47, 1, 1995), p. 3.

104 J. Young, 'The Value in Things': recent advances in the study of folklore and folk life, in Hall and Seemann, *Folk Life and Museums*, p. 105.

105 Bogatyrev, *The Functions of Folk Costume in Moravian Slovakia*, p. 75.

106 Barnes, Textile Design in Southern Lembata, p. 162 and p. 176.

107 Coote and Shelton, *Anthropology, Art and Aesthetics*, p. 7.

108 J. Coote, Marvels of Everyday Vision: the anthropology of aesthetics and the cattle-keeping Nilotes, in Coote and Shelton, *Anthropology, Art and Aesthetics*, pp. 247–248.

109 Shelton, Predicates of Aesthetic Judgement, p. 241.

110 Ibid. p. 240.

111 De Wita, *French Bourgeois Culture*, p. 142.

112 Barnes, Textile Design in Southern Lembata, p. 176.

8 ✧ Approaches using oral history

No more elegant tool exists to describe the human condition than the
personal narrative. (Marjorie Shostak)[1]

Introduction

THE essence of oral history is that it can catch hold of people's
memories through their own voices, a quality that is especially relevant
for those marginalised by or excluded from 'big' history. John Tosh
defines oral history as an approach which gives social history 'a human
face' and recovers 'lost areas of human experience'.[2] Joanna Bornat recognises it as 'treating recollection of experience (as opposed only to the
written word) as valid evidence'.[3] Since clothing is such a fundamental
factor within everyday life and human experience, memories of dress should
be able to make significant contributions to the field of oral history
especially when respondents include both the poorest in society as well
as political, social and cultural elites.

The pity is that within oral history work little focus has yet been placed
on recollection of garments and appearance. Recent emphasis has concentrated on themes such as cultural diversity, or post-colonial oral history.
These focuses are recovering the experiences and opinions of conquered
and marginalised peoples whose eye-view was inevitably left out of the
historical records and memoirs of High Commissioners, District Officers
and military officers. Thus imperial memories are now being counterbal-
anced, for example, by the voices of freedom fighters and of peripheral
communities. The South African sociologist, Belinda Bozzoli, stresses the
benefits to be gained from the 'very intimacy and interactiveness' of interviews with people whose voices have never publicly been heard. Working
on an oral history-based project amongst elderly women in Bophuthatswana
in 1981, she wrote that 'these texts have revealed themselves to be

unsurpassed sources for revealing otherwise hidden forms of consciousness'.[4]
Similar projects amongst ethnic minority communities have also given them
a public voice, often for the first time.[5] Rina Benmayor, Blanca Vázquez,
Ana Juarbe and Celia Alvarez interviewed migrant Puerto Rican workers in
the USA, concluding that 'if these stories prepare us, a younger generation
of listeners for anything, it is to understand how a colonised people survive:
through persistence, perseverance, struggle, ingenuity, and hard work'.[6]

Where the boundaries fall between oral history and period social
analysis is another source of debate. The *Mass-Observation* organisation
headed by the anthropologist, Tom Harrison, used interviews and observation notes through which to investigate social and cultural attitudes in
Britain from the late 1930s into the early 1950s. Dorothy Sheridan, the
curator of these archives, which are under her care at the University of
Sussex, draws a clear methodological line between the oral history processes
of using tape recorded and transcribed oral records and that of the (usually
middle-class) participant-observer who keeps a daily account of events and
feelings or who writes down the spoken words of the respondent *in situ*
or by memory afterwards, the methods used by *Mass-Observation* since the
late 1930s. Thus although these archives contain what some today would
describe as 'oral history' recollection, Sheridan argues that these archives
should not be classified as such.[7] Tosh draws another demarcation line,
this time between *oral history* as 'first-hand recollections of people interviewed by a historian' and *oral tradition*, as 'the narratives and descriptions
of people and events in the past which have been handed down by word
of mouth over several generations'. He notes that much of the formal
content of African history is 'recoverable by no other means'.[8]

Recoverable by no other means are unspeakable memories of war and
genocide, such as the slaughter of Armenians of 1915–22 and Jews in the
Second World War. Naomi Rosh White explains that here 'we are confronted … with the problem of how one might convey experiences and
feelings for which words cannot be found'.[9] Kathleen Blee fears that within
oral history a form of selective amnesia often leads to a dangerously cosy
view of the past and warns that the 'muting of past atrocities may be
endemic to the epistemology of oral history'.[10] Many oral historians are
sharply aware of this, particularly, for example, the French documentary
film maker Claude Lanzmann. He distilled 350 hours of filmed testimony
dealing with the processes of the extermination of Jews in Poland in the
Second World War into his devastating television series *Shoah*. It is evident
that he shares Elie Weisel's view that 'a moral society must have the
strength to [hear] these accounts, just as their authors have the strength
to [give] them. For a moral society must remember … If we stop remembering, we stop being.'[11]

In 1994 Steven Spielberg established *The Shoah Visual History Foundation* in the USA to catch the memories of the last survivors of the concentration camps who are now mostly in their seventies and eighties. So far within the *Holocaust Survivor Digital Archival Project*, 50,000 unedited testimonies have been recorded and 100,000 hours of digitised videotaped memories have been collected, all of which will eventually be available through the Cyberspace Museum. This has taken vast funds and the committed work of more than 3500 interviewers and 4000 volunteers.[12] It will provide lasting evidence of the profound historical importance of oral history.

Lanzmann coaxed most of his respondents into allowing him to film them talking of their memories in front of his camera. Many broke down and begged him to turn off the equipment. One respondent defeated him. Itzhak Zuckermann was the second in command of the Jewish Combat Organisation which led the courageous and suicidal 1943 uprising in the Warsaw Ghetto. He is one of the very few survivors of the uprising. When interviewed Zuckermann could say only two things, that he had started drinking once the war ended and that 'if you licked my heart, it would poison you'.[13]

'Big' history has avoided dealing with such intense personal emotion whereas many proselytisers of oral history see its ability to unleash human feelings as one of its great qualities. Ralph Samuel and Paul Thompson recognised that 'like the novelist, we introduce the emotionality, the fears, the fantasies carried by the metaphors of memory, which historians have been so anxious to write out of their formal accounts'.[14]

Oral history is increasingly used within documentary film making because of the 'potential synergy' of these two research methods. The American historian and film maker, Dan Snipe, comments that

> visual oral history can help lead historians away from the limited conception of moving images as merely an alternative form evoking, communicating, or translating written history. Oral history can demonstrate the power of film and video as evidence while moving images provide a new level of evidence for oral history.[15]

In all of this, recollections of clothing and their cultural meanings have so far rarely been sought. Indeed even the idea that memory of clothing can be used as a primary research tool in oral history has largely been overlooked. Yet many dress historians share the same basic intent as oral historians – to unearth processes of socio-cultural awareness and difference. There is potential synergy here too. The work of Elizabeth Roberts, Director of the Centre for North-West Regional Studies at Lancaster University, is proof of this. Her 1995 study, *Women and Families: an oral history 1940–1970* is centred on assessment of 'attitudes, behaviour and aspects of everyday life'.[16] In examining through oral history interview the social and cultural changes in the lives of working-class British women she makes only brief use of clothing memories. When she does use them, however, they prove to be significant. They provided her, for example, with a note of realism to set against popularly repeated theories of massive increases in working-class consumer spending in the mid-1950s. She notes that even though 'more and more brides married in white' and 'thus yet another middle-class Victorian fashion ... spread down the social scale', expenditure was 'still limited'.[17]

Cheryl Buckley, albeit working on a far more modest scale than Roberts, understands well the significance of clothing memories. Her focus was on home dressmaking. Far from being merely of passing importance, she found that the value of these home-made garments lies in the fact that 'making clothes marked out different stages of [women's] lives; connecting feelings and memories with family and friends. It related intimately to specific places and locations in which they lived, rather than just the chronological, temporal sequence of their lives.'[18] Buckley found that

> older women recalling their lives in the 1920s and 1930s ... could readily describe those events for which clothes held special significance such as what they wore for particular dances, which colour shades their going-away outfits were in, and how their husbands dressed when they first went out together.[19]

Little dress-based oral history research of the quality of Roberts's and Buckley's work has been undertaken. Of all the approaches to dress history cited in this book, the use of oral history is the least developed and practised, though dress historians do recognise its value. Museum curators have always sought out the memories of donors of clothing and all are skilled at such questioning. Few, unfortunately, have the time to undertake in-depth recorded enquiries and little is asked beyond the bare bones of facts about sources, dates and ownership of garments. When probing goes deeper, responses can immediately highlight the cultural significance of a garment to the wearer and why they wish to donate it to a museum collection. In an interview at Brighton Museum in the mid-1970s, the very respectable woman donor of a black lace, mid-1950s nylon corselette, suddenly commented 'my husband and I had such fun with that corset'. Another gave a pretty puff-skirted white nylon and black lace, ready-to-wear dress of about 1958. This had been her first 'grown-up' party dress and she fondly remembered the occasions on which she had worn it.[20] Now there are hopes that donors' object-related memories will be taped or videoed with a view to providing both museums and future researchers with unprecedented material cultural information.

Where dress and clothing do creep into oral history publications, especially community publications, methods are often haphazard, with weak referencing and even less interpretation. *Costume*, the journal of the Costume Society, has, however, featured 'hidden from history' memories since its inception. Most are based on autobiographical written text, but when oral history recollection is included it always provides fresh information. John Reed-Crawford, a couture milliner who set up his own establishment in London in 1954, provided useful memories of the role of the British consumer as a damper on design creativity at this most elite level of fashion manufacture. Confirming the dominating style influence exerted over the creativity of London couturiers by their conventional clients, he commented 'we basically dealt with the gentry. That was always a bit difficult for me, because I wanted to be in the avant-garde of fashion. And of course one had to temper one's products as the French do.'[21]

At the opposite end of the social system, *Costume* featured a detailed account of the memories of Mrs Turner, a corsetière, who worked at, and finally bought out, a corset making business with branches across Lancashire, in Nelson, Colne, Accrington, Burnley and Clitheroe. She remembered that in the early 1920s her customers

> didn't wash corsets, year in, year out. We used to repair them and you can imagine what they were like when they'd been worn for five year. Staff at the corsètieres used to sprinkle them with a carbolic solution in an effort to clean them – which made them literally feel sick … some were cleaned in a local laundry. I'd pick them up in the paper they'd been laid out on, take them straight round to the laundry and hand them in saying 'Mind, they are not mine'.[22]

Even in the traumas of Holocaust testimony, memories of clothing carry an intense significance. Many survivors talked of the Nazis' systematic methods of deliberately degrading and humiliating their victims in the extermination camps. In Auschwitz, Primo Levi's Italian friend, Steinlauf, berated him for not caring any longer about his clothing and appearance.

> We are slaves deprived of every right, exposed to every insult, condemned to certain death, but we possess one power, and we must defend it with all our strength for it is the last – the power to refuse our consent. So we must certainly wash our faces without soap in dirty water and dry ourselves on our jackets. We must polish our shoes, not because regulation states it, but for dignity and propriety … to remain alive, not to begin to die.[23]

Samuel was convinced that the multivalent layers of memory that can be reached through oral history clarify 'the individuality of each life story … a vital document to the construction of consciousness, emphasising both the variety of experience in any social group, and also how each individual story draws on a common culture: a defiance of the rigid categorisation of private and public just as of memory and reality'.[24]

Historiography of oral history

Using interview as a method of seeking out individual opinion and experience was pioneered by Henry Mayhew, Charles Booth and Fabian women researchers, such as Maud Pember Reeves, in the 1848–1913 period. In their investigations into poverty in London,[25] clothing featured constantly in responses to interviews. Looking decent was the last psychological bulwark against the horrors of slipping into destitution and public humiliation. Memories of the struggle to obtain, and then maintain, a respectable outward public appearance led mothers and fathers to struggle against all the odds to keep their families decently dressed. Examples from Mayhew's work illustrate this desperation, which remained a constant feature in poor communities right up to the 1950s and which reappears over and over again in recorded memories.

In Letter VI published in the *Morning Chronicle* on 6 November 1849, Mayhew wrote of a meeting he arranged with twenty-nine needlewomen and slop-workers in the East End of London. Both the emotional reactions of the interviewer (Mayhew) and the opinions of the needlewomen themselves survive the passage of one hundred years with the most moving clarity. Mayhew's own best efforts at objectivity were overwhelmed when he entered the meeting room.

> Never in all history was such a sight seen or such tales heard. There in the dim haze of the large bare room in which they met, sat women and girls, some with babies suckling at their breasts – others in rags – and even these borrowed, in order that they might come and tell their misery to the world.

Mayhew explained to his readers that the needlewomen were aware that two reporters were sitting behind a screen taking their words down verbatim. Mayhew discovered that out of the twenty-nine women present, twenty-six 'had parted with their underclothing to the pawnbroker'. Asked whether they had any other clothes than the ones they sat in, 'one and all declared they had not'. One woman getting to her feet declared, 'I have no frock, because I had to leave it in pawn for sixpence.' Another stated, 'I have been forced to sit up this afternoon and put many a patch on this old frock, for the purpose of making my appearance here this evening.'[26]

During the late 1930s interviews and observation were again used by *Mass-Observation*, whose original aim was 'to produce "an anthropology of ourselves", to discover and publicise how working-class people really felt and behaved at work and at play'.[27] Clothes again feature as an occasional analytical tool. Answering questions about the extent of her wardrobe, the notated words of a working-class woman from Bolton, married and with eight children, survive vividly.

> I've got this dress – an' another old one. I have one coat that's worth wearing – I got that from the Minister's wife – it's black, that's a good colour. Also I've got a change of underclothes – mind it's just a change – an' when I get them given they got to be altered – an I keeps washin' 'em. All the kiddies the same. I cuts an' contrives – They've got Sunday clothes mind – for the sermons – I'm paying for them.[28]

As technology improved, these methods paved the way for formalised processes of recording of memory.

University-, community- and museum-based research

With the widespread availability of cheaper and smaller tape recorders, oral history activities escalated in Britain in the 1950s and 1960s in universities, museums, libraries and on radio. In 1951, the School of Scottish Studies at the University of Edinburgh was set up and by 1969 staff had put together 3000 tapes. The Institute of Dialect and Folk Life Studies at the University of Leeds and the Welsh Folk Museum in Cardiff were also by then committedly recording a wide range of memories of vernacular culture such as patterns of Welsh agriculture, folklore and folksong and dialect speech, where clothing makes only an indirect contribution.[29] The British Institute of Recorded Sound opened in 1955.

From the late 1960s, on both sides of the Atlantic, left-wing interest in working-class history gave oral history a massive injection of new energy. Tosh describes the field as 'a movement', one which in Britain is 'dominated by social historians whose interest is in many cases sustained by an active socialist commitment, evident in their house journal *Oral History*'.[30] The Canadian historian Joan Sangster is clear that 'many of us originally turned to oral history as a methodology with the radical and democratic potential to reclaim the history of ordinary people and raise working-class and women's consciousness'.[31] Staff at the 'new' universities of Kent and Essex in Britain made important pioneering contributions. Paul Thompson of the Department of Sociology at Essex University has spent a lifetime successfully developing oral history in Britain as did the late Raphael Samuel of Ruskin College, who died in 1996. He was a founder member of the History Workshop movement. In December 1969, Thompson organised the first conference of British oral historians. The first international conference was held ten years later.

The American historian Allan Nevins of Columbia University is named in the USA as 'the Father of Modern Oral History'. He worked on his first interview in 1948 and that year set up the Oral History Collection of Columbia University in New York City. By 1990 this contained over 6000 taped interviews and 60,000 pages of transcript[32] dealing with the lives of both working people and of the political and social elite of the USA. Thus oral history has long established its research credibility in the USA.

Oral historians enjoy the challenge their field represents to conventional 'big' history. Tosh sees it as 'a democratic alternative, challenging the monopoly of an academic elite' and offering 'ordinary' people 'a role in the *production* of historical knowledge with important political implications'.[33] Anna Davin, Elizabeth Roberts, Ann Oakley and Leonora Davidoff are amongst a group of women who pioneered work on women's memories and on feminist approaches.

Progress has been phenomenal. The British Institute of Recorded Sound has blossomed into the National Sound Archive of the British Library, a vast and internationally famous oral history archive with a million discs, 160,000 tapes and now videos and laser discs. Current major projects include *The National Life Story Collection* (established by Robert Perks in 1988), *The Living Memory of the Jewish Community* and *Artists' Lives*, a series of interviews with British visual artists which has been run since 1990 in association with the Tate Gallery Archive. Other schemes include *Architects Lives*, *Lives in Steel*, *Retail Lives*, *Legal Lives*, linked to the project *City Lives*, and *Forgotten Feminism*.[34] Financial support has to be found for all such projects and as yet no specific consideration has been given to recording memories about personal clothing or professional fashion interests. Unfortunately no project is in hand to focus on *Fashion Lives*.

Community-based oral history and publishing

In Britain, oral history work ran parallel with the birth of community publishing in the early 1970s. In many cases these organisations were related to university work through the involvement of lecturers in action groups within their own communities. The basic aim was to 'enable people to gain control over their day to day lives'.[35] Thus, for example, in Brighton (successful) community action to turn a derelict early nineteenth-century spa building into a community nursery school rather than a private casino, led to the birth of Queenspark Books in 1974. Early written memoirs included *Daisy Noakes, The Town Beehive – a young girl's lot, Brighton 1910–1934*, first published in 1975. *My First Job: Greenwich pensioners' memories of starting work* was also typical of community oral history. This was compiled in 1984 by local theatre and reminiscence groups working with staff from Essex University to capture the memories of London pensioners. The introduction indicates a non-elitist intent to produce recollection in a form that was 'lively and easy to read, conversational in style ... told in the original words, from transcribed tapes, or pensioners' written contributions'.[36]

Other early community publishing groups which used both oral and written sources for their texts included Centreprise Hackney, where Anna Davin was involved in *The People's Autobiography of Hackney* in the 1970s,[37] and Stepney Books based in Tower Hamlets, whose publications in 1975 included *Ain't It Grand or 'This was Stepney'*, the interwar childhood and adolescent memories of Jim Wolveridge. During the war he worked 'at a small arms factory at Perivale and earned the fantastic wage of £3 10 shillings a week, and a pound a week overtime. After a few weeks I bought the new suit I'd always craved for, and a new tie. Then I went to the West End and squeezed into a front seat at the Windmill, gawd I was a flash johnnie.'[38] By 1988 over 25 groups had linked together to form the National Federation of Worker Writers Movement.[39] All were short of funding. By 1966 the US Oral History Society had also successfully drawn in

> teachers, librarians, archivists, local historians, folklorists, anthropologists, government officials, journalists, and numerous institutions and organisations such as volunteer and professional groups, museums, societies, schools and colleges, business corporations, public and private agencies, and historical organisations of every size.[40]

What is disappointingly evident in all this activity is a lack of interest in the specific recording of clothing memory. Reference to clothing in its personal and domestic setting is especially marginalised. Interviewees and groups acknowledge now that it had not occurred to them deliberately to ask questions about clothing.

Clothing references do crop up occasionally where recorded industrial memory relates to local garment or textile manufacture. Thus a project organised by the Leicester Oral History Archive in preparation for the exhibition *Knitting by Machine* (which marked the 400th anniversary of the invention of the first knitting machine in 1589) resulted in the recording of about forty hours of memories of ex-hosiery workers. Extracts of these were published in Geoffrey Bowles and Siobhan Kirrane's study *Knitting Together: memories of the Leicestershire hosiery industry*[41] and include many references to the making and consuming of clothing. Daisy Ward was a young machine knitter, working six days a week at F. J. Ellis in the late 1920s. She remembered that after a 'marvellous' week, she could earn £2 5s. She gave one pound to her mother and shopped very carefully for her own clothing. She favoured *Marks and Spencer's* where she could 'get a nice skirt for 4s 11d in the old days; it was nothing over five shillings in *Marks and Spencer's*. For ten shillings I was very well dressed, and I could put a bit by to save and, believe me, I was very well off.'[42]

Otherwise comment on clothing only creeps in here and there, more often in the memories of women than of men and more often when the interviews were conducted by women. However, when clothing memories surface they are often startling in their wider social significance. Stepney Books, for example, published the memories of Annie Barnes, an East End suffragette and Labour Party councillor in poverty-stricken Stepney. Annie Barnes worked with the socialist George Lansbury whom she much admired. Lansbury told her of one experience when canvassing as a local council candidate in a very poor area of Bow in the early 1920s.

> He knocked on the door of one house in Devons Road. He was young, full of beans, just starting out in politics. A woman came to the door. She had a sack over her, with a hole for her head and two for her arms. He could hardly believe his eyes. He was so shocked. When she understood what he'd come for she said, 'Canvassing! Do you expect us to bother about anything like that? Everything is in the pawnshop. We've got no money and we're starving.' ... He was so struck he couldn't say anything to her and he went away ... He went to the pawnshop and ordered the things to be sent round to her ... After that he joined the Independent Labour Party and fought for the people. The Lansbury's made Poplar. They fought and fought, the whole family.[43]

Oral history in museums

Following the setting up of the Department of Sound Records at the Imperial War Museum in 1972[44] many museums have undertaken oral history projects. Taped memories are now increasingly used within exhibitions though rarely in fashion and clothing displays. Policy at the Museum of London is in advance of most. The museum hopes to develop a gallery dedicated specifically to the use of oral history. This *Voices Gallery* will offer a new view of hidden history through the use of taped personal interviews supported by photographs, slides and an Internet facility. The Museum selects its major oral history projects in relation to the museum's current exhibitions. Thus Rory O'Connell, Curator of Oral History and Contemporary Collecting, who runs this innovative oral history unit, comments that oral history 'has been almost entirely geared to our exhibition programme which has not featured clothing or related industries very highly'.

When funding became available, however, through the Manpower Services Commission in 1989, seventeen interviews were recorded with the staff of the London couturier, Hardy Amies, including the designer himself, his dressmakers, sales people and the cleaner. O'Connell comments that focus was not only on recording the working practices of this most famous of post-war London fashion houses *per se* but was also 'an experiment in how a museum can document a particular workplace in detail'. The project ended when the funding ended. The tapes were transcribed and although not published are available for public consultation.[45]

Manpower Services Commission funding, which temporarily but effectively boosted oral history activity in Britain in the mid–late 1980s, was also used at the Macclesfield Silk Museum in the late 1980s to fund a project to record family and working lives in relation to the silk weaving industry. Extracts have been used since in exhibition texts and museum publications.[46] The same funding briefly helped support the Leicester Oral History Archives, amongst others.

Recording and transcribing tapes is a skilled, time-consuming and costly process and the current under-funding of museums in Britain has undoubtedly been a force against further progress. It is also evident that oral history projects centred on dress are rarely recognised in museums as worthy of support from their own meagre finances. When funding becomes available, however, the story is different because public interest, certainly amongst women, is strong. In the 1989–95 period many museums set about involving their local communities in activities to mark the fiftieth anniversary of the Second World War. These included oral history schemes where both interviewers and respondents were women. Given free rein, talk was often of clothes: their own clothes, the struggles to dress their families and the whole issue of the morality of fashion in wartime. One innovative scheme was to include tapes and transcribed texts of clothing memories within the Imperial War Museum's exhibition of 1997, *Forties Fashion and the New Look*. Such inclusion of oral history is happily becoming ever more popular, both with museum authorities, curators and with the visiting public.

A typical project was based at Warwickshire Museum in 1989. Both written and spoken memories of wartime clothing were collected from over forty women respondents and published in a small but highly informative booklet, *We Wore What We'd Got*. A much repeated memory was the positive social attitude attached to the remaking of clothing throughout the war. One woman remembered recycling her absent husband's civilian clothes. She went to meet him when he came home on leave. 'I met him at the station in his pants (a bit of lace had made them into knickers), his shirt as a blouse, his pyjama jacket as a blazer and a skirt made from a bleached foodstuff bag and a belt made from cellophane. And he never even noticed.' Another commented that 'mending took up a lot of women's spare time, and a patch was an honourable badge in those days'. The interviews threw up clear differences of attitude to looking stylish during the war. Whilst some felt 'there were more important things to worry about than what you were going to wear tomorrow', another stated firmly that 'going to town every day to work in an office where you were coming into contact with other people, you did make an effort – you had to make an effort'.[47]

None of the themes highlighted by these commemorative projects are new to dress history. They have, however, added a large injection of fresh detail and depth of personal information before the memories of this generation are lost for ever. *We Wore What We'd Got* is typical of popular publications produced by museums and community groups. No attempt at analysis is made beyond grouping the testimonies into chapter headings such as 'Work', 'Weddings' and 'Dressing-up'.

In many of these small museum publications, formal referencing systems such as those used by Elizabeth Roberts are very evidently absent. They seem to be seen as forms of 'popular' history and function outside the formal 'academic' world. Detailed referencing is probably seen as unnecessary. Whilst sympathising with the need for readability, it seems a pity that the provenance of many detailed historical findings is blurred by this vagueness. Despite this weakness, oral history is now safely anchored in the museum world. Indeed Rory O'Connell is convinced that museum authorities now recognise that the general public are being positively drawn into exhibitions which specifically use oral history and are becoming anxious to support it.[48] Its passage into academia has been far more problematic. It was not welcomed in history corridors where suspicion of both its politics and its community links was strong. Tosh noted that in the mid-1980s 'the mainstream of the historical profession remains sceptical and is often not prepared to enter into discussion about the actual merits and drawbacks of oral research'.[49] In 1994 Samuel continued to criticise 'big' history's 'very hierarchical view of the constitution of knowledge'. He listed the many historians 'who despised oral history as dubious' and attacked 'the heavyweights of the profession', who function from 'the unspoken assumption that knowledge filters downwards'.[50]

Areas of interest to oral historians: working-class life

As we have seen, oral history interest has long been firmly set on recording urban and rural working-class history including factory and craft working skills and patterns of manufacture. Many activists, according to Tosh, were driven by a determination that 'the community should discover its own history and develop its social identity free from patronising assumptions of

conventional historical wisdom'.[51] Perhaps because interviewers were often
men, male occupations caught most attention. In the USA by the mid-1950s
Columbia University was already recording the working lives of men in the
Texas petroleum industry, the Ford Motor company and in the Weyerhaeuser
Timber Co.[52] When projects were based on textile and clothing industries,
where women formed, and still form, a high percentage of the workforce,
then aspects of women's work and lives were finally examined. This escalated
as more women became active in oral history work.

One such long-term project at the University of Essex centred on the
significant, local, wholesale manufacture of menswear, a trade that died
out through the 1930s. In 1986 Belinda Westover examined the 1880–1918
period. In 1994 Andrew Phillips researched the 1918–50 period, building
on his belief that 'oral history can shed most light on the social milieu
in which the inter-war industry functioned, its conditions of employment
and how the largely female workforce perceived and interpreted their jobs'.
Aware that judgements should 'not be based on today's standards of living
or social expectations', and somewhat to his own surprise, the answers he
received during his interviews led him to conclude that 'the traditional
view that the rag trade meant unremitting and unhappy labour, a down-
trodden workforce exploited by an authoritarian management, perhaps
needs re-examining'. He even ended his article with the following memory
of a factory worker, 'you could walk through any of those rooms with the
girls in and they were always singing. On a pound a week at that! Always
singing.' In passing, he also discovered that many workers made their own
clothes 'benefiting from factory oddments sold to them cheaply'.[53] Phillips's
focus did not lead him to follow up this revealing fact.

Like Andrew Phillips, Naila Kabeer, a social scientist from the Institute
of Development Studies at the University of Sussex, has also used oral
history as a means of exploring the myths and realities that beset our
understanding of women working in garment manufacturing trades. 'Personal testimonies', she affirms, 'can enrich social science analysis by
providing us with access to the reflections and reactions of social actors
who are directly involved in, and affected by, the structures of oppression'.
Kabeer is careful to explain, however, that she too, like Phillips, has not
relied on oral interview alone but has located her interviewees 'in what I
could find out under the context of their lives'. Her focus is a comparison
of the lives and cultural setting of Bangladeshi women who work in the
Dhaka and East End of London garment manufacturing industries. Kabeer
probes the striking fact that in Bangladesh these women workers are very
publicly evident as they travel to and from their factory-based employment,
whilst in London, because their clothing manufacture work is home-based,
they are far less visible.

Kabeer's carefully systematic study covers the history of the garment trades in both places, emigration into London and then the changing social contexts of both Muslim communities in Dhaka and Tower Hamlets, in London's East End. One of the main focuses of her study is the issue of purdah in the context of current Bangladeshi community debates about the propriety or impropriety of respectable Muslim women undertaking such work. In Dhaka, where garment making is now heavily reliant on female labour, factories have been built in residential areas rather than industrial ones and managers are 'keen to maintain discipline and propriety'. All of this is to encourage women workers, despite the rules of purdah, to feel able to take up work respectably even though it involves leaving home and undertaking a very public journey to and from work. Hena, working in a factory in Dhaka and defending public criticism of her fellow women workers, commented to Kabeer that 'people say that the garments have made girls shameless. But they have the wrong idea. The girls are helping their families by working there. That is courage, not shamelessness.' Kabeer explains that both in Bangladesh and London, these women workers, far from rejecting purdah, were attempting 'to reinterpret it'.

In London, many Bangladeshi women, mostly having arrived a good ten or so years after their husbands, face a closer interpretation of purdah within the close immigrant community of Tower Hamlets, beset as it is by racism, poverty and lack of opportunity. Kabeer, in exposing many myths, makes it clear that there is a need to move beyond generalisations about the position of Asian women in the British context which are 'read' off from a fairly simplified representation of a shared set of restrictions to a more situated understanding of the Bangladeshi community in London's East End. Here almost all the women garment workers work from home, undertaking largely unskilled, simple and badly paid tasks. Kabeer uses interviews to expose the complex cultural nuances they face even though their jobs are home-based. Clothes, as such a public vehicle for the upholding of purdah, are inevitably discussed. One woman living in Tower Hamlets recounts that she

> wore *burkas* in Bangladesh. Here we have cardigans, coats and jumpers, they serve the same purpose as *burkah*. There aren't coats and jackets in Bangladesh, that is why they need to wear the *burkah*. There is one purdah, but people have created many branches of it. For many people, it is believing in God in your heart ... We are breaking purdah even though we may work at home, because we still have to go to the doctor and shopping ... We have never observed purdah the way it was in the very beginning. It is the heart that matters.

Kabeer concludes that there is a very real difference in the situation of the two groups. The London women workers, coming hopefully to London expecting a better life and greater opportunities, find themselves amongst other 'socially excluded' ethnic minority groups. Bangladeshi women have to accept the 'discarded status' of their home-working jobs, jobs that no one else will do. Kabeer maintains that their work is symbolic of the 'excluded status of those who performed them'. The contrast with Dhaka, despite the impoverishment of Bangladesh, could not be greater. There, far from seeing themselves as badly paid sweated slaves, women factory workers 'by contrast aspired to such employment because it moved them from their position at the margins of the labour market to a more central, better paid and more visible place in the economy. Their jobs can be seen as an expression of a new, if problematic, inclusion.'[54]

Kabeer does make use of dress in her study, but it is evident that in most recorded social history-oriented interviews, clothes are only discussed in detail if they are unusually styled in some way or made under unusual circumstances, such as in wartime. Detailed recollections of the specific clothes of ordinary working-class women are therefore rare whilst memories of idiosyncratic working uniforms, such as the trousered pit girls of Wigan or the varied styles of occupational dress worn by fish sellers from Cornwall to Scotland, have survived.[55] Thus the recollections of the son of a fish seller from Newhaven were carefully taken down.

> When my mother went out w' the creel around the the 1890s ... [she wore] a light-coloured shirt and a dark striped skirt ... with a pinny kirtled up over it and wide petticoats. She'd warm stockings too and, over the top of everything else, a dark blue overall.[56]

Ethnic minority research

From the 1950s onwards oral historians have been active in giving voice to marginalised and underprivileged ethnic minorities. In the USA, from the 1960s interest in issues such as the civil rights movement and the present and past of the American Indian was already clear. Willa K. Blum, of the University of California in Berkeley, wrote in 1972 of the ambitious and pioneering *Doris Duke Oral History Project* 'established to give the American Indian an opportunity to express his interpretation of American History and to provide archives of oral history for scholarly use'.[57] Within this context projects which recognise the cultural importance of clothing and domestic textile artefacts as carriers of ethnic identity have been set up mostly by women. One such was an *Oral Traditions Project* in central Pennsylvania which started as part of the Union County's observance of the 1976 Bicentennial. This community was drawn from a variety of ethnic roots, including Polish, Welsh, English and German. Here again, when women were put together, they chose to talk about their home life and, in this case, their quilt-making traditions. 'Nearly 2000 bedcovers were brought to be assessed and owners and quiltmakers were interviewed at length about their skills and attitudes towards quilting.' Oral testimony, as well as photographs, inventories and the quilts themselves, provided evidence for the longevity and dissemination of patterns and techniques and more fully explained 'the cultural and domestic setting'.[58]

The Museum of London collected one hundred hours of tapes from ethnic minority groups in London with interviews undertaken in Urdu and Turkish, amongst other languages, as part of its 1993, *Peopling of London* exhibition. This 'cultural diversity' project continues.[59]

Elite histories

Anthony Seldon and Joanna Pappworth define an elite respondent as 'someone of interest because of the position he or she holds, rather than because he or she is representative or typical of a group'. The recording of such memories has been practised since such a process was first possible, although Seldon and Pappworth still felt in 1983 that such elite oral history was neglected.[60] Nearly twenty years later, the use of elite oral history has become an expected methodology for biographies and period monographs where participants still survive.

In costume museums, however, much of this remains rare. Joanna Marschner, Assistant Curator of Royal Historic Palaces, and Amy de la Haye, curator of twentieth-century dress at the Victoria and Albert Museum until 1998, both acknowledge the dearth of formally recorded oral history related to the clothing of their elite donors. Both stress how time-consuming the recording process is because the need to build up a sense of trust with respondents takes time. Both also emphasised the wary approach of socially elite women over divulging personal details about their lives and their clothes. Marschner noted their expectation of high levels of discretion.[61] Very unusually Stanley Garfinckel had been progressing a major oral history project on the work of the House of Christian Dior. Over a ten-year period he had amassed hours of tapes and video recordings of Dior's clients, friends and staff, prior to a planned publication. Following his death in 1997, these have been placed in the library of Kent State University, USA, as the *Stanley Garfinckel Memorial Archive*. There are plans to place some of this material on the Internet.[62]

Feminist approaches

By the late 1970s, encouraged by the feminist movement, more women undertook oral history research in the belief that it 'offered a means of integrating women into historical scholarship, even contesting the reigning definitions of social, economic and political importance that obscured women's lives'.[63] Joan Sangster, Professor of History and Women's Studies at Trent University, Ontario, is clear that feminist approaches need to be premised on 'the construction of women's historical memory' which in turn 'offers insight into the social and material framework within which they operated, the perceived choices and cultural patterns they face and the complex relationships between individual consciousness and culture'. All oral historians agree on this need for careful interpretation. Feminist oral historians have established their own. 'In order to contextualise oral histories', comments Sangster, 'we also need to survey the dominant ideologies shaping women's worlds; listening to women's words in turn will help us to see how women understood, negotiated and sometimes challenged these dominant ideals'.[64]

Cheryl Buckley, alert to the marginalisation of the history of working-class women, uses feminist analysis in her oral history research, which in part is deeply personal. Her study 'On the Margins: theorizing the history and significance of making and designing clothes at home', in part discusses clothes making and wearing in her own family, from a coal mining community in the West Riding of Yorkshire. Buckley, sharing Sangster's themes, argues that feminist oral historians

> have tried to think differently about their work ... in order to articulate women's voices. Coupled with this is an interest in the places from which women speak – these might be places which have less power or prestige, such as the home, but which are nonetheless crucial in shaping women's experiences as designers, consumers, and historians.

She adds that her motivation in working this way was partly 'to foreground the advantages of "writing and speaking differently" about women's history'.[65]

Nicola Smallbone, following up on Angela McRobbie's earlier work on the place of young women within British subcultures [66] used oral history to research cultural attitudes amongst young Mod women in provincial south-east England in the mid-1960s. Her interviews led her to conclude that these young Mod women 'did not wear pretty blouses to please the boys but instead they dressed like them, and began to assert an equality between them by sharing active common interests in their clothes and social lives'. She concluded that Mod women had 'their own feminine culture within the subculture ... but still the very culture of being a girl was far more ingrained than any other and overrode the more extreme notions of being a Mod'.[67]

Taboo topics

Oral history interviews are able to rescue a whole range of life experiences from oblivion, many relating to the most personal and significant aspects of life. In her study *Women and Families: an oral history, 1940–1970*, of 1995, Elizabeth Roberts includes a chapter on 'The Opposite Sex' which deals with themes of courtship, weddings, the acquisition of sexual knowledge and illegitimacy in the 1918–50 period. She concluded that 'there was continuing ignorance about sexual matters and embarrassment in close social relationships … Premarital sex and especially premarital pregnancy were widely condemned, although they clearly occurred.'[68] Lindsay Falconer's research into the lives and clothes of teenage girls in the 1950s confirms Roberts's conclusions. Margaret Hunter, who was born in 1939, the daughter of a coal miner from Fife, Scotland, told Falconer in 1997

> Oh, no, sex in our day was totally in secret. The subject was taboo except maybe with your best friend. Sex nearly always took place outside, you could never go to a hotel and no way would you and your boyfriend be left alone in the house. No on the surface, good girls didn't, bad girls did.

Annie Hamilton, a former linen weaver, also from Scotland and born in 1940 remembered, 'Sex nearly always led to marriage with or without a baby. You did not do anything for about a year and then you got engaged. You have to remember it was not like it is today.'[69]

Tracey Turner, in her research into the style, manufacture and consumption of sanitary towels, has further opened up an aspect of material culture that has always been 'hidden from history'. One respondent remembering the interwar period told her, 'Mother used to get up in the night to wash out my terry towels so that they could be out away before my father got up.' Another recalled that the same practice continued in the early 1950s. 'My sister and I used to wrap our towels in newspapers and burn them in our bedroom fireplace at night so that Dad would not know what we girls were up to.'[70] Turner's oral history work confirms importantly that the social taboos surrounding the domestic management of menstruation ensured that it was hidden even from its own present.

Methodologies: the pitfalls

In defining their aims and working methods, all oral historians stress the dangers of relying entirely on recorded memory. The dangers of doing so are legion, such as romanticism, every sort of personal, political and gender bias, and the dangers simply of confused dates and jumbled events. The need to be aware that interviewees may also have been influenced by opinions and images gathered or seen later is a further complication. As Samuel and Thompson stress, despite the 'special sense of authenticity ... memory is inherently revisionist, an exercise in selective amnesia. What is forgotten may be as important as what is remembered.'[71]

Specialists have also drawn attention to the different constructions placed on historical memory according to class, gender, race, political viewpoint and ethnicity. 'Cultural values', explains Joan Sangster, 'shape our very ordering and prioritising of events, indeed our notions of what is myth, history, fact or fiction.'[72] Nicola Smallbone became aware of different gender reactions to the interview process.

> Men seemed to be quite reserved about talking about the past, but as soon as they were prompted [with period photographs] they began to pick out images and go into details about their machines [Scooters], who did and did not wear the right clothes ... They seemed to be much more strongly opinionated than the women about exact details.

She found women were more successfully interviewed in pairs when 'they prompted each other and re-lived their memories more freely ... Overall women tended to favour oral communication and were very emotive, recalling personal memories of friendships, romances and minor specific details.'[73]

Rose-coloured memories are another major problem. Samuel and Thompson explain that in many oral histories

> the narrative of hard times becomes a record of courage and endurance. The characteristic note is elegiac, saying goodbye to what will never be seen again, an affectionate leave taking ... Many, maybe most, of the facts will be true. It is the omissions and the shaping which make these stories also a myth.[74]

Methodologies: the value of oral history

Despite the pitfalls, the value of oral history lies in its ability to clarify the individuality of each human life and yet to reveal the contribution of each person within their wider community. Clothing has a major role to play in such approaches because as John Harvey writes 'our clothes have ... a clutch on us. Styles of clothing carry feelings and trusts, investments, faiths and formalized fears.'[75]

This view is exemplified through a testimony used by Anna Davin in her study *Growing Up Poor: home, school and street in London, 1870–1914*. Grace Foakes grew up in Wapping in the early 1900s, and she remembers boots as the horror of her childhood. She wrecked her lightweight, girl's style boots sliding along the street holding on to carts, so her father bought her stouter ones styled for boys: 'My tears had no effect on him.' After buying them, 'as soon as we got home he put studs in the soles. Oh! the noise they made. I felt terrible. The other children laughed, and I cried myself to sleep for many nights.'[76]

Such strong personal emotions are starkly exposed through the immediacy of oral history interviews. The sense of shame at not being able to keep up appearances, so evident in the Mayhew interviews of 1849, is exposed again through an interview conducted by Lynn Griffiths, in Hove, in the south of England in the 1920s. One woman remembered begging her family to delay calling the doctor to certify the death of an elderly relative. 'You can't go down to the doctor yet, you can't go – I have to get everything done.' Getting 'everything done' involved cutting off and hiding the deceased's old corsets because they were 'all done up at the back with knotted bootlaces'.[77]

Under happier circumstances, memories of much loved clothing can highlight profound moments of pleasure, especially amongst younger age groups. As Janice Winship writes 'the dress and appearance through which we are offered the free and glorious expression of ourselves become the metaphor and symbolisation of that freedom'.[78] Smallbone caught the joyous sartorial memories of young male Margate Mods, whose subculture was centred on its specific clothing codes. They took intense pleasure at copying the trend-setting clothing styles of London Mods who visited the seaside town for weekend jaunts on their scooters. 'You got the feel of the clothes, especially living in a holiday town with people coming from around the country and you'd think, wow, look at their dancing ... or it would be, god, I like those trousers.' They also recalled their feelings about girlfriends. Mick Tomlinson explained that girls were only accepted into Mod circles if they had the 'right' clothes, with 'the right hairstyles' and went 'to the right clubs ... image was everything. I'd have known a Mod girl, yes, they'd catch the eye.' Another respondent, Michael Thomas, fondly remembered a girlfriend 'who was at college in London and she used to wear some fantastic clothes. I think that's why I loved her really ... she used to have her hair cut at Vidal Sassoon ... God, I loved her.'[79]

Tosh believes that oral history comes into its own 'when characterising recurrent experience, like the practice of a working skill'.[80] *My First Job* includes an excellent example of work practice memory, that of a young woman working in the wholesale collar making trade in Bermondsey in the East End of London in the 1920s.

All I did was the stitching around the collar ... there were inserters, patent turners, hand turners and stitchers and runners. The runners got the plain material and run that round, the hand turners turned it, the patent turners pressed it; they turned the running you know … Oh, I worked there till I got married. It was piece work at first, and then they got this American idea, which was a conveyer belt, which was the Bido system, and the girls sat each side of it and they all done their bit … Then it went to the end and I done a bit of stitching. They worked in grosses so you had to keep up. We used to sing in the afternoons, till the Manageress used to come and say, 'Now that's enough girls!' This was '28 something like that … You couldn't save much out of what you earnt, years ago. *Rogers* … nice firm to work for.[81]

Here the respondent reveals valuable information on the introduction of US conveyer belt systems into the East End wholesale garment making trade, and the same determination to be positive about working conditions as those found by Phillips in Colchester and by the Leicester Oral History Archive in the same period.

Some sartorial legends are confirmed by oral history. One such is the view that young Mod men and women wore the same style of clothes. Smallbone interviewed Hazel Wright who recalled in the mid-1960s

the time that a boyfriend was meeting her at the bus stop. She got off the bus to find that he was wearing exactly the same outfit as her (Levis and a white crew necked jumper). She said that both refused to walk together, so stayed on opposite sides of the pavement until they reached his house so he could change.[82]

Interpretation

With such inherent problems oral history, as with all the other approaches cited in this book, is of little value in isolation. Memories have to be set within a viable interpretative framework of critical evaluation and these have been formulated by many of the historians cited in this chapter. The first and most obvious bedrock is that the words of the respondents have to be set firmly into her/his personal locality and period. Without that the rest becomes valueless. Thus Tosh supports 'an oral history which is informed by psychological insight and supported with the full resources of historical scholarship'. The role of the interpreter therefore is central to oral history work. As Tosh stresses, 'the end-product is conditioned both by the historian's social position *vis-à-vis* the informant and by the terms in which he or she has learnt to analyse the past and which may well be communicated to the informant'.[83] The folklorist Katherine Borland, a lecturer at the Open University, defines this process of interpretation as one of constructing 'a second-level narrative based upon, but at the same time reshaping the first'.[84] This reshaping process lies at the heart of interpretation and is the most problematic process of all.

Raphael Samuel was already well aware of the delicacy of this issue in 1971: 'The collector of the spoken word is in a privileged position. He is creator, in some sort, of his own archives and he ought to interpret his duties accordingly.'[85] Kathleen Blee, Professor of Sociology at the University of Pittsburgh, comments that feminist scholars have been active in defining 'ways to dissolve the traditional distinction between historian-as-authority and informant-as-subject' and to create an egalitarian process whereby a genuinely reciprocal exchange takes place.[86] Achieving this is not so easy.

Who owns the text?

Joanna Bornat remembers that in the pioneering period of the early 1970s, 'we turned on the tape recorder and we encouraged an outpouring of the past … We were to put interviewees at ease, we were to be sensitive to their needs … It was well intentioned but with one aim in mind: the eliciting of "usable" material.'[87] But then what happens? Who 'owns' the text? What happens if the respondent, whose words and memories form the spine of research, disagrees with the end result, rejecting a feminist or specific political perspective for example? In other words, who owns the interview?

In one project, Katherine Borland shared her conclusions with her interviewee, her grandmother, who took exception to the feminist inter-pretation of her memories. The voids of disagreement were so deep that Borland finally wondered how they had 'managed to misunderstand each other so completely'.[88] Elizabeth Roberts and colleagues seem to have had fewer difficulties with their ninety-six respondents, except for one, a 'Mrs X, who expressed unease about the accuracy of some of our transcriptions … We were satisfied that they were accurate, but to safeguard Mrs X her transcripts are not on public access.' The rest were placed in the Centre for North West Regional Studies and the Library of Lancaster Univer-sity.[89]

After her misunderstandings with her grandmother, Borland proposes a modification of oral history practice, which 'would reveal new ways of understanding our materials to both research partners'. She urges 'lest we as feminist scholars unreflectively appropriate the words of our mothers for our own uses, we must attend to the multiple and sometimes conflicting meanings generated by our framing or contextualizing of the oral narratives in new ways'.[90] The problem stems from the inherent inequalities within the respondent–interviewer relationship. Judith Stacey has expressed anxiety that feminist oral historians often trade on their identity in a system that is 'enmeshed in unequal, intrusive, and potentially explosive relationships, simply by virtue of our positions as researchers'.[91]

And what if there is no final meeting point between subject and interviewer? What of research into issues to which the researcher is actively hostile? The sociologist Kathleen Blee taped the memories of women who had been members of the Klu Klux Klan in the 1920s in order to determine their hitherto unknown role in this organisation. Despite a profound loathing of the Klan's bigoted racism, she found the research valuable because it revealed that far from being minor or passive players, 'women played a significant role in the second Klan's campaigns of rumour, boycotts, and intimidations of African Americans, Catholics, Jews and other minorities'. She was staggered to find that her respondents held a shared revisionist memory of this crusade of evil bigotry as merely 'an ordinary, unremarkable social club'. To her discomfort Blee also acknowledges the dangers of unexpected empathy with informants who 'far from being uniformly reactionary, red-neck, mean, ignorant … many of the people I interviewed were interesting, intelligent and well-informed, … ordinary men and women'. Blee became uneasy on noting that a 'rapport with politically abhorrent informants can be surprisingly, and disturbingly, easy to achieve in oral history interviews'. Blee was forced to admit to herself that her research did empower her racist informants, 'by suggesting to them, and to their political descendants, the importance of the Klan in American history'. Blee finally and convincingly justifies her oral history project because of its contribution to developing 'an accurate and politically effective understanding' of the Klan's extremism.[92]

Clearly, a set of complex ethical issues underlies this use of the memories of living people as a basis for personal research. Blee's specific problems apart, Sangster is quite clear on the ownership issue and on the related responsibilities of the interviewer to the respondent.

> We can honour feminist ethical obligations to make our material accessible to the women interviewed, never to reveal coincidences spoken out of the interview, never to purposely distort or ridicule their lives, but in the last resort, it is our privilege that allows us to interpret, and it is our responsibility as historians to convey their insights using our own.[93]

Rory O'Connell of the Museum of London is convinced that the entire process depends on the oral historian 'taking care' of the people s/he interviews and that this has to be centred quite straightforwardly on the issue of trust.[94]

After all, as Amy de la Haye believes, 'they let us into their lives'.[95]

Examples of good practice

Elizabeth Roberts has used the memories of working-class women as the basis for her two fascinating and exemplary social history studies, *A Woman's Place: an oral history of working class women, 1890–1940* of 1984 and *Women and Families: an oral history, 1940–1970* of 1995. Assessment of clothing comes into both volumes albeit indirectly. Roberts and her colleagues undertook ninety-eight personal interviews for the second volume. Unlike so much of community publishing, Roberts carefully identifies the background of all her respondents, who are mostly referred to by coded numbers, as most wanted to remain anonymous. Thus we know specifically that Mrs A. 3 of Lancaster was born in 1944, that her father was a farm worker and shopkeeper and her mother a mill worker before marriage who helped on the farm and in the shop after marriage. She had three children. Mrs A was 'a nursery nurse before marriage, telephonist after; husband an engineer, two children'. Roberts also sets the specific scene for her oral history interviews, with thorough period analysis of the three towns where her interviewees lived, Barrow, Lancaster and Preston, detailing levels of poverty, changing standards of living and cultural values of the period, including the changing role of the individual and the retention of tradition. She concludes that of all of these, 'only one ... appears to have had a significant impact on the lives of our respondents; the dramatic increase in the number in women in paid work. This is a continuing theme of this study.'

Roberts recognises the important social role played by fashion, though mention is all too brief. She writes that

> fashion was increasingly important and influential, not only through the media but also via friends, the peer group and local shops. It can be argued that fashion was undermining class differences and creating a more homogeneous society; it was certainly more difficult to assess people's status and occupation by the way they dressed. Set against this trend however was the tendency of individuals to decide for themselves whether or not to reject certain norms and to retain others.

Most of Roberts's sparse references to dress are related to weddings and so 'Mrs Morrison' recalled that her bridesmaids had 'cherry red, for the winter wedding, you see. And then we had our reception at the Co-op because that was the place at the time.'[96]

Ann Wise, Assistant Curator of Costumes and Textiles at Worthing Museum, East Sussex, which has a famously strong dress collection, has carefully built up examples of locally worn, 'ordinary' garments, of which there were few when she took over the collection in 1987. In doing so she set out to make the collection more reflective of the historical social reality of the community. Linked to the popular women's journal *Woman's Weekly* and through oral history interviews she has systematically collected bathing dress, underwear and garments worn by women from the 1920s to the 1960s.

This work led Wise, too, to take a keen interest in assessing the contribution of the private and the home dressmaker to the style and manufacture of clothing. She illicited information, through tape and direct transcription on working practices and conditions. These enabled her to identify the 'class' of the establishments where her respondents worked in the 1920s. Gladyis Stonier, for one, worked from her apprenticeship at the age of fourteen through to the age of thirty, for Joan Laurie of Rowlands Road, Worthing, who also owned a premises in Brighton. Both shops were managed by *Madam Barnett* (aka Mrs Fletcher). In 1929, aged twenty-two and by then a skilled fitter, Gladyis Stonier earned £2 a week, around twice as much as the factory workers in Colchester. Her working conditions, however, seem to have been far less happy. Far from singing at work, Gladyis recalled

> I worked all hours God made for that two pounds ... the thing is they had our life. I mean you were absolutely glued to it, you didn't dare take your eyes off it to look up, if anyone was talking in the workroom – say the boss for instance came up and you were talking to the head of the workroom and you happened to stop work – Oh my goodness me, 'you can work another hour for that' she'd say to us![97]

Conclusion

The basic case presented in this book is that an understanding of the historical and cultural meanings of clothing can enhance our understanding of the human condition. Samuel believed that

> the individuality of each life story ... becomes ... a vital document to the construction of consciousness, emphasising both the variety of experience in any social group, and also how each individual story draws on a common culture: a defiance of the rigid categorisation of private and public just as of memory and reality.[98]

There is no doubt that recollections of clothing can help in drawing out exactly these themes. In general terms, there is also no doubt of the ever-growing interest in oral history work. Indeed, Brian Lewis, who set up *Yorkshire Art Circus* in 1980, which concentrates on memories of coal mining communities, believes the recording processes may be getting out of hand. 'There are thousands of oral history projects. It's a cottage industry to give PhDs to academics. But nobody transcribes the tapes. If you've got a book, they've got something to keep and be proud of.'[99] Evidence from the careful, accessible and transcribed work undertaken by many oral history units, such as that of the Museum of London, indicates an overly cynical viewpoint here.

However, amongst dress historians, who lack the means but not the will to undertake oral history research, even taping is still rare. There are, however, now more positive signs of the inclusion of oral history both within museum research and display as well as within university design and dress history programmes on both sides of the Atlantic. Amongst oral historians great skill exists in conducting and interpreting interviews, but asking focused questions about their respondents' clothing recollections still largely remains a missing ingredient. The value of dress history within this field merits higher levels of recognition.

Notes

1 M. Shostak, 'What the Wind Won't Take Away', the genesis of Nisa – the life and words of a !Kung Woman, reprinted from Personal Narratives Group (ed.), *Interpreting Women's Lives: feminist theory and personal narratives* (Bloomington, Indiana University Press, 1989), pp. 228–240, in R. Perks and A. Thomson, *The Oral History Reader* (Routledge, London, 1998), p. 413.

2 J. Tosh, *The Pursuit of History: aims methods and new directions in the study of modern history* (Longman, London, reprint 1991), p. 227 and p. 211.

3 J. Bornat, Oral History as a Social Movement, Reminiscence and Older People, in Perks and Thomson, *The Oral History Reader*, p. 189.

4 B. Bozzoli, Interviewing the Women of Phokeng, extracted from Belinda Bozzoli with Mmantho Nkotsoe, Women of Phokeng: consciousness, life strategy and migrancy in South Africa, 1900–1983 (*African Studies Oral Documentation Project*, University of Witwatersrand African Studies Institute, James Curry, London, 1991), in Perks and Thomson, *The Oral History Reader*, p. 148.

5 Tower Hamlets Arts Project, *Across Seven Seas and Thirteen Rivers: life stories of pioneer Syletti settlers in Britain* (Tower Hamlets Arts Project, London, 1987).

6 R. Benmayor, B. Vázquez, A. Juarbe and C. Alvarez, Continuity and Change in Three Generations of Puerto Rican Women, in R. Samuel and P. Thompson, *The Myths We Live By* (Routledge, London, 1990), p. 198.

7 With thanks to Dorothy Sheridan; see J. Richards and D. Sheridan (eds), *Mass-Observation at the Movies* (Routledge and Kegan Paul, London, 1991); idem, *The Tom Harrisson Mass-Observation Archive: a guide for researchers* (University of Sussex, Brighton, 1991) and D. Sheridan, *Mass-Observation and Literacy Practices* (Hampton, London, 1996).

8 Tosh, *The Pursuit of History*, p. 206 and p. 209.

9 N. Rosh White, Marking Absences, Holocaust Testimony and History (reprinted from *Oral History Association of Australia Journal*, 1996), pp. 12–18, in Perks and Thomson, *The Oral History Reader*, pp. 172–173.

10 K. Blee, Evidence, Empathy and Ethics: lessons from oral histories of the Clan (reprinted from *Journal of American History*, 2, 1993), pp. 596–606, in Perks and Thomson, *The Oral History Reader*, p. 337.

11 Rosh White, Marking Absences, quoting Elie Wiesel, One Generation After, in Perks and Thomson, *The Oral History Reader*, p. 181.

12 See http://www.vhf.org/and http://www.intergraph.com/gis.

13 *Shoah*, Part 3, directed by Claude Lanzmann, 1985.

14 Samuel and Thompson, *Myths We Live By*, p. 2.

15 D. Snipe, The Future of Oral History and Moving Images (reprinted from *Oral History Review*, 19, 1/2, Spring/Fall 1991), pp. 75–87, in Perks and Thomson, *The Oral History Reader*, p. 381.

16 E. Roberts, *Women and Families: an oral history, 1940–1970* (Blackwell, Oxford, 1995), p. 21.

17 Ibid. p. 73.

18 C. Buckley, On the Margins: theorizing the history and significance of making and designing clothes at home (*Journal of Design History*, 11, 2, 1998), p. 158.

19 Ibid. p. 160.

20 Interview conducted by the author when Curator of Costume at Brighton Museum.

21 D. Henderson, A Hat-Maker Remembers: a conversation with John Reed-Crawford (*Costume*, 32, 1998), p. 87.

22 P. and R. A. MacTaggart, Half a Century of Corset Making: Mrs Turner's recollections (*Costume*, 11, 1977), p. 127.

23 P. Levi, *If This is a Man* (Bodley Head, London, 1960), p. 47.

24 Samuel and Thompson, *Myths We Live By*, p. 2.

25 M. Pember Reeves, *Round About a Pound a Week* (Virago, London, 1979), which details the report written by the Fabian Women's Group on their street survey recording the daily budgets and daily lives of working-class families in Lambeth, first published in 1913. See also Charles Booth, *Life and Labour of the People of London* (reprint, A. E. Kelley, New York, 1969).

26 E. P. Thompson and E. Yeo, *The Unknown Mayhew* (Penguin, London, 1973), p. 200, p. 215 and p. 213, quoting from Henry Mayhew's letters in *The Morning Chronicle*, published between 19 October 1849 and 12 December 1850.

27 P. Gurney (ed.), *Bolton Working-Class Life in the 1930s: a Mass-Observation anthology* (University of Sussex Library, Falmer, 1988), p. i.

28 Ibid. p. 2.

29 Report on the conference held at the British Institute of Recorded Sound, 13 December 1969 (*Oral History*, 1, 1, 1970), p. 1, p. 6, p. 8.

30 Tosh, *The Pursuit of History*, pp. 207–208.

31 J. Sangster, Telling our Stories: feminist debates and the use of oral history (reprinted from *Women's History Review*, 3, 1994), pp. 5–28, in Perks and Thomson, *The Oral History Reader*, p. 92.

32 R. Polsky, Interviewing Craftspeople in the USA: an oral history project (*Oral History*, Autumn 1990), p. 47.

33 Tosh, *The Pursuit of History*, p. 212.

34 Information drawn from current publicity material from the British Library National Sound Archive, 96 Euston Road, London NW1, where a Listening and Viewing Service is available by appointment.

35 A. Paul, *Poverty, Hardship But Happiness – those were the days: 1903–1917* (Queenspark Books, Brighton, 2nd edition, 1975), p. 3.

36 P. Schweitzer (ed.), *My First Job: Greenwich pensioners' memories of starting work* (Age Exchange Theatre Company, London, 1984).

37 A. Davin, *Growing Up Poor: home, school and street in London, 1870–1914* (Rivers Oram Press, London, 1996), p. 270.

38 J. Wolveridge, *Ain't It Grand: or this was Stepney* (Stepney Books, London, 1976), p. 73.

39 Consortium of London Publishing Groups, *Booknews*, a newsletter for people in Education (no. 2, April 1988).

40 T. Sitton, G. L. Mehaffy, O. L. Davis, Jr, *Oral History: a guide for teachers (and others)* (University of Texas Press, Austin, 1983), p. 128.

41 G. Bowles and S. Kirrane, *Knitting Together: memories of the Leicestershire hosiery industry* (Leicestershire Museums Publication, no. 108, 1990).

42 Ibid. p. 36.

43 Annie Barnes in conversation with Kate Garding and Caroline Gibbs, *Tough Annie: from suffragette to Stepney councillor* (Stepney Books, London, 1980), p. 29.

44 A. Seldon and J. Pappworth, *By Word of Mouth: elite oral history* (Methuen, London, 1983), p. 9.

45 In conversation with the author, August 1998.

46 With thanks to Louann Collins, Curator of the Macclesfield Silk Museum.

47 M. Wood, *We Wore What We'd Got: women's clothes in World War 2* (Warwickshire Books, Exeter, 1989), p. 28, p. 29 and p. 10.

48 Interview with Rory O'Connell, 12 May 1999.

49 Tosh, *The Pursuit of History*, p. 207.

50 R. Samuel, *Theatre of Memory: past and present in contemporary culture*, vol. 1 (Verso, London, 1994), pp. 4–5.

51 Tosh, *The Pursuit of History*, p. 212.

52 W. K. Blum, Oral History in the United States (*Oral History*, 1, 3, 1972), p. 18.

53 A. Phillips, Women on the Shop Floor: the Colchester rag trade, 1918–1950 (*Oral History*, Spring 1994), p. 57 and p. 61.

54 N. Kabeer, *The Power To Choose: Bangladeshi women and the labour market – decisions in London and Dhaka* (Verso, London, 2000), pp. 51–52, p. 73, p. 92, p. 278, p. 236, pp. 403–404, with thanks to Polly Jones.

55 See for example: S. Levitt and J. Tozer, *The Fabric of Society: a century of people and their clothes, 1770–1870* (Laura Ashley, Carno, 1983) and L. Hamer, The Cullercoats Fishwife (*Costume*, 18, 1984), pp. 66–74.

56 A. Blair, *Croft and Creel: a century of coastal memories* (Shepeard-Walwyn, London, 1987), p. 144.

57 Blum, Oral History in the United States, pp. 23–25.

58 J. Lasansky, *In the Heart of Pennsylvania: 19th and 20th century quiltmaking traditions* (Union County Historical Society, Lewisburg, 1985), reviewed in *Textile History* (vol. 17, Autumn 1986), pp. 215–216.

59 Interview with Rory O'Connell, 12 May 1999.

60 Seldon and Pappworth, *By Word of Mouth*, p. 6.

61 Interviewed on 7 August 1998.

62 With thanks to Geraldine Howell of the University of Westminster for this information.

63 Sangster, Telling Our Stories, p. 88.

64 Ibid. p. 91.

65 Buckley, On the Margins, p. 158.

66 A. McRobbie, *Feminism and Youth Culture: from Jackie to Just 17* (Macmillan, London, 1991).

67 N. Smallbone, *A Girl in the Sixties – Mod, Rocker or nobody* (B.A. Hons Design History dissertation, University of Brighton, 1996), p. 70.

68 Roberts, *Women and Families*, p. 75.

69 L. Falconer, *'This Teenage Thing is Getting Out of Hand': the working class teenage girl, 1955–1965* (B.A. Hons Design History dissertation, University of Brighton, 1997), p. 13.

70 T. Turner, *Making and Consuming Female Sanitary Protection from 1890–1993* (B.A. Hons Design History dissertation, University of Brighton, 1993), p. 52 and p. 54.

71 Samuel and Thompson, *Myths We Live By*, pp. 7–8.

72 Sangster, Telling Our Stories, p. 89.

73 Smallbone, *A Girl in the Sixties*, p. 8.

74 Samuel and Thompson, *Myths We Live By*, p. 9.

75 J. Harvey, *Men in Black* (Reaktion, London, 1995), p. 19.

76 Davin, *Growing Up Poor*, p. 76, quoting Grace Foakes, Between High Walls: a London childhood (no publisher given, 1972).

77 L. Griffiths, *Women's Underwear 1919–1930* (B.A. Hons Design History dissertation, Brighton Polytechnic, 1988), p. 88.

78 J. Winship, *Woman Becomes An Individual – femininity and consumption in women's magazines, 1954–1969* (Centre for Contemporary Cultural Studies, University of Birmingham, 1981), p. 1.

79 Smallbone, *A Girl in the Sixties*, p. 23 and p. 25.

80 Tosh, *The Pursuit of History*, p. 210.

81 Schweitzer, *My First Job*, p. 28.

82 Smallbone, *A Girl in the Sixties*, p. 34.

83 Tosh, *The Pursuit of History*, pp. 213–217.

84 K. Borland, That's Not What I Said: interpretive conflict in oral narrative research, in Perks and Thomson, *The Oral History Reader*, p. 321.

85 R. Samuel, Perils of the Transcript (reproduced from *Oral History*, 1, 2, 1971), pp. 19–22, in Perks and Thomson, *The Oral History Reader*, pp. 389–392.

86 K. Blee, Evidence, Empathy and Ethics (reprinted from *Journal of American History*, 80, 2, 1930), pp. 596–606, in Perks and Thomson, *The Oral History Reader*, p. 333.

87 Bornat, Oral History as Social Movement, p. 191.

88 Borland, That's Not What I Said, p. 329.

89 Roberts, *Women and Families*, p. 241.

90 Borland, That's Not What I Said, p. 330.

91 Sangster, Telling Our Stories, quoting J. Stacey, Can There be a Feminist Ethnography?, in S. B. Gluck and D. Patai (eds), *Women's Words: the feminist practice of oral history* (Routledge, London, 1991), p. 92.

92 Blee, Evidence, Empathy and Ethics, pp. 336–343.

93 Sangster, Telling Our Stories, p. 93.

94 Interview, 13 May 1999.

95 Interview with Amy de la Haye, Curator of Twentieth Century Dress, Victoria and Albert Museum, 7 August 1998.

96 Roberts, *Women and Families*, p. 241, p. 21, p. 4 and p. 74.

97 A. Wise, Dressmakers in Worthing, 1920–1950 (*Costume*, 32, 1998), p. 86.

98 Samuel and Thompson, *Myths We Live By*, p. 2.

99 Chris Arnot, The History of Life as We Know It, *The Independent*, 8 August 1998, p. 8.

Conclusion

TIM Breen's conviction that things acquire meaning only once woven into 'a complex cultural conversation'[1] about the structure of society can be taken as the end point of this journey. Such cultural conversations, however, are dependent upon open-minded interdisciplinary approaches that are not skewed by personal prejudice, by obsessive reliance on one field of study or by over-reliance on the latest theoretical fad.

This book has sought to show the danger of leaving out pieces of the puzzle so that the overall picture becomes flawed. It is evident that object-based dress historians need now to deal properly with the wider new theoretical approaches to their subject identified here. It also remains true that many historians and cultural studies specialists still suffer from an inability (or will) to 'read' from the actuality of clothing objects. The approaches debated here emphasise the need for historians looking at dress to read across a whole range of books and specialist journals which deal with aspects of dress, material culture, oral history, ethnography, feminist and social history and so on.

Examples of the fascinating research which exemplifies the new open approach to dress and textile history analysis which is currently suffusing its way through academia are to be found in a wide range of specialist journals. It is significant that much of such research is the work of women historians and analysts. The 1998 edition of the *Journal of Historical Sociology*, for example, published a compelling and seminal study by Ruth Watson focusing on issues of colonial authoritarianism enacted through the design and use of cloth. Watson gives an account of the ban imposed by the British authorities on the selling of a specially designed, blue damask fabric imported into Nigeria in 1939. This featured a striking jacquard-woven, repeat portrait design of the *Olubadan abasi*, Ibadan's head-chief, with a crown and the words *Olubadan d'Oba Abuse Buse*. The British colonial authorities took the unusual course of legally banning the sale and wearing of this cloth in 1939. They argued that if it was worn as intended at a

conference of Yoruba Chiefs to be held in the new Town Hall of the great
city of Ibadan, civil unrest would occur because of rivalry between regional
power groupings. Thus sale was denied, and records show that the unfortunate importer, the Aladayemi Adeoba Stores in Ibadan, were 'still
requesting permission to sell the cloth and they were still being refused,
as late as 1950, nine years after the death of Olubandan Abasi'.[2]

As an example of complex cultural meanings to be found within
clothing and textiles, this example, published in a sociology journal, is
hard to better. It reinforces Anthea Jarvis's belief that 'the gulf between
academics and curators has not been fully closed but bridges have been
built and communication prospers'.[3] Watson's research also reinforces
Styles's view that

> No longer is it possible to sustain a history of dress that considers its
> principal tasks to be those of establishing the time line of high fashion, or
> the chronology of changes in the construction of clothing. Questions of
> meanings and interpretation now dominate the intellectual agenda.[4]

Whilst being wary of the 'fetishization of theory', there is no doubt
of the positive excitement and innovation to be found within the cross-
currents now whirling through dress history/dress studies, as this book has
sought to show. Many voids still remain to be filled. The 'new' dress
history, whilst redressing the weight of research away from endless publications on couture clothing, has still largely failed to assess in any serious
depth issues surrounding the design, manufacture, retailing and consumption of urban working-class dress in Western cultures in the nineteenth
and twentieth centuries. The design and consumption of the fabrics of
fashion across all levels of manufacture have also only been paid cursory
attention. There is much left to be done and no one person can be expected
to be expert across so many fields. Indeed Styles comments that 'a crude
pooling of approaches' will not solve the problem. He believes that 'we
need a willingness to monitor and reflect on other approaches. Acknow-
ledgement of this diversity is the key to putting the study of dress back
into history.'[5] Respect for each others' specialisms is the final essential
ingredient.

Notes

1 T. Breen, The Meaning of Things: interpreting the consumer economy in the 18th
  century, in J. Brewer and R. Porter, *Consumption and the World of Goods* (Routledge,
  London, 1993), pp. 249–260.

2 R. Watson, Material Culture and Civic Power in Colonial Ibadan (*Journal of Historical
  Sociology*, 11, 4, December 1998), p. 464, quoting Nigerian National Archives, Ibadan,

A. A. Williams for the Chief Secretary to Messrs Aladayemi Adeoba and Son, 20 March 1950, NAI, CSO.26/35943.

3 A. Jarvis, Letter from the Editor (*Fashion Theory*, Special Issue: Methodology, 2, 4, 1998), p. 300.

4 J. Styles, Dress in History: reflections on a contested terrain (*Fashion Theory*, 2, 4, 1998), pp. 387–388.

5 Styles, Dress in History.

Index